WRITE

▶ YOUR

BUSINESS

PLAN

get your plan in place and your business off the ground

EP
Entrepreneur
PRESS®

BY THE STAFF OF ENTREPRENEUR MEDIA, INC.

Entrepreneur Press, Publisher
Cover Design: Andrew Welyczko
Production and Composition: Eliot House Productions

Library of Congress Cataloging-in-Publication Data

      Write your business plan: get your plan in place and your business off the
ground / by The Staff of Entrepreneur Media, Inc.

        pages.   cm.

        Includes index.

        ISBN-13: 978-1-59918-557-6 (alk. paper)

        ISBN-10: 1-59918-557-1 (alk. paper)

        1. Business planning. 2. New business enterprises—Management. 3. Small
business—Management. I. Entrepreneur Media, Inc.

      HD30.28.W754 2015

      658.4'012—dc23   2014035844

Printed in the United States of America

19 18 17 16   10 9 8 7 6 5 4 3

Contents

SECTION I
Before Writing Your Plan

C H A P T E R 1

C H A P T E R 2

SECTION II

Writing Your Business Plan

CHAPTER 11

How Does Your Business Work?. **185**

CHAPTER 12

Expressing Your Ideas in Financial Terms **201**

SECTION III

Enhancing Your Business Plan

CHAPTER 13

Enlightening Extras: Appendices **237**

CHAPTER 14

You Only Make a First Impression Once. **247**

SECTION IV
Appendices

Preface

In the early 1950s, all Ray Kroc could think about was selling food mixers. By 1954, he had failed at just about every job he had had—piano player, paper-cup salesman, ambulance driver. And at the age of 52, he wanted to do something different.

One of his customers, a small hamburger joint in San Bernardino, California, caught his eye. Instead of buying a single mixer, this tiny restaurant, owned by brothers Dick and Mac McDonald, bought eight. The restaurant was simple. It didn't serve much more than a hamburger, fries, and some drinks.

The McDonald brothers were content. Ray Kroc wasn't.

So he put together a plan.

Kroc believed the hamburger restaurant's success could be exported around the country. He saw what the McDonald brothers didn't—a network of restaurants using the best practices of the San Bernardino location to sell burgers and fries. So he calculated the potential, wrote a proposal, and within a year had formed the McDonald's Corporation, eventually transforming a roadside hamburger joint into an international powerhouse.

It wasn't because Kroc was simply an idea man, an entrepreneur, or visionary. A lot of us have good ideas. Some of us have great ones. But that doesn't mean we can turn those ideas into businesses. What sets the dreamer apart from the doer is the plan. The business plan.

That's why this book is so important. Entrepreneurship is the lifeblood of the world economy, the process of innovation, disruption, and risk that creates companies each day and drives otherwise normal people to leave their jobs and turn their own inventions or concepts into moneymaking enterprises.

To build a company, though, you need a plan. A real one. A plan that lays out your product, your strategy, your market, your team, and your opportunity. It is your vision. It is the blueprint for your business.

Why do you need a plan? Well, for one thing, someone needs to fund your business, and people don't like parting with dollars unless they're pretty confident you know what you're doing. That is certainly true of venture capitalists and bankers. It's also true of friends and family. Whether you are borrowing $50,000 or $5 million, your backers want to see real numbers, real projections, and real strategy. Can you blame them? After all, it may be your idea, but it's their money.

Still, business plans go beyond simply getting funding. A good leader formulates a plan for herself, making it a living document to help drive the business. It is a sounding board to strategy. Projections change and opportunities and missteps happen. The plan is the course correction, a chart off which to plot next moves, pivots, or future objectives. A good business plan can help you evaluate whether the time is right for an acquisition. It can be a tool in deciding whether to hire or cut staff. It can be a barometer to measure your performance against that of your competitors.

This book will walk you through how to craft the best business plan for your business. From determining the needs of your customer, to explaining your technology, to laying out your strategy, this book is the most comprehensive how-to manual for building your business. We walk you through which financials are important, how to analyze your competition, and what technology is available to assist you in understanding where your company is and where it can go. What's more, we give you real-world examples of plans that worked, helping to raise money or hone strategy.

Not every business will succeed. In truth, far more businesses fail than succeed. The differentiator is always in the planning. This book gives you that competitive edge.

Ray Kroc saw two things. First, he saw an opportunity that was unmet. More important, he saw a business in need of a plan—and a leader. Every day, someone wakes up with an idea. You have taken the next, more important step of buying this book to make that idea into a business. I hope you profit from that experience.

—Ray Hennessey, Editor, *Write Your Business Plan* and
Editorial Director, Entrepreneur.com

Before Writing Your Plan

Plan to Prosper
Business Plan Basics

A business plan is a written description of the future of your business. It is a document that tells the story of what you plan to do and how you plan to do it. If you jot down a paragraph on the back of an envelope describing your business strategy, you've written a plan, or at least the germ of a plan.

Business plans are inherently strategic. You start here, today, with certain resources and abilities. You want to get to a "there," a point in the future (usually three to five years out) at which time your business will have a different set of resources and abilities as well as greater profitability and increased assets. Your plan shows how you will get from here to there. In essence it is a road map from where you are now to where you want to be later on.

There are some generally accepted conventions about what a full-blown business plan should include and how it should be presented. A plan should cover all the important matters that will contribute to making your business a success. These include the following:

1. *Your basic business concept.* This is where you discuss the industry, your business structure, your particular product or service, and how you plan to make your business a success.

2. *Your strategy and the specific actions you plan to take to implement it.* What goals do you have for your business? When and how will you reach your goals?

3. *Your products and services and their competitive advantages.* Here is your chance to dazzle the readers with good, solid information about your products or services and why customers will want to purchase your products and services and not those of your competitors.

4. *The markets you'll pursue. Now you have to lay out your marketing plan.* Who will your customers be? What is your demographic audience? How will you attract and retain enough customers to make a profit? What methods will you use to capture your audience? What sets your business apart from the competition?

5. *The background of your management team and key employees.* Having information about key personnel is an important but often misrepresented portion of a business plan. It's not a long and detailed biography of each person involved but an accurate account of what they have done and what they bring to the table for this specific business opportunity.

6. *Your financing needs.* These will be based on your projected financial statements. These statements provide a model of how your ideas about the company, its markets, and its strategies will play out.

As you write your business plan, stick to facts instead of feelings, projections instead of hopes, and realistic expectations of profit instead of unrealistic dreams of wealth. Facts—checkable, demonstrable facts—will invest your plan with the most important component of all: credibility.

How Long Should Your Plan Be?

A useful business plan can be any length, from that scrawl on the back of an envelope to more than 100 pages for an especially detailed plan describing a complex enterprise. A typical business plan runs 15 to 25 pages, created and (usually) sent electronically, sometimes accompanied by forms the receiver requests that you fill out. Occasionally you may still be asked for a hard copy of your plan.

Miniplans of five to ten pages are the popular concise models that may stand on their own for smaller businesses. Larger businesses, seeking major funding, will often have miniplans as well, but the full business plan will be waiting in the wings. It's to your advantage to run long when creating your plan and then narrow it down for presentation purposes.

The size of the plan will also depend on the nature of your business and your reason for writing the plan. If you have a simple concept, you may be able to express it in very few words. On the other hand, if you are proposing a new kind of business or even a new industry, it may require quite a bit of explanation to get the message across. If you are writing a plan for a division of a large organization, you may be given a set format and prescribed length.

The purpose of your plan also determines its length. If you are looking for millions of dollars in seed capital to start a risky venture, you will usually (although not always) have to do a lot of explaining and convincing. If you already have relationships with potential investors, they may simply want a miniplan. If you are just going to use your plan for internal purposes to manage an ongoing business, a much more abbreviated version may suffice.

Many business plan presentations are made with PowerPoint decks, using 10 to 12 slides to tell your story. This is a great starting point, but you should have at least a miniplan available, especially if you are seeking millions of dollars. More on PowerPoint presentations later.

buzzword

Competitive advantage is what makes you different from, and better than, your competition. Lower price, higher quality, and better name recognition are examples of competitive advantages. By studying your competition, you can devise your own competitive advantage by providing something (or several things) that it does not offer.

>> Cocktail Napkin Business Plan

Business plans don't have to be complicated, lengthy documents. They just have to capture the essence of what the business will do and why it will be a success.

The business plan for one of the most successful startups ever began with a triangle scrawled on a cocktail napkin. The year was 1971, and Herb Kelleher and Rollin King were formulating their idea for an airline serving Houston, Dallas, and San Antonio. The triangle connecting the cities was their route map—and the basis of the business plan for Southwest Airlines.

The two entrepreneurs soon expressed their vision for Southwest Airlines more fully in a full-fledged business plan and raised millions in initial capital to get off the ground. Eventually they went public. Along the way, the airline expanded beyond the three cities to include other Texas destinations, and now it serves 84 destination in 41 states plus Washington, DC, and Puerto Rico with 3,200 flights daily and revenues of $17.1 billion. Southwest specializes in low-cost, no-frills, high-frequency service, which, if you just add some lines to the original triangle, is the same strategy mapped out on that cocktail napkin.

When Should You Write It?

The fact that you're reading this book means you suspect it's about time to write a business plan. Odds are you are at or near one of the many occasions when a business plan will prove useful.

- A business plan is a good way to explore the feasibility of a new business without actually having to start it and run it. A good plan can help you see serious flaws in your business concept. You may uncover tough competition when researching the market section, or you may find that your financial projections simply aren't realistic.

- Any venture that faces major changes (and that means almost all businesses) needs a business plan. If the demographics of your market are rapidly changing, strong new competitive products challenge your profitability, you expect your business to grow or shrink dramatically, or the economic climate is improving or slipping rapidly, you'll need a business plan. This will allow you to make changes accordingly.

- If you are contemplating buying or selling a business, your business plan can provide you with a handy tool to establish a value—and to support that value if challenged.

- You will need a business plan if you are seeking financing. Your business plan is the backbone of your financing proposal. Bankers, venture capitalists, and other financiers rarely provide money without seeing a plan.

buzzword

Business concept is a term referring to the basic idea around which you build your business. For instance, FedEx is built on the idea of overnight delivery, and Amazon was originally based on the idea of selling books over the internet.

>> Pumping Up a Puny Plan

Jay Valentine doesn't like business plans, doesn't believe in them, and doesn't write them for startups he's involved in. "It's ridiculous for a startup to make these plans and projections," he says. Valentine prefers to wait until he's conferred with a number of customers and booked a few sales. Then he knows how he'll sell his product and what the revenues are likely to be.

Still, Valentine was the CEO of InfoGlide Inc., a database-technology startup, so he was responsible for coming up with a plan that would please the venture capitalists. InfoGlide was asking for several million dollars to bring the technology to market. So he wrote one. "It was maybe 15 pages," says Valentine. "Just me writing about the company and what we were trying to do."

That wouldn't please number-crunching venture capitalists, Valentine knew. So he hired a consultant to prepare a five-year financial forecast. Then he sent it in, sight unseen. "I never even looked at the financials," he says. "But it was thick—and that's what the venture capitalists like to see." Crazy? Maybe. But the pumped-up plan landed $3 million from a big venture capital firm.

Less sophisticated investors or friends and family may not require a business plan, but they deserve one. Even if you're funding the business with your own savings, you owe it to yourself to plan how you'll expend the resources you're committing.

Writing a business plan is not a one-time exercise. Just because you wrote a plan when you were starting out or raising money to get under way doesn't mean you are finished. Many companies look for additional rounds of funding. By updating business plans to let investors know how the funding has been used to date, and the results of such efforts, the chances of procuring such funding is improved. A business plan should be rewritten or revised regularly to get maximum benefit from it. Commonly, business plans are revised yearly, more frequently if conditions have changed enough to make the previous plan unrealistic.

Who Needs a Business Plan?

About the only person who doesn't need a business plan is one who's not going into business. You don't need a plan to start a hobby or to moonlight from your regular job. But anybody beginning or extending a venture that will consume significant resources of money, energy, or time and that is expected to return a profit should take the time to draft some kind of plan.

Startups

The classic business plan writer is an entrepreneur seeking funds to help start a new venture. Many, many great companies had their starts in the form of a plan that was used to convince investors to put up the capital necessary to get them under way.

However, it's a mistake to think that only startups need business plans. Companies

fact or fiction

The typical image of a business planner is an entrepreneur seeking to lure investors to a hot startup. But most plans are not written by entrepreneurs or even business owners. Nor are they always seen by anyone outside the company involved. They're often created by corporate managers for corporate managers and are used for internal planning and control.

>> No Plan, No Problem

When the folks behind LawyerUp, an online service for people in need of an attorney quickly, started the business it was called Morange Workshops, and they had no formal plan. They just did what they knew they were good at and let the business "plan" itself. By using skills that were inherently theirs, they created a business on less than a shoestring budget. The business grew slowly but steadily for nine years, and by 2010, they had reached $250,000 in revenues. The company was named a national finalist in the Make Mine A Million $ Business Competition, run by Count Me In and sponsored by American Express Open.

While this strategy worked well for LawyerUp, it is the exception to the rule. Your idea may be very strong to get you off the ground without complicated spreadsheets and market analysis, but most companies benefit from having at least a rudimentary business plan to guide them when they start and over time. One thing about a business plan is that you can (and should) always be updating it as your business evolves in an ever-changing business climate.

and managers find plans useful at all stages of their existence, whether they're seeking financing or trying to figure out how to invest a surplus.

Established Firms Seeking Help

Many business plans are written by and for companies that are long past the startup stage but also well short of large-corporation status. These middle-stage enterprises may draft plans to help them find funding for growth just as the startups do, although the amounts they seek may be larger and the investors more willing because the company already has a track record. They may feel the need for a written plan to help manage an already rapidly growing business. A business

fact or fiction

Legend says FedEx founder Fred Smith wrote the company's business plan as a term paper while he was a student at Yale. Not so, says Smith. His Yale paper outlined some possibilities of a centralized package-distribution system but was far from a full-fledged business plan.

>> Free Movies—A New Business Idea

One way to establish a competitive edge is to beat the competition's prices. That's particularly simple when you charge nothing. And that was the foundation of the business plan written by Kristen and Doherty Davis of Easthampton, Long Island, New York. Their business, Popcorn Noir, would make money on food and drinks that went beyond typical movie fare by featuring beer, wine, and sumptuous snacks served at tables. This business model fit in nicely with the relaxed vacation community that is Easthampton.

While this was not intended to become a multinational conglomerate but rather a small part of the town's growing art scene, the couple carefully planned their unique cinema/cocktail lounge experience. They also included some membership plans to accommodate single-day customers with $25 VIP memberships.

Concepts like this can benefit significantly from a business plan by presenting new and innovative ideas in an easy-to-follow format.

plan may be seen as a valuable tool to convey the mission and prospects of the business to customers, suppliers, or other interested parties.

Just as the initial plan maps how to get from one leg of the journey to the next, an updated plan for additional funding adds another leg of your journey. It's not unlike traveling from the United States to Paris and then deciding to visit London or Barcelona or both along the way. You would then need to add to, or update, your plans. A business plan can, therefore, address the next stage in the life process of a business.

Why Should You Write a Business Plan?

Business plans could be considered cheap insurance. Just as many people don't buy

plan pointer

Check with your local Small Business Development Center (www. sba.gov) if you need help developing your business plan. Many colleges and universities also have small-business experts available to lend a hand.

>> Focus on Value

Kodiak Venture Partners, a venture capital firm that invests in high-tech, early-stage companies, focusing on communications, semiconductors, and software, believes that a business plan is important. "The business plan is an important tool in keeping an early-stage company focused. The key is not to treat it as a static item: produced once, polished, and set on the shelf," says Luciana Castro, marketing director.

For the early-stage company, the business plan is often viewed solely as a key part of obtaining financing. A business plan that effectively helps the company obtain financing will clearly communicate the company's value, the customer problems solved by the company's product, and the important investments required to bring those products to market. Maintaining your focus on these items is critical to the growth of a strong company, so a plan that clearly articulates these items should also be used in the management of the growing company.

fire insurance on their homes and rely on good fortune to protect their investment, many successful business owners do not rely on written business plans but trust their own instincts. However, your business plan is more than insurance. It reflects your ideas, intuitions, instincts, and insights about your business and its future—and provides the cheap insurance of testing them out before you are committed to a course of action.

What Are Your Objectives?

You need to think of what you want and whether your plan's findings suggest you'll get it. For instance, is your objective to gain freedom from control by other people? If your plan shows that you'll have to take on several equity partners, each of whom will desire a chunk of ownership, you may need to come up with a business that does not require capital needs that are very intensive.

Perhaps you want a company that will let you do your work and get home at a reasonable hour, even a business you can start from home.

There are so many options when it comes to starting a business, including the size, location, and, of course, the reason for existence. You will be able to determine all of these and so many more aspects of business with the help of your business plan. It forces you to think through all of the areas that form the main concept to the smallest details. This way you don't find yourself remembering at the last minute that your website is still not developed or that you still have most of your inventory in a warehouse and no way to ship it.

What Your Business Plan Can't Do

The author of a book on business plans is likely to dream up a lot of benefits to writing one. And a business plan can do a lot for you. But it would be a disservice to claim that a good business plan is all you need to succeed. Even a perfectly planned business can fail if fortune fails to smile on it.

Predict the Future

It may seem dishonest to say that a business plan can't predict the future. What are all those projections and forecasts for if they are not attempts to predict the future? The fact is, no projection or forecast is really a hard-and-fast prediction of the future. Not even the French seer Nostradamus could tell you for sure how your business will be doing in five years. The best you can do is have a plan in which you logically and systematically attempt to show what will happen if a particular scenario occurs. That scenario has been determined by your research and analysis to be the most likely one of the many that may occur. But it's still just a probability, not a guarantee.

You can, however, use your research, sales forecasts, market trends, and competitive analysis to make well thought-out predictions of how you see your business developing if you are able to follow a specified course. To some extent, you can create your future rather than simply trying to predict it by the decisions you make. For example, you may not have a multimillion-dollar business in ten years if you are trying to start and run a small family business. Your decision on growth would therefore factor into your predictions and the outcome.

Guarantee Funding

There are all kinds of reasons why a venture capitalist, banker, or other investor may refuse to fund your company. It may be that there's no money to give out at the moment. It may be that the investor just backed a company very similar to your own and now wants something different. Perhaps the investor has just promised to back her brother-in-law's firm or is merely having a bad day and saying no to everything that crosses her desk. The point is, the quality of your plan may have little or nothing to do with your prospects for getting funded by a particular investor.

But what about the investment community as a whole? Surely if you show a well-prepared plan to a lot of people, someone will be willing to back you, right? Again, not necessarily. Communities, as well as people, are subject to fads, and your idea may be yesterday's fad. Conversely, it may be too far ahead of its time. It also may be an idea that comes about in a shaky economy or a saturated market. Timing is sometimes a factor that is out of your control.

The same is true of the availability of funds. At times, banks everywhere seem to clamp down on lending, refusing to back even clearly superior borrowers. In many countries, there is no network of venture capitalists to back fledgling companies.

Raise All the Money You'll Need

A business plan cannot guarantee that you will raise all the money you need at any given time, especially during the startup phase. Even if you are successful in finding an investor, odds are good that you won't get quite what you asked for. There may be a big difference in what you have to give up, such as majority ownership or control, to get the funds. Or you may be able to make minor adjustments if you cannot snare as large a chunk of cash as you want.

In a sense, a business plan used for seeking funding is part of a negotiation taking place between you and your prospective financial backers. The part of the plan where you describe your financial needs can be considered your opening bid in this negotiation. The other information it contains, from market research to management bios, can be considered supporting arguments. If you look at it in that way, a business plan is an excellent opening bid. It's definite, comprehensive, and clear.

But it's still just a bid, and you know what happens to bids in negotiations. They get whittled away, the terms get changed, and, sometimes, the whole negotiation breaks down under the force of an ultimatum from one of the parties involved. Does this mean you should ask for a good deal more money than you actually need in your plan? Actually, that may not be the best strategy either. Investors who see a lot of plans are going to notice if you're asking for way too much money. Such a move stands a good chance of alienating those who might otherwise be enthusiastic backers of your plan. It's probably a better idea to ask for a little more than you think you can live with, plus slightly better terms than you really expect.

Fool People

A professional financier such as a bank loan officer or a venture capitalist will see literally hundreds of business plans in the course of a year. After this has gone on for several years, and the financier has backed some percentage of those plans and seen how events have turned out, he or she becomes very good at weeding out plans with inconsistencies or overblown projections and zeroing in on weaknesses, including some you'd probably rather not see highlighted.

If you've seen the television show *Shark Tank,* you'll understand how shrewd those individuals with the dollars can be. In short, most financiers are expert plan analyzers. You have little chance of fooling one of them with an overly optimistic or even downright dishonest plan. That doesn't mean you shouldn't make the best case you honestly can for your business. But the key word is "honestly."

You certainly shouldn't play down your strengths in a plan, but don't try to hide your weaknesses either. Intelligent, experienced financiers will see them anyway. Let's say you propose to open a small healthy food store at an address a block away from a Whole Foods. An investor who knows this fact but doesn't see any mention of it in your plan may suspect you've lost your senses—and who could blame her?

Now think about the effect if your plan notes the existence of that big grocery store. That gives you a chance to differentiate yourself explicitly, pointing out that you'll be dealing only in locally produced foods—which the superstore doesn't carry but many of its customers may want. Suddenly that high-volume operator becomes a helpful traffic builder, not a dangerous competitor.

So recognize and deal appropriately with the weaknesses in your plan, rather than sweeping them under the rug. If you do it right, this troubleshooting can become one of the strongest parts of the whole plan.

> *"You certainly shouldn't play down your strengths in a plan, but don't try to hide your weaknesses either."*

Business Planning Risks

There are risks associated with writing a business plan. That's right: While one of the main purposes of a business plan is to help you avoid risk, the act of creating one does create a few risks as well. These risks include:

- *The possible disclosure of confidential material.* Although most of the people who see your plan will respect its confidentiality, a few may (either deliberately or by mistake) disclose proprietary information. For this reason you may want to have a non-disclosure agreement, or NDA, signed before sending it to others. See Figure 1–1 on page 16.

- *Leading yourself astray.* You may come to believe too strongly in the many forecasts and projects in your business plan.

- *Ruining your reputation . . . or worse.* If you fill the plan with purposely overly optimistic prognostication, exaggeration, or even falsehoods you will do yourself a disservice. Some plans prepared for the purpose of seeking funds may run afoul of securities laws if they appear to be serving as prospectuses unblessed by the regulators.

- *Spending too much effort planning.* You then may not have enough energy or time to actually run your business. Some call it "analysis paralysis." It's a syndrome that occurs when you spend so much time planning that you never do anything. For a lot of businesspeople, this is a nonissue—they detest planning so much that there's no

---

MUTUAL NON-DISCLOSURE AGREEMENT

   THIS MUTUAL NON-DISCLOSURE AGREEMENT ("Agreement") is made and entered into between _____, whose address is _____ _____, and _____, whose address is _____. This Agreement shall take effect on the date last executed.

1.   **Purpose.** The parties hereto wish to do the following: _____

_____

_____
_____.

Consistent with and in furtherance of the aforementioned purpose, each said party may disclose ("Disclosing Party") to the other party ("Recipient") certain technical and business information, which the Disclosing Party desires the Recipient to treat as the Disclosing Party's trade secrets and confidential information as defined in Section 2 below (collectively, "Confidential Information").

2.   **"Confidential Information"** means any information disclosed by either party to the other party, either directly or indirectly, in writing, orally or by inspection of tangible objects (including without limitation documents, prototypes, samples, plant and equipment). Confidential Information shall include without limitation technical data, trade secrets and know-how, including, but not limited to, research, product plans, products, services, suppliers, customer lists and customers, prices and costs, markets, software, developments, inventions, laboratory notebooks, processes, formulas, technology, designs, drawings, engineering, hardware configuration information, marketing, licenses, finances, budgets and other business information. Confidential Information shall not, however, include any information which: (i) was publicly known and made generally available in the public domain prior to the time of disclosure by the Disclosing Party; (ii) becomes publicly known and generally available after disclosure by the Disclosing Party to the Recipient through no wrongful action by the Recipient; (iii) is already in the possession of the Recipient at the time of disclosure by the Disclosing Party, as shown by the Recipient's files and records immediately prior to the time of disclosures; (iv) is obtained by the Recipient from a third party without a breach of such third party's obligations of confidentiality; (v) is independently developed by the Recipient without use of or reference to the Disclosing Party's Confidential Information, as shown by documents and other competent evidence in the Recipient's possession; or (vi) is required by law to be disclosed by the Recipient, provided that the Recipient gives the Disclosing Party prompt written notice of such required disclosure prior to such disclosure and assistance in obtaining an order protecting said Confidential Information from public disclosure.

3.   **Non-Use and Non-Disclosure.** The Recipient of any Confidential Information from the Disclosing Party agrees not to use said Information for any purpose except to evaluate and engage in discussions concerning a potential business relationship between the parties. The Recipient further agrees not to disclose the Disclosing Party's Confidential Information (i) to any third party without the prior written consent of the Disclosing Party, or (ii) to those employees or agents of Recipient, who are **not** required to have that Information in order to evaluate or engage in discussions concerning the purpose of this Agreement as set forth in Section 1 above. The Recipient shall not reverse engineer, disassemble or decompile any prototypes, software or other tangible objects, which embody the Disclosing Party's Confidential Information and which are provided to the Recipient hereunder.

4.   **Maintenance of Confidentiality.** The Recipient agrees to take reasonable measures to protect the secrecy, and avoid disclosure and unauthorized use, of any of the Disclosing Party's Confidential

Figure 1-1. Sample Non-Disclosure Agreement

chance at all they'd forgo actually doing business and merely plan it.

   Business planning can take on a life of its own. It's possible to spend so much time planning a startup that you miss your window of opportunity or to schedule such frequent updates of a plan for an established business that it becomes difficult to administer its other

Information disclosed hereunder. Without limiting the foregoing, each party shall take at least those measures that it/they take to protect its/their own most highly confidential information.

5. **No Obligation.** Nothing herein shall obligate either party to proceed with any transaction between them, and each said party reserves the right, in its/their sole discretion, to terminate the discussions contemplated by this Agreement concerning the purpose set forth above.

6. **Return of Materials.** All documents and other tangible objects containing or representing Confidential Information which has been disclosed by the Disclosing Party to the Recipient hereunder, and all copies thereof which are in the possession of the Recipient, shall be and remain the property of the Disclosing Party and shall be promptly returned to the Disclosing Party upon the Disclosing Party's written request.

7. **No License.** Nothing in this Agreement is intended to grant Recipient any rights in or to any Confidential Information disclosed hereunder and belonging to the Disclosing Party, except as expressly set forth herein.

8. **Term.** The obligations of the Recipient to protect the confidentiality of any Confidential Information disclosed hereunder by the Disclosing Party shall survive until such time as such Confidential Information becomes publicly known or otherwise ceases to be confidential through no breach of this Agreement by the Recipient.

9. **Remedies.** Each party agrees that any violation or threatened violation of this Agreement may cause irreparable injury to the other party, entitling the other party to seek injunctive relief in addition to all legal remedies.

10. **Miscellaneous.** This Agreement shall bind and inure to the benefit of the parties hereto and their successors and assigns. This Agreement shall be governed by the laws of the State of _____, without reference to that State's conflict of laws and principles. Any and all claims or disputes between the parties hereto arising out of, or in any manner concerning, this Agreement shall be exclusively litigated in a court located in or having jurisdiction over _____County, in the State of _____, which both parties agree shall have personal jurisdiction over them. This document contains the entire agreement between the parties with respect to the subject matter hereof, and supersedes and replaces any and all prior or contemporaneous agreements and understandings, whether written or oral, concerning said subject matter. No provision of this Agreement shall be deemed waived, nor may this Agreement be amended or otherwise modified, except by a writing signed by all of the parties hereto.

IN WITNESS WHEREOF, the parties have duly executed this Agreement on the dates indicated below.

By:_____   By:_____

_____   _____
(Printed Name/Title)   (Printed Name/Title)

Dated:_____   Dated:_____

Figure 1-1. Sample Non-Disclosure Agreement, continued

details. Big corporations have large staffs, which can be devoted to year-round planning. As a small-business owner, you have to be more selective.

Your planning may be approaching the paralysis stage if you find yourself soothing your nerves about starting a business by delaying the startup date so you can plan more. If you notice yourself putting off crucial meetings so you can dig up more information for a plan update, suspect that planning has become overly important.

■ *Diluting the effectiveness of your plan.* If you put too much detail into your plan, you run the risk of overburdening anybody who reads it with irrelevant, obscuring detail. A plan isn't supposed to be a potboiler, but it should tell a story—the story of your business. Therefore, it should be as easy as possible to read. That means keeping technical jargon under control and making it readable in one sitting.

Explain any terms that may be unfamiliar to a reader who's not an expert on your industry. And never make the mistake of trying to overawe a reader with your expertise. There's a good chance someone reading your plan will know more than you do. If you come across as an overblown pretender, you can bet your plan will get short shrift.

It's easy to believe that a longer, more detailed plan is always better than a short, concise one. But financiers and others to whom you may send your plan are busy people. They do not have time to plow through an inches-thick plan and may in fact be put off by its imposing appearance. Better to keep it to a couple dozen pages and stick to the truly important material.

■ *Expediting your plan.* While some insist on endless planning, others try to speed up the process. In an effort to get a plan written quickly to show a potential investor, you may find yourself cutting corners or leaving out vital information. You don't want to take forever to prepare a business

> *"If you put too much detail into your plan, you run the risk of overburdening anybody who reads it with irrelevant, obscuring detail. Shorter plans or PowerPoint presentations are cleaner, easier ways to keep it simple."*

plan, but using some of the business plan software programs can make it so easy that you find yourself letting the programs do more of the work. Remember, the tools are there to guide you and not the other way around. Give yourself enough time to make sure that:

1. Each section says what you want it to say.
2. All of your numbers add up and make sense.
3. You have answers to anything readers could possibly ask you.

>> **Expert Advice** <<

Kaye Vivian, an expert in writing business plans, offers this advice on how you can improve your content and presentation.

Content

> *Know your competition.* Be prepared to name them and tell what makes you different from (and better than) each of them. But do not disparage your competition.
> *Know your audience.* You'll probably want several versions of your business plan—one for bankers or venture capitalists, one for individual investors, one for companies that may want to do a joint venture with you rather than fund you, etc.
> *Have proof to back up every claim you make.* If you expect to be the leader in your field in six months, you have to say why you think so. If you say your product will take the market by storm, you have to support this statement with facts. If you say your management team is fully qualified to make the business a success, be sure staff resumes demonstrate the experience needed.
> *Be conservative in all financial estimates and projections.* If you feel certain you will capture 50 percent of the market in the first year, you can say why you think so and hint at what those numbers may be. But make your financial projections more conservative—for example, a 10 percent market share is much more credible.
> *Be realistic with time and resources available.* If you are working with a big company now, you may think things will happen faster than they will once you have to buy the supplies, write the checks,

and answer the phones yourself. Being overly optimistic with time and resources is a common error entrepreneurs make. Being realistic is important because it lends credibility to your presentation. Always assume things will take 15 percent longer than you anticipated. Therefore, 20 weeks is now 23 weeks.

> *Be logical.* Think like a banker, and write what he/she would want to see.

> *Have a strong management team.* Make sure it has good credentials and expertise. Your team members don't have to have worked in the field, but you do need to draw parallels between what they have done and the skills needed to make your venture succeed. Don't have all the skills you need? Consider adding an advisory board of people skilled in your field, and include their resumes.

> *Document why your idea will work.* Have others done something similar that was successful? Have you made a prototype? Include all the variables that can have an impact on the result or outcome of your idea. Show why some of the variables don't apply to your situation or explain how you intend to overcome them or make them better.

> *Describe your facilities and location for performing the work.* If you will need to expand, discuss when, where, and why.

> *Discuss payout options for the investors.* Some investors want a hands-on role; some want to put associates on your board of directors; some don't want to be involved in day-to-day activities. All investors want to know when they can get their money back and at what rate of return. Most want out within three to five years. Provide a brief description of options for investors, or at least mention that you are ready to discuss options with any serious prospect.

Presentation

> *Appearance counts.* Most software programs give you some design options. Choose those that best represent your needs. If you are not using business plan software, look for ways to be creative and imaginative with your graphics, but don't overdo it. Then, double-check everything before you hit "send."

> *Use informative headings in the document.* Use lots of subtitles, and let them sell your idea. Think of websites or *USA Today,* with its short paragraphs and headlines that convey information even if you don't read the article. Make it easy for your readers to find what they want to know. They won't read it from start to finish anyway.

> *Answer the five Ws.* Good journalists tell who, what, where, when, why, and how in their articles. Be sure your business plan does the same.

> *Keep it short.* No matter how complex your technology or how abstract your concept.

> *Package it nicely.* Two-column documents are easier to read than full pages of text. Use charts or tables or graphics or illustrations to break up long passages of words. Add a spot of color on the pages if you have the option—a colored line on the pages or a colored logo or other "spot" color. Readability studies say that adding a second color increases retention of the information.

What Not to Include in a Business Plan

> *Form over substance.* If it looks good but doesn't have a solid basis in fact and research, you might as well save your energy.

> *Empty claims.* If you make a statement without supporting it, you may as well leave it out. You need to follow-up what you say in the

>> Adding Icing to the Cake . . . or Plan

They say rules are made to be broken. While you don't want to go out of your way to go against the grain, sometimes that is just what needs to be done. A recent business plan for a chain of coffee shops, for example, included photos of the proposed location, mock-ups of menus, and maps of the competition's locations. The graphics made the plan longer, but they added real value. Product shots, location shots, blueprints, floor plans, logos, and screenshots of your website can be useful for any type of retail business even if they make the plan a little longer than the norm.

next sentence with a statistic, fact, or even a quote from a knowledgeable source that supports the claim.

> *Rumors about the competition.* If you know for sure a competitor is going out of business, you can allude to it but avoid listing its weaknesses or hearsay. Stick to facts.

> *Superlatives and strong adjectives.* Words like "major," "incredible," "amazing," "outstanding," "unbelievable," "terrific," "great," "most," "best," and "fabulous" don't have a place in a business plan. Avoid "unique" unless you can demonstrate with facts that the product or service is truly one of a kind. (Hint: Chances are, it isn't.) The same goes for hyperbole. Let the positives of your business speak for themselves.

> *Long documents.* If they want more, they will ask.

> *Overestimating on your financial projections.* Sure you want to look good, but resist optimism here. Use half what you think is reasonable. Better to underestimate than set expectations that aren't fulfilled.

> *Overly optimistic time frames.* Ask around or do research on the internet. If it takes most companies 6 to 12 months to get up and running, that is what it will take yours. If you think it will take three months to develop your prototype, double it. You will face delays you don't know about yet—ones you can't control. Remember to be conservative in your time predictions.

> *Gimmicks.* Serious investors want facts, not gimmicks. They may eat the chocolate rose that accompanies the business plan for your new florist shop, but it won't make them any more interested in investing in the venture.

> *Amateurish financial projections.* Spend some money and get an accountant to do these for you. They'll help you think through the financial side of your venture, plus put the numbers into a standard business format that a businessperson expects.

(Above sections © Kaye Vivian.)

>> Ten Keys to a Successful Business Plan

Now that we've discussed business plans in general and explored what should and should not be included, how to present your plan, and some of the risks involved, here is an infographic overview of why you should write a business plan in the first place thanks to Washington State University. The overall basic concepts behind the vast business plan experience are summed up clearly in the following: Ten Keys to a Successful Business Plan.

Steps 1 and 2 to a successful business plan.
Reprinted with permission of Washington State University.
©2014 Washington State University. All rights reserved.

>> Ten Keys to a Successful Business Plan, continued

3 RECOGNIZE HOW YOUR BUSINESS IS UNIQUE

▷ Outline a business model that details the advantages of your organization, in order to ascertain how your business will survive

▷ Scrutinize the strengths and weaknesses of your competition, as well

▷ Distinguish yourself from the crowd to boost your shot at investment capital

▷ 36% of surveyed business owners with a business plan obtained investment capital

▷ Only 18% of those without business plans secured it

4 NAME YOUR KEY STAKEHOLDERS

▷ Identify your management team, board, and advisers

▷ Include the details of their value-add

5 KNOW THE SIZE OF YOUR MARKET

▷ Analyze the market conditions: how big it is, how much is it growing, how fast is it growing and what is its profit potential?

6 KNOW WHO MAKES UP YOUR TARGET MARKET

▷ Your marketing strategies should be clearly aimed at your target market

▷ If not, you're wasting time, effort, and money

CUSTOMER SERVICE

Steps 3 through 6 to a successful business plan.
Reprinted with permission of Washington State University.
©2014 Washington State University. All rights reserved.

>> Ten Keys to a Successful Business Plan, continued

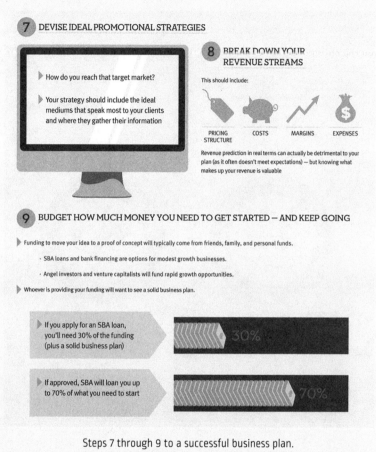

7 DEVISE IDEAL PROMOTIONAL STRATEGIES

▶ How do you reach that target market?

▶ Your strategy should include the ideal mediums that speak most to your clients and where they gather their information

8 BREAK DOWN YOUR REVENUE STREAMS

This should include:

PRICING STRUCTURE   COSTS   MARGINS   EXPENSES

Revenue prediction in real terms can actually be detrimental to your plan (as it often doesn't meet expectations) — but knowing what makes up your revenue is valuable

9 BUDGET HOW MUCH MONEY YOU NEED TO GET STARTED — AND KEEP GOING

▶ Funding to move your idea to a proof of concept will typically come from friends, family, and personal funds.
  · SBA loans and bank financing are options for modest growth businesses.
  · Angel investors and venture capitalists will fund rapid growth opportunities.
▶ Whoever is providing your funding will want to see a solid business plan.

▶ If you apply for an SBA loan, you'll need 30% of the funding (plus a solid business plan)

30%

▶ If approved, SBA will loan you up to 70% of what you need to start

70%

Steps 7 through 9 to a successful business plan.
Reprinted with permission of Washington State University.
©2014 Washington State University. All rights reserved.

>> **Ten Keys to a Successful Business Plan,** continued

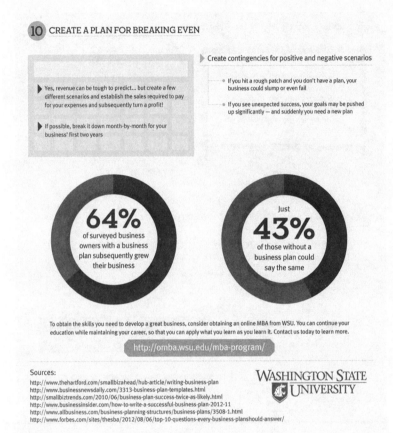

10 CREATE A PLAN FOR BREAKING EVEN

▶ Create contingencies for positive and negative scenarios

▶ Yes, revenue can be tough to predict... but create a few different scenarios and establish the sales required to pay for your expenses and subsequently turn a profit!

▶ If possible, break it down month-by-month for your business' first two years

- If you hit a rough patch and you don't have a plan, your business could slump or even fail

- If you see unexpected success, your goals may be pushed up significantly — and suddenly you need a new plan

64% of surveyed business owners with a business plan subsequently grew their business

Just **43%** of those without a business plan could say the same

To obtain the skills you need to develop a great business, consider obtaining an online MBA from WSU. You can continue your education while maintaining your career, so that you can apply what you learn as you learn it. Contact us today to learn more.

http://omba.wsu.edu/mba-program/

Sources:
http://www.thehartford.com/smallbizahead/hub-article/writing-business-plan
http://www.businessnewsdaily.com/3313-business-plan-templates.html
http://smallbiztrends.com/2010/06/business-plan-success-twice-as-likely.html
http://www.businessinsider.com/how-to-write-a-successful-business-plan-2012-11
http://www.allbusiness.com/business-planning-structures/business-plans/3508-1.html
http://www.forbes.com/sites/thesba/2012/08/06/top-10-questions-every-business-planshould-answer/

WASHINGTON STATE
UNIVERSITY

Step 10 to a successful business plan.
Reprinted with permission of Washington State University.
©2014 Washington State University. All rights reserved.

Before
Beginning
Your Plan

You've decided to write a business plan, and you're ready to get started. Congratulations. You've just greatly increased the chances that your business venture will succeed. But before you draft your plan, you need to focus on several areas from conceptual to "concrete." One of the most important reasons to plan your plan is that you are accountable for the projections and proposals it contains. That's especially true if you use your plan to raise money to finance your company.

Business plans can be complicated documents. You'll be making lots of decisions as you draft your plan, on serious matters, such as what strategy you'll pursue, as well as less important ones like what color paper to print it on. Thinking about these decisions

> *"Your plan may look beautiful, but without a solid under- standing of your own intentions in business, it is likely to lack coherence and, ultimately, prove ineffective."*

in advance is an important way to minimize the time you spend planning and to maximize the time you spend generating income.

Determine Your Goals and Objectives

Close your eyes. Imagine that it's five years from now. Where do you want to be? What will the business look like? Will you be running a business that hasn't increased significantly in size? Will you command a rapidly growing empire? Will you have already cashed out and be relaxing on a beach somewhere, enjoying your hard-won gains?

Now is a good time to free-associate a little bit—let your mind roam, exploring every avenue that you would like your business to go down. Try writing a personal essay on your business goals. It could take the form of a letter to yourself, written from five years in the future, describing all you have accomplished and how it came about.

As you read such a document, you may make a surprising discovery, such as that you don't really want to own a large, fast-growing enterprise but would be content with a stable small business. Even if you don't learn anything new, getting a firm handle on your goals and objectives is a big help in deciding how you'll plan your business. Answering the questions in Figure 2–1 is an important part of building a successful business plan. If you don't have a destination in mind, it's not possible to plan at all.

Your plan may look beautiful, but without a solid understanding of your own intentions in business, it is likely to lack

buzzword

Goals: Business goals are typically long-term calcu- lated plans that you are working toward. They may encompass one or several shorter objectives and can be measured along the way, often by setting up milestones. Goals should be realistic and include a timeframe.

Goals and Objectives Worksheet

If you're having trouble deciding what your goals and objectives are, here are some questions to ask yourself.

1. How determined am I to see this venture succeed? _____

   _____

2. Am I willing to invest my own money and to work long hours for no pay, sacrificing personal time and lifestyle, maybe for years? _____

   _____

3. What's going to happen to me if this venture doesn't work? _____

   _____

4. If it does succeed, how many employees will this company eventually have? _____

   _____

5. What will be its annual sales in a year? Five years? _____

   _____

6. What will be its market share in that time frame? _____

   _____

7. Will it be a niche marketer, or will it sell a broad spectrum of goods and services? _____

   _____

8. What are the plans for geographic expansion? Local? National? Global?

   _____

9. Am I going to be a hands-on manager, or will I delegate a large proportion of tasks to others? _____

   _____

Figure 2-1. Goals and Objectives Worksheet

Goals and Objectives Worksheet

10. If I delegate, what sorts of tasks will I share? Sales? Technical? Others?

_____

11. How comfortable am I taking direction from others? Could I work with partners or investors who demand input into the company's management? _____

_____

12. Is this venture going to remain independent and privately owned, or will it eventually be acquired or go public? _____

_____

Figure 2-1. Goals and Objectives Worksheet, continued

>> Business Planning without a Net

When former Lotus Development CEO Jim Manzi joined a young company called Industry Net Corporation, he had big plans. He helped raise $25 million for the Pittsburgh-based online seller of industrial products, promising to turn it into the leader in internet marketing.

But the company, renamed Nets Inc., wasn't able to fulfill its projections. Employment doubled to 300 as Manzi simultaneously tried to develop a market and the technology to handle complex online transactions. Soon the company was running through its investors' stake at the rate of $3 million a month. Meanwhile, revenues were less than $10 million a month.

After less than two years, Nets Inc. still hadn't developed either its technology or its market in the way its plans had forecast. And investors had tired of waiting. They refused to provide more funding, and Nets Inc. had to file for bankruptcy protection. The experience illustrates the importance of coming up with a plan that not only offers promise but can fulfill that promise as well.

coherence and, ultimately, prove ineffective. Let's say in one section you describe a mushrooming enterprise on a fast-growth track, then elsewhere endorse a strategy of slow and steady expansion. Any business-plan reader worth his or her salt is going to be bothered by inconsistencies like these. They suggest that you haven't thought through your intentions. Avoid inconsistency by deciding in advance what your goals and objectives will be and sticking with them.

>> Business Plan Dog and Cat Story

Noah's Arf

Her friends and family thought Kris Price had lost her mind when she sold her house and left a successful 23-year career with Nike to launch her own business. But after four years of hard work and research, Price achieved her dream.

In June 2002, she opened Noah's Arf, a full-service pet care facility in Portland, Oregon. Her company provided a safe, clean, and fun environment for pets, whether you left them at the Arf or hired the company to visit your pet at your home.

As an exhibit manager for Nike, Price spent a lot of time traveling for business, and finding a good facility at which to leave her dog was challenging. This gave her the idea for the business. She visited dog day-care centers and dog washes all over the country, but she never found one that had all the services she imagined her business would. Her first step was to create a business plan.

"I hadn't written a business plan before. I am not good at writing, so I struggled with it. But I just kept at it and kept at it, and then went back and forth with the SBA and took about a year getting my numbers right. The exercise of writing my business plan totally opened my eyes. Business Plan Pro asked questions that made me think about what was involved and made me do my research," explained Price.

Armed with her business plan, Price approached the SBA for a $200,000 loan. "I had to come up with $70,000 of my own contribution, so I sold my house,

>> **Business Plan Dog and Cat Story,** continued

and gave my car to the business. I lease this place—I wish I owned it. I have put a lot of money into the building considering it's not mine, but I had a vision of what I wanted it to look like. I don't think it would have worked if I had not put the money in. A lot of people asked me, 'Don't you think you are getting in over your head. Why don't you try to launch one thing at a time?' And I replied, 'That's not the concept.' A lot of people have day cares and kitty condos and dog washes, but they don't have all in one. There is nothing else in Oregon like this."

Price's vision turned out to be one that her customers shared. In July 2002 the company broke even and six months after the launch had built up a regular clientele of 20 dogs whose owners drop them off at the Arf every day. The facility had a capacity of 40 day-care dogs and 26 overnight stays, as well as nine kitty condos.

Seven years later, Kris made the last payment on the $200,000 loan she received years earlier to start the business. She acknowledges that without her business plan there is no way she would have been given the loan. "If a person can get through the plan, then they can get anywhere," says Kris.

Today, Noah's Arf is the leading luxury location for dogs and cats in the Portland area.

Focus on Financing

It doesn't necessarily take a lot of money to make a lot of money, but it does take some. That's especially true if, as part of examining your goals and objectives, you envision very rapid growth.

Energetic, optimistic entrepreneurs tend to believe that sales growth will take care of everything, that they will be able to fund their own growth by generating profits. However, this is rarely the case, for one simple reason: You usually have to pay your own suppliers **before** your customers pay you. This cash-flow conundrum is the reason so many fast-growing companies have to seek bank financing or sell equity to finance their growth. They are growing faster than they can afford.

Sometimes the cash-flow gap is very large. Pharmaceutical companies may spend hundreds of millions of dollars in a multiyear project to develop and bring to market a new drug. These companies must have large cash flows from other products to fill the gap or seek loans or other forms of financing to avoid running out of money before having a market-ready product.

Other companies require much smaller amounts of capital to finance their ongoing operations. Small service firms such as local web-design companies or carpet cleaners frequently operate on a cash basis, getting paid with cash, check, or credit card at the time they perform their services after making only small outlays for supplies in advance. But as a general rule, your business will most likely have to consider some kind of financing, as discussed in the next chapter. Now is

buzzword

Objectives: In business, objectives are specific results you are seeking to achieve within a specific time. They are usually short term and are easily measurable. Minimizing expenses, increasing revenue, and rolling out a new product are examples of objectives. They can also help you meet long-term goals.

>> Low-Budget Businesses

You can start a very low-budget business and write a business plan as it evolves to bring in capital for advertising marketing and/or expansion. Many service businesses revolve primarily around using your time, motivation, knowledge, ingenuity, communication skills, and other factors that do not necessitate much outlay of funds. Consultants, counselors, coaches, cleaning services, web designers, writers, organizers, and many other possible businesses can be started by you, in your home, with very little funding.

The main cost will be promoting what you do, and much of that can be done online and by word of mouth. Websites are inexpensive to build, and once you get started you can put your initial income back into the business for a while. Then, when you have a list of clients and even some testimonials from them, you can begin working on your business plan to build up your business.

plan of action

Many enterprises can be started with the help of modest amounts of cash, no more than the contents of a small savings account. You'll find suggestions for hundreds of businesses you can start for amounts as little as nothing plus general startup suggestions in the *Ultimate Start-Up Directory* (Entrepreneur Press, 2007) by James Stephenson, or *Start Your Own Business: The Only Startup Book You'll Ever Need* (Entrepreneur Press) by The Staff of Entrepreneur Media, Inc.

the time to think about some of the issues that will surface.

Start by asking yourself what kinds of financing you are likely to need—and what you'd be willing to accept. It's easy when you're short of cash, or expect to be short of cash, to take the attitude that almost any source of funding is just fine. But each kind of financing has different characteristics that you should take into consideration when planning your future. These characteristics take three primary forms.

First, there's the amount of control you'll have to surrender. An equal-equity partner may, quite naturally, demand approximately equal control. Venture capitalists often demand significant input into management decisions by placing one or more people on your board of directors. Angel investors may be very involved or not involved at all, depending on personal style. Bankers, at the other end of the scale, are likely to offer no advice whatsoever as long as you make payments of principal and interest on time and are not in violation of any other terms of your loan. Second, consider the amount of money you are likely to need. This means carefully considering your startup needs as well as your ongoing operational needs projected for several years.

Once you have determined whether you can launch and run a business for $20,000, $200,000, $2 million, or $200 million, you will be able to consider the various funding sources. You may need to consider several funding sources. See Figure 2–2 for comparisons.

Almost any source of funds, from a bank to a venture capital firm, has some guidelines about the size of financing it prefers. Anticipating the size of your needs now will guide you in preparing your plan.

The third consideration is cost. This can be measured in terms of interest rates and shares of ownership, as well as in time, paperwork, and

Financing Source	Control Issues	Funds Available	Cost
Friends & family	Varies	Usually small	Low or none
Bank loan	Little	Varies	Varies
Partner	Potentially large	Varies	Low
Government-backed loan	Little	Usually small	Low
Venture capital	Large	Moderate to large	Low
Angel investor	Varies	Small to moderate	Low
Stock offering	Large	Large	Large

More on these forms of financing will show up in the next chapter.

Figure 2-2. Financing Characteristics Comparison

plain old hassle. At the top of the list are public offerings of stock, which may cost several hundred thousand dollars in legal and accounting fees to put together and require a great deal of your own time and attention.

Planning: The Purpose of Your Plan

Your business plan can be used for several things, from monitoring your company's progress toward goals to enticing key employees to join your firm. Deciding how you intend to use yours is an important part of preparing to write it.

- *Do you intend to use your plan to help raise money?* In that case, you'll have to focus very carefully on the executive summary, management, and marketing and financial aspects. You'll need to have a clearly focused vision of how your company is going to make money. If you're looking for a bank loan, you'll need to stress your ability to generate sufficient cash flow to service loans. Equity investors, especially venture capitalists, must be shown how they can cash out of your company and generate a rate of return they'll find acceptable.

- *Do you intend to use your plan to attract talented employees?* Then you'll want to emphasize such things as stock options and other aspects of compensation, as well as location, work environment, corporate culture, and opportunities for growth and advancement. If you're a high-tech startup, top employees are likely to ask to see your plans for attracting venture capital and later selling out to a bigger firm or going public so they can realize the value of their stock options.

- *Do you anticipate showing your plan to suppliers to demonstrate that you are a worthy customer?* A solid business plan may convince a supplier of some precious commodity to favor you over your rivals. It may also help you to arrange supplier credit—one of the most useful forms of financing to a small business. You may want to stress your blue-ribbon customer list and spotless record of repaying trade debts in this plan.

- *Do you hope to convince big customers that you will be a dependable supplier?* Then you'll want to emphasize your staying power, innovation, and special capabilities. In this plan, unlike the supplier-targeted one, you may want to play down relationships with other big customers, especially if they are foes of the one you're wooing.

buzzword

Working capital is the amount of money a business has in cash, accounts receivable, inventory, and other current assets. (Current assets are assets likely to be turned into cash within a year.) Net working capital, which is what this term usually refers to, is current assets minus current liabilities. (Current liabilities are things like accounts payable to suppliers and short-term loans due in less than a year.) The higher the amount of net working capital you require, the greater your financing needs are likely to be.

>> When Is a Negative a Positive?

Cash is one of the major constraints on the growth of any business. It's the reason why even highly profitable, fast-growing companies frequently have to go hat in hand to borrowers, seeking money to allow them to fill their orders so they can turn sales into cash. There's one type of company, however, that doesn't have a problem with cash. It's one with a negative cash conversion cycle, which means a company collects the cash several days before having to pay its suppliers.

Amazon.com is an example of a company working with a negative cash flow conversion cycle. Its inventory can be held for nearly 30 days plus roughly another 10 days to collect receivables. That totals 40 days, and it pays receivable in 54 days, allowing it a negative cash conversion cycle of 14 days. In the end, doing business this way means you have the cash before you are spending it. Not many businesses have the success and reputation to make something like this work.

■ *Do you expect to use your plan only for internal purposes?* Then you'll want to build in many milestones, benchmarks, and other tools for measuring and comparing your future performance against the plan. Such things may be of little interest to a banker evaluating your loan-worthiness but could make all the difference between a useful plan and one that's no good at all for monitoring corporate performance.

These distinctions are not merely academic. A plan that's well-suited for internal purposes would probably be completely wrong for taking to a potential Fortune 500 customer. Actually, the marketplace of business-plan consumers is even more finely segmented than that. A plan for a bank, for instance, wouldn't accomplish much by including a strategy for selling the company to a large conglomerate several years down the road, whereas a venture capitalist would look for your exit strategy very early on.

Think about all this, and keep it in mind as you create your plan. Along the way, you'll have to make many decisions about what to include

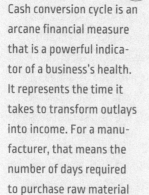

buzzword

Cash conversion cycle is an arcane financial measure that is a powerful indicator of a business's health. It represents the time it takes to transform outlays into income. For a manufacturer, that means the number of days required to purchase raw material and turn it into inventory, then sales, and, finally, collections. The shorter your cash conversion cycle, the better.

or leave out and what to stress or play down. Setting some direction now about how you intend to use your plan will make those later decisions faster and more accurate.

Because many entrepreneurs utilize business plans for various purposes, you'll want to have several versions available. By carefully editing and rewriting certain sections with your audience in mind, you can have plans ready for different occasions. The plan for raising funding will likely be more extensive and detailed than the plan for attracting new employees, who may not want to read as much but will want some answers to the question, "Why should I work at your company?" While the business plan is the sum of various sections, how you massage and edit those sections can help you utilize it for a variety of purposes.

Consider that once you've created a good business plan, you should use it in as many ways as possible, including self-motivation and guidance as you make business decisions and undergo changes.

Get the Software You Need

Now that you've thought about your goals, focused on your financing, and determined the purpose of your plan (and considered to whom you will send it), you'll want to take a practical approach and consider some of the software tools of the trade.

While you remain in the driver's seat, writing the plan and doing all the heavy thinking, your business plan software can handle research, organization, calculations, and more.

Of course, you don't have to use specific business plan software to write your plan. Microsoft Office or any similar software on which you can write each section of your plan can serve your purpose. You can even use Excel, Lotus 1-2-3, or other spreadsheets software to handle the financial pages.

However, should you want to the guidance of a software program, you'll want to find one that meets your computer capabilities, has tech support readily available, and is highly rated. You should also ask other business owners, perhaps in your local chamber of commerce, which ones they used and what they have to say about the software.

The difference between a $59 and $99 software program is typically the features. Some you may want while others may not be applicable for your plan. Looking at business-plan-software-review.toptenreviews.com, you'll find product comparisons, including research tools provided, printing and publishing, support, and more. Look over the plans over and decide which one has what you need.

The functionality of the software and how much instruction is provided are key to making an informed decision. Many have the same or similar features, but those that you can learn without tearing your hair out are the best choices. The latest in software is designed to walk you through the process. However, some walk you more directly while others walk you in a circle before getting you to where you want to go. Do your research.

The bottom line with software, however, is that it can only provide what you ask for. Too often, people misunderstand the capabilities of software. Remember, it cannot write the business plan for you.

Among the various software options, three of the more popular programs to consider are Business Plan Pro, BizPlanBuilder, and Ultimate Business Planner.

Business Plan Pro

Business Plan Pro is very user friendly with split-screen availability that lets you create your plan while following instructions as you go using

plan pitfall

Thanks to plan-writing software's built-in financial formulas, you just have to plug in the data. Because you don't enter the formulas yourself, however, you won't have the same understanding of your financial statements as if you had to think about and manually enter them. So if you use plan-writing software, look under the hood and see what is going on inside all those spreadsheets.

either the online or the desktop version. There are more than 500 complete sample business plans in a variety of industries to help the typical small-business owner formulate a plan.

Business profiles of more than 9,000 industries help narrow down research. You'll find tools that make it easy to create your much-needed forecasts and easily make changes as necessary. You can then design any number of charts and customize them to meet your needs.

The Plan-As-You-Go outline option allows you to use the plan to create your management strategy as you go. This way you can start out with the basics for your own purposes and then build slowly, adding more details to present your plan to lenders or investors.

On the market for more 15 years, with over one million sold, Business Plan Pro has been continuously updated by Palo Alto, the parent company, which also provides excellent customer service.

BizPlanBuilder

Another popular software program, BizPlanBuilder, which offers a Cloud-based online version and a Windows-based app, has menus to guide the writer through the entire process of creating a plan. In addition, much of the research can be found within the software.

You will find many specific features in BizPlanBuilder for the more complex business plan, such as budget analysis with best/worst case scenarios and color-coded tabs to help navigate spreadsheets. There are also business forecasting tools as well as nondisclosure agreements, surveys, worksheets, and business logs.

Easy drop-and-drag navigation lets you customize your plan as you go. You can also interface with Excel and import from PowerPoint applications as well as Word, but not Quickbooks or Peachtree systems. BizPlanBuilder also provides plenty of support as you go.

Ultimate Business Planner

Another strong competitor is Ultimate Business Planner from Atlas Business Solutions, possibly the most user friendly. It is designed to take the stress out of writing a business plan. The Windows-based program has more than 1,000 sample business plans to review and interfaces with

Microsoft Excel, Adobe PDF, and QuickBooks using an easy-to-import wizard to guide you through. There are also plenty of resources for starting your business and that make it easy to create the many forms and documents you'll need, including those with projections and forecasts.

Ultimate Business Planner has plenty of available resources, including valuable data from the SBA. There is also free technical support for a limited time.

Digging for Dollars

A business plan is almost essential for entrepreneurs seeking to raise money to help fund their companies. In fact, business plans are so closely tied to fundraising that many entrepreneurs look at them as suited only for presenting to investors and overlook the management benefits of planning. But for those entrepreneurs who are seeking funding, a business plan accomplishes several things. First, it helps convince potential sources of funding that the entrepreneur has thought the idea through. It also gives any actual investors a set of financial benchmarks for which the entrepreneur can be held accountable.

In a sense, a business plan is a ticket to enter the financial dance. It would be overly simplistic to say that you must have a plan to get funding. But it's not too simplistic to say that a good plan will help you to raise your funds more quickly, more easily, and more completely than you could without it.

Justification of Your Ideas

Before seeking investors, you need to know exactly what you are seeking and where that money will be spent. Not unlike justifying expenses when sending your taxes to the IRS, you need to justify the amounts you are asking for and be specific. Investors are not simply writing out checks with no idea of where the money will be spent. Sure you can ask for a little more than you need in hopes that the negotiating brings you down to the amount you truly need for funding . . . or something reasonably close. It's also important to maintain your credibility because you will probably need additional funding as your company grows. Therefore, if you squander the money your investors have provided, you can be pretty sure you won't get a round two when you need additional funding.

Having justification for what you put in your plan is essential for winning over someone reading it. Random ideas get random results. Well-thought-out, justified ideas get serious consideration.

Assessing Your Company's Potential

It's also advantageous to take a few minutes to make sure that your company has the potential to succeed before digging for those hard-to-get dollars. For most of us, our desires about where we would like to go are not as important as our businesses' ability to take us there. Put another way, if you choose the wrong business, you're going nowhere.

Luckily, one of the most valuable uses of a business plan is to help you decide whether the venture you have your heart set on is really likely to fulfill your dreams. Many, many businesses never make it past the planning stage because their would-be founders, as part of a logical and coherent planning process, test their assumptions and find them wanting.

Test your idea against at least two variables. First, financial, to make sure this business makes economic sense. Second, lifestyle, because who wants a successful business that they hate? Figure 3–1 can help you focus on your financial and lifestyle goals.

Assessing Your Company's Potential

Answer the following questions to help you outline your company's potential. There are no wrong answers. The objective is simply to help you decide how well your proposed venture is likely to match your goals and objectives.

Financial

1. What initial investment will the business require? _____

_____

2. How much control are you willing to relinquish to investors? _____

_____

3. When will the business turn a profit? _____

_____

4. When can investors, including you, expect a return on their money?

_____

5. What are the projected profits of the business over time? _____

_____

6. Will you be able to devote yourself full time to the business financially?

_____

7. What kind of salary or profit distribution can you expect to take home?

_____

8. What are the chances the business will fail? _____

_____

9. What will happen if it does? _____

_____

10. Do you have a backup or alternative plan? _____

_____

Figure 3-1. Assessing Your Company's Potential

>> Tips to Help You Win Funding

Keep these tips in mind to help you win the funding you are searching for:

- Spend extra time working on the executive summary. (See Chapter 6.) Because bankers and professional investors receive so many business plans, they sometimes go right to the executive summary for an overall view of what your plan is all about. If you can't seize their interest in your executive summary, go back to the drawing board and try again.

- Make sure your business plan is complete. You would be surprised at how many business plans are submitted with important data missing. You need to double- and triple-check to make sure all of the important components are included. Even when using business plan software, people skip sections or decide an area is not important. Leave nothing to chance. A well-written and complete business plan gives you a higher chance of success and better odds of getting the financing you are seeking.

- Be able to back up anything you have on paper if asked for more details. While the business plan should have all the answers, investors, bankers, and venture capitalists are shrewd and ask questions that may not be answered in the plan. Be ready to answer anything they can possibly throw at you. Expect the unexpected and prepare for it.

Direct Funding Sources

When you're looking for money, it may seem that investors are scarce. But the real problem may be that you're not looking in enough places for potential financiers. You may find investors as close as your immediate family and as far away as professional venture capitalists on the other side of the world.

Investors come in many shapes and sizes, as well as with various needs and intentions. Odds are you can find someone to help you with your financing needs if you cast your net wide enough.

Your Own Resources

Your own resources, savings, investments, and other valuable assets are the beginning of your financing efforts. One reason to write a business plan is to provide reassurance that you are making a sensible investment. Note that you will be investing serious nonfinancial assets in your business: your time, effort, hopes, and reputation.

As for your own financial assets, make sure the money is not earmarked for tuition or part of your necessary family spending, such as your mortgage, rent, and the like. If you're in debt, it is also advisable to get out from under before starting a business. But, you can start writing your business plan while getting your financial affairs in order.

Even though hopefully you will be investing assets from investors, you should be prepared to invest some of your own money in your business venture. Rule of thumb says if you want other people to invest in you, then you also have to invest in yourself.

Why should other people take a gamble on your business if you won't?

Friends and Family

The most likely source of financing is the group of people closest to you. Spouses, parents, grandparents, aunts, uncles, and in-laws, as well as friends and colleagues, have reasons to help you that arm's-length financiers lack. For that reason, they may back you when no one else will.

One seldom-noticed aspect of asking family and friends to invest in your venture is that other investors (especially bankers and venture capitalists) often ask if you have approached friends and family to raise initial capital. If you say you haven't, they'll then ask why not. If your deal is so appealing, why wouldn't you let your friends in on the ground floor? If you say yes, but they couldn't come through for you, at least the banker or VC will know you tried.

plan of action

Business planning is all about making decisions: How big to grow? How to deal with obstacles? *101 Creative Problem Solving Techniques* (New Management Publishing), by James Higgins, is a book offering a disciplined, effective approach to making the most of all kinds of decisions.

Willingness to take a risk doesn't make friends and family foolish investors. Money from family and friends has backed many very successful business ventures. Here are a few:

- Albertson's Inc. Cofounder Joe Albertson borrowed $7,500 from his aunt to make his $12,500 contribution to the partnership that began the grocery store that grew to have sales of more than $2 billion a year.
- Pizza Hut Inc. Cofounders Frank and Dan Carney borrowed $600 from an insurance fund left by their late father to start the pizza chain.
- Eckerd Corporation. Jack Eckerd raised $150,000 from family members to purchase three failing Florida drugstores, the cornerstone of a company whose sales would one day top $9 billion a year.

buzzword

Direct funding sources invest directly in your business. These include funds from individuals, banks, government agencies, and various levels of professional investors. Indirect funding sources provide trade credit and financing mechanisms such as extended terms on purchases. These are important sources of working capital, but they do not put funds directly into your business.

Friends and family may not be able to raise millions of dollars, but they can provide long-term financing for highly speculative endeavors that more mainstream financiers wouldn't touch.

Even Families Need a Plan

If you're financing your venture with family money, you may think all you need is a smile and a polite request to raise what you need. In the short

>> Familiar Financiers

According to a Babson and Baruch Colleges report, 87 percent of startups still get a financial lift from family members, work colleagues, or friends and neighbors. The report also noted that the median investment amount is $15,000.

term, that may work and produce the funds you need to start out. But over the long term, even family-financed enterprises will benefit from having a business plan.

Such a plan shows family members who are putting up the money what they can expect for their contribution. And it helps keep the entrepreneur—you—mindful of responsibilities to the family members who backed you and on track to fulfill your obligations.

fact or fiction

Think Daddy's money is no way to start a business? Consider that Eddie Bauer had to have his father cosign a $500 loan to open his first tennis shop in Seattle. Spiegel purchased Bauer's catalog operation in 1988 for $260 million.

Pros and Cons of Family Funding

On the positive side, family and friends will let you know if your idea appeals to them. Typically they will also give you the time and a less stressful environment in which to present your plan. Family members may be more readily available to lend a helping hand when you need one and may be there to take over the business down the road.

The flip side is that you are closer to your family and friends. Losing the money of someone close to you can create a lot of tension between you and your family or friends. Family members and friends may also want to get more involved and try to oversee aspects of the business or push you to make changes that other investors would not. They may even expect to be on your management team, which would not be the case with a bank.

In order to make investor agreements work with friends and family, you need to spell out everything clearly and make sure you can separate your business from your personal relationships. This is not necessarily as easy as it sounds. You need to go into any such deals playing some defense and making it clear that people may lose their investments. Provide plenty of warning, and, if they insist on being part of your business, make sure there are boundaries set out in advance that everyone can agree upon.

Crowdfunding

A rather recent entry into the world of procuring funds for projects is crowdfunding. This is a means of gathering funds from a diverse group of investors using internet technology.

plan pitfall

Family members offer tempting capital sources. But emotions can interfere with judgment when dealing with relatives and can lead to hurt feelings as well as possible lawsuits and other entanglements. Minimize the risk of such misunderstandings by fully documenting terms, possible interest rates, and other details for loans and equity investments from family.

If you do not document the terms of such loans in writing, the IRS can either treat the loan as permanent capital or impute a stiff interest rate to the loan. Neither of these options is desirable.

The idea is broad based with some investors on crowdfunding sites getting rewards for investing money while others become investors with a stake in the business. As a result, some of these sites are, like PBS, seeking support from generous people with a passion for a type of business or short-term project or for a cause behind that business or project. Other sites are looking for investors in more full-blown long-term business ventures.

Massolution, a research firm specializing in crowdfunding, reported that the overall industry raised more than $2.7 billion in 2012, across more than 1 million individual campaigns globally and then went on to top that mark in 2013.

Sir Richard Branson, who has invested in the crowdfunding platform Indiegogo, told the *Telegraph* (UK) newspaper that he would have used crowdfunding to start his Virgin empire if it had existed in the 1960s.

Adam Chapnick, former head of Indiegogo, notes that an abbreviated business plan works best for most crowdfunding sites. "Make a big fat business plan—then throw it away," says Chapnick, adding that it is important to go through the process of creating a business plan and then necessary to simplify it and make it quick to convey for crowdfunding.

MicroVentures Marketplace Inc. starts off with a snapshot questionnaire to which you can attach a business plan if you so choose, but it's not required. Like Indiegogo, it would also look for the abridged version of your longer plan.

There are more crowdfunding services coming of age, with new parameters and guidelines, many of which meet specific niche groups.

Rules are changing, in part because of federal and SEC regulations and in part because the crowdfunding services are seeing new ways of doing business. For example, Kickstarter, the early trendsetter in this industry, which has raised over $300 million dollars for over 1,800 projects, will give the new business venture the money that has been raised only if the total amount requested has been reached. Therefore, if you request $10,000 to start a business, and you raise only $7,500 from interested parties, you get nothing. Other services, though, would give you the $7,500. Kickstarter is also more selective about what projects end up on its website, looking for more "trendy" ideas to keep the company in the limelight.

By reviewing the various crowdfunding websites, you can determine which one might be best for your efforts. Look at what the investors will get in return. This can be anything from a gift, not unlike pledging money to PBS, a return on the investment with interest, or, on equity investment crowdfunding websites, a share in the business.

Also keep in mind that many people invest in crowdfunding ventures with their hearts and/or emotions. It is a daring means of investing, but one that drives many crowdfunding investors to put money into something in which they personally believe, such as an environmentally sound business.

Of course there are downsides to crowdfunding, such as putting an idea out there that can be easily stolen or having backers that offer money only while not giving you either the network you need, good business advice, or second rounds of funding. There is also a lot of time spent on marketing to raise your funds. In addition, the SEC is closely watching this new investment opportunity, so you need to be abreast of the latest rules governing crowdfunding.

While Kickstarter and Indiegogo are more frequently used for creative projects, business owners have found success with Crowdfunder.com, Somolend.com, AngelList.com, MicroVentures.com, or CircleUp.com. But there are so many more that you can find by googling "crowdfunding for business."

Banks

Many of the most successful businesses are financed by banks, which can provide small to moderate amounts of capital at market costs. They don't want control—at least beyond the control exerted in the covenants of a loan document. And they don't want ownership. Bankers make loans, not investments, and as a general rule they don't want to wind up owning your company.

Bankers primarily provide debt financing. You take out a loan and pay it back, perhaps in installments consisting of principal and interest, perhaps in payments of interest only, followed by a balloon payment of the principal. One of the nice things about debt financing is that the entrepreneur doesn't have to give up ownership of his company to get it. The cost is clearly stated.

Bankers can usually be counted on to want minimal, if any, input into how the business is run. Most often, as long as you remain current on payments, you can do as you like. Get behind on the payment schedule, and you're likely to find a host of covenants buried in your loan documentation.

Loan covenants, however, may require you to do all sorts of things, from setting a minimum amount of working capital you must maintain to prohibiting you from making certain purchases or signing leases without approval from the bank. In fact, most bank loans contain so many covenants that it's difficult for a borrower to avoid being technically in default on one or more of them at a given time. For this reason, you want your accountant, financial advisor, or attorney to review your loan documents and spell out everything for you very carefully.

Your loan officer is likely to ignore many covenant violations unless you stop, or seem likely to stop, making timely payments. Even then you'll probably get a chance to work out the problem. But if you remain in violation, you may find yourself declared in default in short order, and the bank may demand all of its money immediately, perhaps seizing your collateral and even forcing you to protect yourself by declaring bankruptcy.

What Bankers Want

A banker's first concern is getting the bank's money back plus a reasonable return. To increase the odds of this, bankers look for certain things in the businesses they lend to. Those include everything from a solid explanation of why you need the money and what you're going to use it for to details about any other borrowing or leasing deals you've entered into.

Bank loan applications can be voluminous, almost as long and complete as a full-fledged business plan. Plans and loan applications aren't interchangeable, however. A banker may not be interested in your rosy projections of future growth. In fact, when confronted with the kind of growth projection required to interest a venture capitalist, a banker may be turned off. On the other hand, a banker is likely to be quite interested in seeing a contingency plan that will let you pay back the loan, even in the event of a worst-case scenario. The things a banker will look for you to address are:

- *Cash flow.* One of the most convincing things you can show a banker is the existence of a strong, well-documented flow of cash that will be more than adequate to repay a loan's scheduled principal and interest. Basically, you're going to have to show where you're going to get the money to pay back what you're borrowing.

  You'll need more than a projection of future cash flow, by the way. Most bankers will want to see cash flow statements as well as balance sheets and income statements for the past three or so years. And don't forget your tax returns for the same period.

- *Collateral.* If you're just starting out in business or if you're dealing with a banker you don't know well, you're unlikely to be able to borrow from a bank without collateral. (That's doubly true if, as is the case with many entrepreneurs, both descriptions apply to you.) Collateral is just something the banker can seize and sell to get back some or all of the money you've borrowed in the event that everything goes wrong and you can't pay it back with profits from operations. It may consist of machinery, equipment, inventory, or all too often, the equity you own in your home. It's advisable NOT to put your home up for collateral—it's simply too big a risk.

> **buzzword**
>
> A balloon payment is a single, usually final, payment on a loan that is much greater than the payments preceding it. Some business loans, for example, require interest-only payments the first year or two, followed by a single large payment that repays all the principal.

But it's a good idea to take the initiative here and propose something that will be used if you suspect a banker will require it. Often the collateral will consist of whatever you're borrowing money to buy—production equipment, computers, a building, etc.

Why do bankers seek collateral? They have no desire to own second-hand equipment or your house. Experience has taught them that entrepreneurs who have their own assets at risk are more likely to stick to a business than those who have none of their own assets at risk.

plan pitfall

It seems sensible to plan to put up as collateral the exact item you're borrowing money to buy. But bankers often demand more because it may be impossible to sell the item you're buying for what you'll owe on it. So plan to use purchased equipment for part of your collateral, but be ready to offer more.

- *Cosigners.* They provide an added layer of protection for lenders. If your own capacity for taking on additional debt is shaky, a cosigner (who is essentially lending you his or her creditworthiness) may make the difference.

- *Marketing plans.* More than ever before, bankers are taking a closer look at the marketing plans embedded in business plans. Strong competitors, price wars, me-too products, the fickle habits of the buying public, and other market-related risks must be addressed. There are also very web-savvy marketers out there, and it helps if you are tapped into online marketing, such as social media.

  Your banker (and most other investors) have to know that you recognize these risks and have well-thought-out ways to deal with them. Besides, it's the cash flow from operations that pays off bank loans.

- *Management.* Bankers like to stress the personal aspect of their services. Many state that they are interested in making loans based on a borrower's character as well as her financial strength. In fact, the borrower's track record and management ability are concerns for bankers evaluating a loan application. If you can show you've run one or more other companies successfully, it will increase your chances of landing a loan to get a startup going.

Getting Your House in Order

As an entrepreneur seeking a bank loan, or any type of funding for that matter, you'll want to make sure you have everything in place, including all of your financial documentation as well as your credit history. And, if you need to improve your credit history and rating, you should do so in advance. Even if you have previous experience running a business, you'll need to get your personal credit information in order. Start by contacting one of the three major credit bureaus:

- Equifax: 1-800-685-1111, PO Box 740241, Atlanta, GA 30374; www.equifax.com
- Experian: 1-888-397-3742, PO Box 2002, Allen, TX 75013, www.experian.com
- TransUnion: 1-800-888-4213, PO Box 2000, Chester, PA 19022; www.transunion.com

Do this once because loan officers will also inquire and the more your credit ratings are checked, the more suspicious it may appear to lenders. Also, read your credit reports over *very carefully*, especially if your rating is not as good as you expected it to be. Credit bureaus make more mistakes than you would ever imagine. Make sure there are no errors on your credit reports. If there are errors, call the credit bureau to have them corrected.

fact or fiction

One, two, three strikes you're out. Most small business owners give up after trying three banks. You should be more persistent. Those entrepreneurs that have persisted have found that the fifth, tenth, or even 20th banker has been impressed enough to give them a loan. Of course, tweaking the business plan based on criticism you receive can, and often does, help improve your odds as you continue going from bank to bank. Listen and learn from feedback and criticism, make changes if you feel the comments are relevant, and keep on going. Be persistent.

When Bank Financing Is Appropriate

Bank financing is most appropriate for up-and-running enterprises that can show adequate cash flow and collateral to service and secure the loan. Bankers are less likely to provide startup money to turn a concept into a business, and they are even less likely to put up seed money to prove a concept unless you have a track record of launching previous businesses with successful results. Even then, each concept will stand on its own merits.

Bankers are sensitive to the term or length of a loan. Most bank loans are short to intermediate term, meaning they are due in anywhere from less than a year to five years. A short-term loan may be for 90 days and used to finance receivables so you can get a big order out the door. A longer-term loan, up to 20 years, may be used to purchase a piece of long-lasting capital equipment.

Borrowing When You Really Need It

The old saying about bankers lending only to people who don't need to borrow is almost true. Bankers prefer to lend to companies that are almost, but not quite, financially robust enough to pursue their objective without the loan. Bankers are lenders, not investors. Unlike a venture capitalist who takes an equity position, bankers don't get a higher return on their loan if you happen to be more successful than expected. Their natural tendency is to be conservative.

This is important to understand because it affects how and when you will borrow. You should try to foresee times you'll need to borrow money and arrange a line of credit or other loan before you need it. That will make it easier and, in many cases, cheaper in terms of interest rates than if you wait until you're a needier and, in bankers' eyes, less-attractive borrower.

Credit Unions

Another option when seeking funding is to join a credit union. According to the National Credit Union, there are more than 7,000 credit unions in the country with nearly 100 million members. Because credit unions are not-for-profit financial institutions, their focus is serving the financial needs of their members and not on making a profit. As a result, once you have applied and joined a credit union, it may be easier to get a lower interest rate with fewer

plan of action
When looking for sources of financing go to Entrepreneur's website, www.entrepreneur.com/bestbanks, and check out their up-to-date listing of best banks for entrepreneurs.

fees than can be found at a bank when procuring a loan. However, like a bank, you will still need to prove your credit worthiness and that you can repay the loan or have someone cosign for it.

Because banks have gotten a lot of bad press in recent years for attaching fees to all sorts of activities, many people have switched over to credit unions. One reason is that credit unions typically offer more personalized service, which can include helping you get your house in order before applying for a loan. Credit unions may also offer a sense of camaraderie because they are typically sponsored by a business, a community, or some group of people of which you are one. This can be advantageous because you may find other people interested in your business ideas.

While credit unions are not protected like banks by the FDIC, they are covered by the National Credit Union Share Insurance Fund (NCUSIF). This fund provides federal and most state-chartered credit union members with up to $250,000 of insurance per individual depositor, per federally insured credit union.

Small Business Administration and Other Government Agencies

Sometimes the government really does want to help. The Small Business Administration (SBA) is devoted to helping small-business people get started and run successful businesses. One of its most valuable offerings is a set of financial assistance programs that aim to help you raise the money you need to get started and keep going.

The most popular of several SBA-loan programs is the 7(a) General Small Business Loans. The maximum loan amount is $5 million, but as of 2012, the average loan was $337,730. Loans guaranteed by the SBA are assessed a guaranty fee. This fee is based on the loan's maturity and the dollar amount guaranteed, not the total loan amount. The lender initially pays the guaranty fee, and it has the option to pass that expense on to the borrower at closing. The funds to reimburse the lender can be included in the overall loan proceeds.

The SBA website provides a very comprehensive overview of all its loan programs and provides answers to many typical questions. Along

plan pointer

Lenders look for borrowers exhibiting the four Cs of credit:

1. *Character.* What's your reputation and record?

2. *Capacity or cash flow.* Do you have sufficient cash flow to repay principal and interest?

3. *Capital.* Does your business have enough capital to keep going if you can't pay the debt from earnings?

4. *Collateral.* Do you own something valuable the banker can take if you can't pay the loan back?

with standard business loans, you'll find disaster loans, microloan programs, and real estate and equipment loans.

The SBA can also provide some guarantees. The 7(a) loans, for example, are backed by the full faith and credit of the U.S. government, which guarantees a lender will get back most—but not all—of the money lent out, even if the borrower can't pay. A typical loan guarantee covers 80 percent of the loan. You will find it easier to borrow money and usually get a lower finance rate if you can get an SBA guarantee.

While the SBA sometimes lends money directly to small businesses, most of its financing help is in the form of loan guarantees. To avail yourself of these programs, you need to meet the SBA's definition of a small business and put up pretty much all the business's assets as collateral. Most banks handle SBA-backed loans and can tell you more about the programs. It's easier to learn by going to the SBA.gov website and reviewing its loans. You can also visit one of the SBA district offices.

Angel Investors

If you are having trouble getting funding for your venture under the right terms, or under any terms at all, you'll be glad to know about the existence of angels in the investment world. Angels are individuals who invest their own money, as opposed to institutions or professional money managers, who invest other people's money. Many angels are well-off professionals, such as doctors and lawyers. Some are retired but have tremendous expertise to share in a specific field. Others are successful small-business owners who have made a bundle with their own entrepreneurial efforts and are now interested in letting their money work for them in someone else's venture.

>> Finding an Angel

Angel investors used to be a difficult group to find. Not so any longer. There are groups formed by angels and other organizations, such as Funding Post (fundingpost.com), that arrange for special angel and venture-capitalist showcases in various parts of the country. You can sign up and pay to attend an event at which up-and-coming entrepreneurs, like yourself, get to meet with many angel investors and VCs in one place. Have your short elevator pitch (discussed at the end of the book) ready, and demonstrate the enthusiasm you have for your new business.

Because angels invest their own money, you might think they are the most discriminating, difficult-to-please investors. In fact, they are as a rule much more willing to take a flier on a risky, unproven idea than are professional investors and lenders.

Angels often take a personal interest in a project and may simply believe strongly in the person behind it . . . that's you! They are usually swayed more by personal concerns than by financial ones.

While angel investors used to be located primarily by word of mouth, they are easier to find in the electronic age. ACE-Net is an electronic network of angel investors developed by the SBA. It helps angel investors and small businesses seeking capital meet online. To learn more, visit www.angel-investor-network.com/ACE-Net.html, or call it in White Plains, New York, at (914) 682-2025.

There is an annual fee to enroll in ACE-Net, which varies by state. You can also find the ACE-Net branch in your state on the website.

The Angel Capital Association is another place to learn about angels and seek out an

buzzword

Due diligence refers to all the things an investor should do to check out an investment. It has a legal definition when applied to the responsibilities of financial professionals, such as stockbrokers. In general, it includes such things as requiring audited financial statements and checking warehouses for claimed inventory stocks.

>> Small Business Investment Company Program

The SBA has a program that bridges the capital gap between loans (direct or guaranteed) and equity investments, which are the most difficult to find. Most banks are unwilling to offer very long-term loans (sometimes called "quasi-capital"), and most venture capital firms are unwilling to invest under $3 million in businesses that are unlikely to go public or be acquired for a fancy multiple within three to five years. Enter the Small Business Investment Company (SBIC).

Congress created the SBIC Program in 1958 to fill the gap between the availability of venture capital and the needs of small businesses in startup and growth situations. SBICs, licensed and regulated by the SBA, are privately owned and managed investment firms that use their own capital plus funds borrowed at favorable rates with an SBA guarantee, to make venture-capital investments in small businesses.

Virtually all SBICs are profit-motivated businesses. They provide equity capital, long-term loans, debt-equity investments, and management assistance to qualifying small businesses. Their incentive is the chance to share in the success of the small business as it grows and prospers.

There are two types of SBICs: regular SBICs and specialized SBICs, also known as 301(d) SBICs. Specialized SBICs invest in small businesses owned by entrepreneurs who are socially or economically disadvantaged, mainly members of minority groups.

The program makes funding available to all types of manufacturing and service industries. Many investment companies seek out small businesses with new products or services because of the strong growth potential of such firms. Some SBICs specialize in the field in which their management has special knowledge or competency. Most, however, consider a wide variety of investment opportunities. Go to www.sba.gov/INV/liclink.html for a listing of SBICs.

angel network—a local group of angel investors in your area. Visit them at www.angelcapitalassociation.org. It can also be reached at (913) 894-4700.

Keep in mind that angels are, above all else, unconventional. Many have little training in evaluating business ideas. If 20 angels turn you down, it doesn't mean a thing. Until you've gone through the last name in your Rolodex, you still have a chance of landing an angel backer.

You may also fit angel guidelines if you don't need a whole lot of money. Institutional venture capitalists can, by pooling the funds of several different groups, raise vast sums. It's not unheard of for venture capitalists to invest nine-figure sums—more than $100 million—in relatively new, unproven ventures. Even Bill Gates or Warren Buffett is unlikely to feel comfortable sinking that kind of

plan pitfall

Be careful how much you plan to rely on trade credit. It can be expensive. When all is said and done, you could end up paying as much as 36 percent in annual interest

>> A Pie-Eyed Plan

Gordon Weinberger of Londonderry, New Hampshire, likes to call himself the 6-foot, 9-inch Pie Guy. A better name for the founder and CEO of Top of the Tree Baking Co. might be the dollar-at-a-time guy.

Weinberger started his company as a bakery, making and marketing all-natural apple and other pies. After a few years, he decided he needed to concentrate on the marketing alone, and he contracted out the manufacturing of the pies to larger commercial bakeries. The only problem was, it would take money to reposition his company from being a manufacturer to being a marketer of already-cooked pies. So he took to the road in a gaudily painted school bus. He traveled to spots as disparate as Aspen, Colorado, and wealthy Connecticut suburbs in search of the haunts of the rich and investment-minded. When he rolled up, he presented his business plan and asked for backers.

By the time he pulled out his thumb, Weinberger had raised several hundred thousand dollars, primarily in small amounts. And he was well on the way to a successful restructuring of his ten-person company.

plan pointer

If you're after angels, it's in your interest to guard their interests. Unsophisticated angels may, for instance, give you money without specifying exactly what they are buying, such as percentage of ownership. Such angels can be taken advantage of. But you may want more help someday, and angels tend to talk with each other. So make it legal, make terms clear, and take care of their interests.

money into anything uncertain. Your angels' capacity will vary, of course, but angels tend to start small and see how you are doing before adding to the pot. One of the nicest things about the angel networks that have formed in recent years is that they can pool their resources, giving you a few angel investors in one place at one time. This also makes it easier when you are preparing to meet with angel investors. Rather than meeting one at a time, you can meet several in one angel network or even a couple who will spread the word among their partners so that they can decide as a group.

Venture Capitalists

Venture capitalists represent the most glamorous and appealing form of financing to many entrepreneurs. They are known for backing high-risk companies in the early stages, and a lot of the best-known entrepreneurial success stories owe their early financing to venture capitalists.

When many entrepreneurs write a business plan, obtaining venture-capital backing is what they have in mind. That's understandable. Venture capitalists are associated with business success. They can provide large sums of money, valuable advice, priceless contacts, and considerable prestige by their mere presence. Just the fact that you've obtained venture-capital backing means your business has, in their

fact or fiction

The term "angel investor" sounds like it was bestowed by a happy entrepreneur whose venture was saved by the arrival of one of these well-heeled, risk-welcoming investors. Actually, however, the term comes from the theater, where the label was applied to backers who rescued shows that no one else was willing to finance.

>> When Venture Capital Is an Option

Venture capital is most often used to finance companies that are young without being babies and that are established without being mature. But it can also help struggling firms as well as those that are on the edge of breaking into the big time.

The following are the major types and sources of capital, along with distinguishing characteristics of each.

· *Seed money.* Seed money is the initial capital required to transform a business from an idea into an enterprise. Venture capitalists are not as likely to provide seed money as some other, less tough-minded financing sources, such as family investors. However, venture capitalists will back seedlings if the idea is strong enough and the prospects promising enough. If they see something new and exciting (usually an aspect of technology) and foresee rapid growth (and a strong potential for high earnings), they may jump in and back a fledgling startup. It's a long shot, but it does happen.

VCs, however, are less likely to provide equity capital to a seed-money-stage entrepreneur than they are to provide debt financing. This may come in the form of a straight loan, usually some kind of subordinated debt. It may also involve a purchase of bonds issued by the company. Frequently these will be convertible bonds that can be exchanged for shares of stock. Venture capitalists may also purchase shares of preferred stock in a startup. Holders of preferred shares receive dividends before common stockholders and also get paid before other shareholders if the company is dissolved.

Seed money is usually a relatively small amount of cash, up to $250,000 or so, that is used to prove a business concept has merit. It may be earmarked for producing working prototypes, doing market research, or otherwise testing the waters before committing to a full-scale endeavor.

>> **When Venture Capital Is an Option,** continued

- *Startup capital.* Startup capital is financing used to get a business with a proven idea up and running. For example, a manufacturer might use startup capital to get production under way, set up marketing, and create some actual sales. This amount may reach $1 million.

  Venture capitalists frequently are enthusiastic financiers of startups because they carry less risk than companies at the seed-money stage but still offer the prospect of the high return on investment that VCs require.

- *Later-round financing.* Venture capitalists may also come in on some later rounds of financing. First-stage financing is usually used to set up full-scale production and market development. Second-stage financing is used to expand the operations of an already up-and-running enterprise, often through financing receivables, adding production capacity, or boosting marketing. Mezzanine financing, an even later stage, may be required for a major expansion of profitable and robust enterprises. Bridge financing is often the last stage before a company goes public. It may be used to sustain a growing company during the often lengthy process of preparing and completing a public offering of stock.

  Venture capitalists even invest in companies that are in trouble. These turnaround investments can be riskier than startups and therefore even more expensive to the entrepreneurs involved.

  Venture capital isn't for everybody, but it provides a very important financing option for some young firms. When you're writing a business plan to raise money, you may want to consider venture capitalists and their unique needs.

eyes at least, considerable potential for rapid and profitable growth.

Venture capitalists both lend to and make equity investments in young companies. The loans are often expensive, carrying rates of up to 20 percent. They sometimes also provide what may seem like very cheap capital.

That means you don't have to pay out hard-to-get cash in the form of interest and principal installments. Instead, you give a portion of your or other owners' interest in the company in exchange for the VC's backing.

What Venture Capitalists Want

While venture capitalists come in many forms, they have similar goals. They want their money back, and they want it back with a lot of interest and capital growth.

VCs typically invest in companies that they foresee being sold either to the public or to larger firms within the next several years. As part owners of the firm, they'll get their rewards when such sales go through. Of course, if there's no sale or if the company goes bankrupt, they don't even get their initial money back.

VCs aren't quite the plungers they may seem. They're willing to assume risk, but they want to minimize it as much as possible. Therefore, they typically look for certain features in companies they are going to invest in. Those include:

plan pitfall

Many VCs insist on placing one or more directors on the boards of companies they finance. And these directors are rarely there just to observe. They take an active role in running the company.

VCs also are reluctant to provide financing without obtaining an interest in the companies they back, sometimes a very significant and controlling interest. This can make them just as influential as if they had a majority of the directors on the board, or more so.

- Rapid sales growth
- A proprietary new technology or dominant position in an emerging market
- A sound management team
- The potential to be acquired by a larger company or be taken public in a stock offering within three to five years
- High rates of return on their investment

Rates of Return

Like most financiers, venture capitalists want the return of any funds they lend or use to purchase equity interest in companies. But VCs have some

buzzword

Turnaround is the term used to describe a reversal in a company's fortunes that takes it from near death to robust health. For example, in the 1970s, Chrysler had to be bailed out by the federal government. Then in the 1990s, Daimler-Benz bought the turned-around Chrysler in what was at the time history's biggest industrial buyout. Some turnarounds are faster, taking months or weeks. Some never happen at all.

very special requirements when it comes to the terms they want and, especially, the rates of return they demand.

Venture capitalists require that their investments have the likelihood of generating very high rates of return. A 30 percent to 50 percent annual rate of return is a benchmark many venture capitalists seek. That means if a venture capitalist invested $1 million in your firm and expected to sell out in three years with a 35 percent annual gain, he or she would have to be able to sell the stake for approximately $2.5 million.

These are high rates of return compared with the 2.5 percent or so usually offered by ten-year U.S. Treasury notes and the nearly 10 percent historical return of the U.S. stock market. Venture capitalists justify their desires for such high rates of return by the fact that their investments are high-risk.

Most venture-backed companies, in fact, are not successful and generate losses for their investors. Venture capitalists hedge their bets by taking a portfolio approach: If one in ten of their investments takes off and six do OK, then the three that stutter or fail will be a minor nuisance rather than an economic cold bath.

Cashing-Out Options

One key concern of venture capitalists is a way to cash out their investment. This is typically done through a sale of all or part of the company, either to a larger firm through an acquisition or to the public through an initial offering of stock.

In effect, this need for cashing-out options means that if your company isn't

buzzword

Rate of return is the income or profit earned by an investor on capital invested in a company. It is usually expressed as an annual percentage.

seen as a likely candidate for a buyout or an initial public offering (IPO) in the next five years or so, VCs aren't going to be interested.

Being Acquired

A common way for venture capitalists to cash out is for the company to be acquired, usually by a larger firm. An acquisition can occur through a merger or by means of a payment of cash, stock, debt, or some combination.

Mergers and acquisitions don't have to meet the strict regulatory requirements of public stock offerings, so they can be completed much more quickly, easily, and cheaply than an IPO. Buyers will want to see audited financials, but you—or the financiers who may wind up controlling your company—can literally strike a deal to sell the company over lunch or a game of golf. About the only roadblocks that could be thrown up would be if you couldn't finalize the terms of the deal, if it turned out that your company wasn't what it seemed, or, rarely, if the buyout resulted in a monopoly that generated resistance from regulators.

Venture capitalists assessing your firm's acquisition chances are going to look for characteristics like proprietary technology, distribution systems, or product lines that other companies might want to possess. They also like to see larger, preferably acquisition-minded, firms in your industry. For instance, Microsoft, the world's largest software firm, frequently acquires small personal-computer-software firms with talented personnel or unique technology. Venture capitalists looking at funding a software company are almost certain to include an assessment of whether Microsoft might be interested in buying out the company someday.

Going Public: Initial Public Offerings (IPOs)

Some fantastic fortunes have been created in recent years by venture-funded startups that went public. Initial public offerings of their stock

plan pitfall

Some VCs specialize in a field, such as retail, bio-technology, or high-tech. Others have a regional focus. But whatever his or her special interests, almost any venture capitalist will admit to desiring the basic charac-teristics of steady growth, market dominance, sound management, and poten-tial for going public in an investment.

plan of action

The National Association of Certified Valuation Analysts is the trade group for people whose business is deciding what businesses are worth. It can help you find a valuation analyst as well as learn the basics of figuring a business's worth. Contact NACVA at NACVA.com or call it at (801) 486-0600.

have made numerous millionaires, seemingly overnight. For example, when Twitter made its initial public offering at a price of $26 in November 2013, the stock took off, gaining as much as 93 percent within a day and creating 1,600 millionaires. Wow! IPOs have made many millions for the venture investors who provided early-stage financing.

The 2012 passage of the Jumpstart Our Small Business Startups (JOBS) Act allows for confidential filing of IPO-related documents. This has made it easier for small business owners who do not want their numbers getting out to the public too soon. There was often concern about investors getting too much preliminary information that could influence their decision to commit to the company. Confidentiality has increased the number of IPO filings in the small business community.

Nonetheless, an IPO takes lots of time. You'll need to add outside directors to your board and clean up the terms of any sweetheart deals with managers, family, or board members as well as have a major accounting firm audit your operations for several years before going public. If you need money today, in other words, an IPO isn't going to provide it.

An IPO is also probably the most expensive way to raise money in terms of the amount you have to lay out up front. The bills for accountants, lawyers, printing, and miscellaneous fees for even a modest IPO will easily reach six figures. For this reason, IPOs are best used to raise amounts at least equal to millions of dollars in equity capital. Venture capitalists keep all these requirements in mind when assessing an investment's potential for going public. Keep in mind that the number of new businesses that go public is quite small.

Bonds

There are two kinds of debt financing: straight loans and bonds. Bonds give you a way to borrow from a number of people without having to do separate deals with each of them. If you need to borrow $500,000, for instance, you can issue 500 bonds in $1,000 denominations. Then you can sell those bonds to anyone who'll buy them, including family, friends, venture capitalists, and other investors subject to stringent legal constraints.

Corporations use a bewildering variety of bonds for financing, but the most common type simply calls for you to pay a stated amount of interest on the face amount for a certain period. After that time, usually five years, you pay back the face amount to the buyer.

Bonds give you the great advantage of being able to set the interest rate and terms and amount you're trying to raise instead of having to take whatever a lender offers. The problem with bonds is that they are regulated similarly to public stock offerings. So although they're widely used by big companies, very few small companies issue them.

fact or fiction

Many entrepreneurs dream of going public. But IPOs are not for every firm. The ideal IPO candidate has a record of rapidly growing sales and earnings and operates in a high-profile industry. Some have a lot of one and not much of the other. Low earnings but lots of interest characterize many biotech and internet-related IPOs. These tech companies are usually the ones that generate the huge IPOs and instant millionaires we read about.

There is an exception to this general rule. Some states pool together long-term loans in state-guaranteed industrial bonds for industrial (read: job-creating) businesses. This has the advantage of lowering the issuing costs for the companies involved while providing the patient quasi-capital they need to succeed. Check with your state's economic development department.

Indirect Funding Sources

Direct funding sources put money into your business. Indirect funding sources postpone taking money out of the business, thus conserving working capital. Trade credit is far and away the most important indirect source of funding.

Trade Credit

You don't need a loan application, permission from the Securities and Exchange Commission, or even a note from your mother to take advantage of one of the most useful and popular forms of financing around. Trade credit, the credit extended to you by suppliers who let you buy now and pay later, can make a substantial difference to your cash flow.

You can measure the amount of trade credit you have outstanding by simply adding up all your accounts payable, or the amount outstanding of bills on your desk. Any time you take delivery of materials, equipment, or other valuables without paying cash on the spot, you're using trade credit.

For many businesses, trade credit is an essential form of financing. For instance, the owner of a clothing store who receives a shipment of bathing suits in April may not have to pay for them until June. By that time, she can hope to have sold enough of the suits to pay for the shipment. Without the trade credit, she'd have to look to a bank or another source for financing.

> **buzzword**
>
> Factoring is the flip side of trade credit. It's what happens when a supplier sells its accounts receivables to a financial specialist, called a factor. The factor immediately pays the amount of the receivables, less a discount, and receives the payments when they arrive from customers. Factoring is an important form of finance in many industries.

>> **Expert Advice** <<

Jim Casparie, the founder and CEO of The Venture Alliance, a national firm based in Irvine, California, dedicated to getting companies funded, talked to several professional investors at VentureNet, a conference run by the Software Council of Southern California.

The individuals he interviewed included David Cremin, managing director of DFJ Frontier; Michael Song, a partner with Rustic Canyon; Bill Collins, managing partner of Publex Ventures; and Robert Kibble, managing partner of Mission Ventures. Some additional comments and insights were also provided by Jon Kraft, chair of the Software Council of Southern California.

So what do these gentlemen prefer to see in a company before they get excited enough to write a check?

1. *Seasoning.* They're looking for more experienced, older entrepreneurs who have "been there, done that." The time of investing in the 19-year-old kid who's a tech genius isn't necessarily gone, but the kid had better be able to find an older, seasoned executive to join his team.

2. *Customers.* Rather than putting the emphasis on *the team* or *the revenue numbers*, there seemed to be a new emphasis on the customer:
   - What compels them to buy *this* product or service?
   - What problems does this product or service solve? Why is it better than the alternatives?
   - Why is it worth the price?
   - Does it compel you to tell others about your experience?
   - Are your customers asking if they can invest in your company?

3. *Team.* The team is still an important part of the equation, but the entrepreneur is just as important. Here's what the investors are looking for in both:
   - *Passion:* The entrepreneur must demonstrate a contagious excitement about his vision for the company.
   - *Tenacity:* The entrepreneur must prove he has the stamina and willpower to stay with his vision through thick and thin.
   - *Flexibility:* The entrepreneur must be willing to reevaluate and refocus his plans when things don't work out as anticipated.
   - *Commitment:* The entrepreneur must be willing to invest enough of his own money into this project to convince investors he is serious.
   - *Teamwork:* The entrepreneur's team must prove it can work effectively together.
   - *Coachability:* The entrepreneur and the team must be coachable. No team knows everything they need to know to succeed.
   - *Knowledge:* Investors prefer to back teams that really know their market and have a combined background that is rich and impressive in the niche for which the company is engaged.

4. *Opportunity.* Investors want *big* ideas, those that can change the world. Ideas that change our behavior, culture, or way of thinking. Ideas that can build $100-million-size companies. Anything less is too speculative. The risks of investing in a company are so great—and the chances of a reward so small—that investors can't afford to bet on opportunities that won't surely have huge payoffs. And one of the biggest problems when addressing opportunity is, "Am I too early?" Investing in a huge opportunity five years before the market will recognize and embrace it is a very frustrating thing. Not only will you lose your investment, you'll have to suffer the extreme frustration of watching someone else make a lot of money on the foundation you helped build.

5. *Business Model.* Will the numbers map out? In other words, once someone takes a sharp pencil and starts tracing where every revenue dollar comes from and then seriously challenges every expense it'll take to generate that revenue dollar, will you have

- a *profitable* model?
- a *repeatable* model?
- an *expandable* model?
- a *predictable* model?
- a *defensible* model?

> *"It's also important to remember that very, very few investors will decide to work with a company based just on a business plan."*

Many entrepreneurs fail because they don't know how to do this type of exercise with a "real world" view.

Well, there you have it: the latest and deepest thinking from a sample of professional investors. How do you and your company match up? If you were honest and found areas where you were lacking, *please* find someone who can help you fix them *before* you approach anyone to invest. Your extra investment of time will significantly improve your chances for funding.

Put
Your Plan
to Work

The process of writing your business plan helps you take a thorough, careful, and comprehensive look at the most important facets of your business, including the contexts in which it operates. Just raising questions can sometimes lead to a solution, or at least ensure that if conditions change you won't be forced to make decisions hastily. The ongoing "what if this or that happens?" inherent in the planning process keeps you alert. In other words, the planning process itself makes you a far more capable manager and entrepreneur than you would be without it. For many, this is a more valuable result than securing funding.

In many ways, writing a business plan is an end in itself. The process will teach you a lot about your business that you are unlikely to learn by any other process. You'll spot future trouble areas, identify opportunities, build confidence in the strength of your ideas, and help your organization run smoothly, simply through the act of writing a plan.

Evaluating a New Venture

Lisa Angowski Rogak is an entrepreneur who started several newsletters in much the same way. She devised a plan focusing on marketing strategy and cash-flow projections to see if she could come up with a way to sell the newsletters while keeping her bills paid. She then prepared a sample issue to be used in a direct-mail and publicity campaign. "Planning is the key to the success of your newsletter," says Rogak. "It's the single most important thing you can do to ensure the success of your newsletter."

That's the kind of encouragement that helps entrepreneurs persevere, whether they have an existing concern that's hitting a rough spot or a startup concept that nobody else seems to believe in. Numbers can lie, of course, and nobody can create a spreadsheet that really tells the future. But evaluating financial data is to entrepreneurship what evaluating lab results is to a medical doctor. If your vital signs are good, odds are your future will be as well.

But what if the odds don't look so favorable? What if the first pass through your cash-flow projection or income pro formas contains more red than a fire-station paint locker? Sure, you can go back and look for an error or an overly pessimistic or conservative assumption. You can even try altering a few of the inevitable numbers that you really have no way of estimating accurately to see where the pressure points are, if nothing else.

But what if you do that, even pushing your alterations past the point of credibility, and your plan still doesn't make sense? Well, in that case, you've probably done yourself the really big favor of finding out something isn't going to work before you sink your money into it. Nobody knows exactly how often this happens, but it's safe to say that a lot of businesses are never attempted because the plan convincingly says that they shouldn't be.

Is that bad? Well, it may feel bad. But think how much worse you would feel if you went ahead with the venture, and things turned out as the plan forecast. Business planning is a powerful tool for evaluating the feasibility of business ventures. Use it.

It would be a shame to keep the benefits of a well-done plan to yourself. And you shouldn't. You can use your plan to find funding. But a good plan can also help sell your products, services, and your whole company to prospects and suppliers. Furthermore, a plan is a valuable tool for communicating your visions, goals, and objectives to other managers and key employees in your firm.

> *"Business planning is a powerful tool for evaluating the feasibility of business ventures."*

Informing Suppliers and Customers

Increasingly, companies large and small have been trying to trim the number of suppliers and customers they deal with and develop deeper and stronger relationships with the ones they keep. An essential part of this is getting to know more about existing and prospective vendors and clients. So don't be surprised if one day, when you're trying to set up a new supplier relationship or pitch a deal to a big company, the person you're negotiating with asks to see your business plan.

Why do suppliers care about business plans? Suppliers want to sell only to people who can pay, which is one important reason a new supplier could ask to see your business plan before taking a big order. Remember, if a supplier is selling to you on credit—letting you take delivery of goods and pay for them later—that supplier is, in effect, your lender. Suppliers who sell for other than cash on delivery have the same legitimate interest in your business's strategy and soundness as does a banker.

Say a supplier's analysis of customer records shows it has a knack for developing long-term profitable relationships with moderate-sized companies that emphasize excellent service, price at a premium level, and provide only the best merchandise. Business plans provide all the information such a company will need to find and clone its best customers. So if a supplier asks to see your plan, be willing to share it. It could be the start of a long and mutually beneficial relationship.

Customers are likely to be concerned about how well your respective strategies fit with theirs. For instance, say your mission statement says that you intend to produce the best-in-the-world example of your product no matter what the cost. Your customer, meanwhile, is a high-volume, low-price reseller of the type of products you make. Even if your offering fits the customer's need this time, odds are good that the relationship won't work out over the long haul. If, on the other hand, a look at your business plan reveals that your companies share the same kind of strategies and have similar objectives in type if not scope, it's an encouraging sign.

Managing with Your Plan

The spread of the open-book management theory means a lot more employees are seeing their companies' business plans than ever before. When employees get the key information managers are using to make decisions, they understand management better and make better decisions themselves, and efficiency and profitability often increase as a result. This is transparency in business.

Many companies hold annual meetings at which they present an edited version of the business plan and discuss it with their employees. You can also use bulletin boards or company newsletters to publish smaller sections of your plan, such as your mission statement or some details of financial objectives and how you're progressing.

One drawback to using excerpts of a business plan to help inform and manage your employees is that some people won't understand it, especially taken out of context. Often, companies have some materials to email employees about reading financial reports, etc.

Monitoring the Performance of Your Business

Using a business plan to monitor your performance has many benefits. If your cash flow is running much shorter than projected at the moment, even though you're not currently in trouble, that information may help you to spot disaster before it occurs. By comparing plan projections with actual results, you gain a deeper understanding of your business's pressure points or the components of your operation that have the most effect on results.

Spotting Trouble Early

You don't have to be a wizard to get some solid hints about the future beyond tomorrow, especially when it comes to the operations of your own business. You can look at virtually any page of your business plan and find an important concept or number describing some expected future event that, if it turns out to be diverging from reality, may hint at future trouble.

Say your profit margins are shrinking slowly but steadily, and the trend seems irreversible. If you notice that within a few months, your declining margins will push your break-even point too high to live with, you can take action now to fix the problem. You may need to add a new, higher-margin product, get rid of an old one, or begin stressing marketing to a more profitable clientele. All these moves, and many more you could take, have a good chance of working if your careful comparison of plan projections with actual results warns you of impending danger. Use the projections in your business plan as guideposts as you move forward.

Understanding Pressure Points

Not all tips that come from comparing plans with results have to do with avoiding danger. Some help you to identify profit opportunities. Others may show how seemingly minor tweaks can produce outsized improvements in sales or profitability. For example, the plan for a one-person professional service business indicated that rising sales were not, in general, accompanied by rising costs. Fixed items such as office rent and insurance stayed the same, and even semivariable costs such as electric bills will vary only slightly. The bulk of any extra business went straight to the bottom line, showing up as profit improvement. But one cost that didn't seem especially variable went up sharply as business volume climbed. That was the number of transactions.

Ordinarily this would be a given and not necessarily a matter of grave concern. A large enterprise would simply hire a few more modestly paid customer service reps, credit department staff members, or bookkeepers to handle the added orders, invoices, and the like. For this single professional, however, added paperwork comes at a very high cost—her own time.

Somehow in her projections of steadily rising sales volume, she had neglected to note that more business meant more invoices to be sent out, more account statements to be mailed or emailed, more customers to be reminded to pay, more time spent on banking needs, and so on. All this work, while not necessarily unpleasant, was taking up more and more of her time.

As a part of checking her plan against results, she noticed this unexpected increase in transactions and figured out what it meant. She calculated that, when taking all paperwork into account, she spent roughly an hour on each transaction no matter how large or small. She realized that one of the most important pressure points in her business was related to the size of a transaction. By refusing small engagements and seeking clients who could offer big jobs, she would reduce the amount of time spent on otherwise unproductive paperwork and increase the time she could spend completing client requirements.

Ultimately, she was able to trim what had been 100 annual transactions down to 75, while increasing the amount of her dollar revenue. The result was a free 25 hours to spend working on more business or even vacationing. If you can see and relieve a pressure point like that, you can really keep your business from boiling over.

There are few things to equal the sensation of filling in all the numbers on a cash-flow projection, hitting the recalculate button, and scrolling to the bottom of your spreadsheet to see what the future holds. If the news is good

plan pitfall

Caveat time. The fact that your business is unlikely to perform exactly as planned is no reason to skip planning! A plan isn't worthless just because it doesn't present the future with perfect accuracy. At worst it can help you monitor how reality is stacking up to your plan. If your plan seems way off base, you may need a fix—or another plan.

and you see a steady string of positive cash balances across the bottom row, you know that, assuming your data is good and your assumptions reasonable, your business has a good chance of making it.

Do the Numbers Add Up?

Many businesses fail because of events that are impossible to foresee. If you'd begun a car dealership specializing in yacht-sized gas guzzlers right before the Arab oil embargo in the 1970s, you would probably have been out of business in less time than one had to sit on the resulting lines at gas stations, through no fault of your own. The same might go for a software startup that comes out with a new program just before Microsoft unveils a top-secret, long-term development effort to create something that does the same job for a lot less money.

It's probably not a bad idea, as part of your business-planning process, to include some information in your business plan about the activities or intentions of potential embargos. If nothing else, crafting a backup plan is a good idea should something happen that is out of your control. Preparation for unexpected disasters can make or break your business. The companies that had off-site backup of their documents after Katrina hit New Orleans in 2005 had far better chances of restarting their businesses than those that had to begin from scratch. Of course, some things are just wild cards and can't be predicted. For these you just have to trust the luck of the draw.

So what numbers have to add up? Certainly you have to be selling your products and services at a profit that will let you sustain the business long-term. You'll also have to have a financial structure, including payables-and-receivables systems and financing, that will keep you from running out of cash even once. If you have investors who want to sell the company someday, you may need a plan with a big number in the field for shareholders' equity on the projected balance sheet.

When you're asking yourself whether the numbers add up, keep the needs of your

plan of action

While putting together your numbers, include a capital reserve fund to spend on special projects or to be used for unforeseen emergencies.

>> Fitting with Ford

The automobile industry provides one of the clearest examples of the extent to which big companies are trying to cut the number of suppliers they do business with. Ford Motor Co. has gone especially far in reducing the number of its suppliers. "In one of our vehicles, we now have one overall supplier, plus four other suppliers, for a total of five," says C. W. Graning, procurement strategy manager for purchasing and supply development and strategy at Ford. "In the past, we had a total of 27."

When you look at the bigger picture, it's even more startling. In 1983, Ford had more than 1,800 suppliers. By 1993, it had 825. By 1998, the number had shrunk to 600. What that meant for the losing suppliers, of course, was that they had to replace the sales to the Dearborn, Michigan, giant or perish. Ford once again increased its number of suppliers in the new century and was up to 1,260 by 2012, but once again, they had to start cutting down and within a year had dropped the number back to 750.

As is the case when businesses cull the number of suppliers, those who made the cut get even more business from Ford than before. How did they pass Ford's muster? The answer is by fitting into Ford's management system. That means lots of reports, lots of analysis, and lots of planning. In fact, a comprehensive business plan describing how the supplier will work with Ford in every aspect of the supplier-customer relationship is one of the key criteria of the automaker in selecting companies to become its long-term bosom buddies.

It's not exactly going with the low bid, but for those who have the ability to prepare convincing plans, seeking business from big companies that are cutting the number of their suppliers can be rewarding indeed.

business and your business partners in mind. Even if it looks like it'll take an air strike to keep your business from getting started, you don't want to do it if the numbers say that long-term it's headed nowhere. Therefore, you need to look carefully at the trends in your industry and try to determine where it will be in 5, 10, or 20 years. No, it's not easy to do, but you can see where innovation and new ideas are coming from and how they might change the face of your industry.

Attracting Good People

First, "good people" is a very subjective term. A person with a great resume, treated poorly by management, is no longer very motivated and likely NOT to be a "good person." Conversely a "bad person," based on what you have on paper, may, with some training, trust, and fair treatment, turn out to be a very good hire.

Nonetheless, a good business plan can help you attract what are considered to be "good people," from managers and other employees to vendors, suppliers, and partners. It gives people the idea that you have a well-thought-out plan of action so they have more confidence that you have credibility and feel they are not jumping onboard what may soon be a sinking ship. It can also give up-and-comers the idea that you offer training and advancement.

What you offer as an entrepreneur will determine whom you will attract. In any economy, good or bad, people want to be treated with respect and are more likely to become part of your team if they see advancement and a corporate culture they can embrace. Therefore, just like dating, you need to present yourself and your business in a way that will give others a positive impression.

Prospective Partners

Partners are like any other investor, and it would be a rare one who would come on board without some kind of plan. Partners want to know your basic business concept, the market, and your strategy for attacking it; who else is on your team; what your financial

fact or fiction

Every business is different, so every plan should be different, right? Not necessarily. Ken Olsen raised money to start Digital Equipment Corporation with the help of a plan copied out of a textbook. He just changed the name and a few numbers and other facts. That said, be careful. Templates can make your business plan appear similar to those of other companies, some of which could be competitors. If you are utilizing other plans for guidance, at least be creative in your writing and presentation.

>> Is Success Easy?

A January 2014 study by *Entrepreneur Weekly*, Small Business Development Center, Bradley University, and University of Tennessee Research shows that

- 25 percent of startups will fail after one year,
- 50 percent of startups will fail after four years, and
- 63 percent of startups will fail after seven years.

The findings also showed success by industry (i.e., were still in business) after four years:

- Finance, insurance, and real estate had a 58 percent chance.
- Health, education, and agriculture had a 56 percent chance.
- Manufacturing business had a 49 percent chance.
- Both retail and construction had a 47 percent chance.

plan of action

The Employee Benefit Research Institute (EBRI) conducts regular studies and surveys to find out what employees want and what employers are giving them. To learn more about what benefits you should offer to attract the best, go to EBRI.org or call it at (202) 659-0670.

performance, strengths, and needs are; and what's in it for them. Luckily, these are exactly the same questions a business plan is designed to address, so you're likely to please even a demanding prospective partner by simply showing him or her a well-prepared plan. The one difference is a plan probably won't contain the details of a partnership agreement. And you'll need one of these to spell out the conditions of your partnership, no matter how well you and your prospective partner know, understand, and trust one another. Have an attorney who is familiar with partnerships help draft the paperwork so you are on the same page from the start and know exactly what is expected of each partner.

Take a Conservative Stance

While you don't want to fail, there is a point when writing a business plan that you admit the possibility of failure. It's only natural to create a plan that will describe a roaring success, but you have to be careful not to present an overly optimistic view, especially of such elements as sales, costs, and profit margins.

It's tempting to noodle around with the numbers until you come up with the desired result. And if you make only small changes here and there, it may seem all right. What difference does it make? Say you increase your projected market share by 1 percent

> *"If your plan indicates that the business idea isn't sound, by all means look for errors."*

here, reduce expected costs by 2 percent there, and lower your estimate of required startup capital by a few percentage points as well.

A number of similarly small changes, in sum, can make a big difference in the bottom line of your plan and turn what otherwise looks like a loser into a projected winner. But don't be seduced. You may be asking for investments from friends and family you care about as well as putting your own life savings into the enterprise. The feelings of arm's-length investors may not be so important, but if you mislead them in your plan, you may open yourself up to accusation of misrepresentation.

Looking at things in your plan through rose-colored glasses may even doom your business to failure if it causes you to seek insufficient startup capital, underprice your product or service, or expect unrealistically rapid growth. Temper your enthusiasm. If your plan indicates that the business idea isn't sound, by all means look for errors. But don't make the mistake of skewing your plan to fit an idea that isn't sound.

Updating Your Plan

Writing a business plan is one of those skills that improve with practice. The first one or two times you create a plan you may feel a little unsure of yourself and even less certain that what you're doing has value.

If you go on to start several ventures during your career, you'll naturally write several business plans, and each one will be better than the last. It's likely as well that with better planning skills will come improved business skills, boosting the odds that each successive company you start will do better than the previous one.

But there's no reason that only serial entrepreneurs should get the benefit of regular business-planning sessions. If you start just one company, or even if you never start a company at all, you should be constantly honing your business-planning skills by updating your business plan.

Updating a plan is normally easier than starting from scratch. Instead of trying to figure out what your basic business concept is, you only have to decide whether it's changing. You'll usually be able to reuse the financial

>> Will You Need to Update Your Plan?

Here are eight reasons to think about updating your plan. If one applies to you, it's time for an update.

1. A new financial period is about to begin. You may update your plan annually, quarterly, or even monthly if your industry changes quickly.

2. You need financing. Lenders and other financiers need an updated plan to make financing decisions.

3. Significant markets change. Shifting client tastes, consolidation trends among customers, and altered regulatory climates can trigger a need for plan updates.

4. New or stronger competitors are looking to your customers for their growth.

5. Your firm develops a new product, technology, service, or skill. If your business has changed a lot since you wrote your plan, it's time for an update.

6. You have had a change in management. New managers should get fresh information.

7. Your company has crossed a threshold, such as moving out of your home office, reaching $1 million in sales, or employing 100 people.

8. Your old plan doesn't seem to reflect reality anymore. Maybe you did a poor job last time. Maybe things have just changed faster than you expected. But if your plan seems irrelevant, redo it.

formulas, spreadsheets, management biographies, and other more or less evergreen contents of your plan.

It's important, however, that a plan update not be a mechanical task, limited to plugging in the most recent sales figures. Take the time to challenge some of the core assumptions of your prior plan to see if they still hold up. Have profit margins been higher than you expected? Then start planning how to make the most of any extra cash you generate. Is your new retail store unit not performing as well as others or you expected? Then now's the time to figure out why. Has competition for your new product arisen sooner than you guessed? Take a look at other products with an eye to seeing if they are also more vulnerable than you think.

In large corporations with strict planning routines requiring annual, semiannual, and quarterly plans and plan updates, managers spend at least part of their time working on or thinking about a new plan or plan update. All that information flowing up to senior managers in the form of plans helps keep the brass informed. It helps those in the trenches, too. It's a fact that everybody is judged by past performance. And the best way to ensure that a year from now you'll be looking back on your performance with satisfaction and pride is to plan now and often.

>> Expert Advice <<

What are the most important parts of a business plan?

"This changes with the stage of the company," says Robert Roeper, managing director of venture capital firm VIMAC. "In a very early-stage company, the key components are the definition of the need/projected market, the buyer, and the product/technology that will be used to fulfill the need. Next comes the business model that speculates on the cost to acquire a customer and the anticipated revenue from that customer."

"Then comes a rational review of potential competition. Finally is a presentation of the management team that will get you to the next stage of growth. The reason for this order is that, in general, if the potential market isn't big enough, all the other things don't matter, and if the market's big enough but you can't identify the buying chain, then you don't know enough yet to position the product/technology, etc. Bad positioning is epidemic in early stage companies, but it can be corrected."

Donna Maria Coles Johnson, author, speaker, and founder/CEO of the Indie Business Network, thinks it depends on for whom the plan is prepared. "If it's for a venture capitalist, the most important part would be the financials because they want to know how they will make money and how quickly they will make money," she says. "Same if you are seeking a bank loan or investors. Also important, no matter who the audience is, is the executive summary because it's often the first thing people read. If the executive summary does not succinctly and enthusiastically convey the business concept, the reader will move on quickly to something else."

"Attention has to be captured quickly and held in order to obtain funding. If the plan is geared toward attracting top management to become part of the team, the financials are important. But the executive summary is also important because it's the part of the plan that demonstrates the idea that the management team will be part of a new, exciting, innovative venture with maximum chances of success. Everyone wants to be a part of success!"

"Overall, there really is no 'most important part.' A business plan has to tell a story. It has to flow with a fluidity and consistency throughout. If it does not, and even one section falls flat, the entire story can be called into question. Each section should build on the other and refer specifically to the other when appropriate. There must be no inconsistencies that would call your planning and management expertise into question. A business plan should create a synergy, where the whole is greater and more credible than the mere sum of its parts."

Scott Simpson, a former associate at Battery Ventures Associates, thinks there are three important parts of a business plan: the problem statement, the explanation of your solution to the problem, and the explanation of your differentiation from your competitors. "The best plans clearly explain the reason for the proposed product or service's existence," he says. For example, "My software will allow large manufacturers to integrate with their suppliers, which is something that they cannot do today and is necessary for them going forward." The explanation of a product or solution should clearly explain exactly what the product, service, or business is going to produce or sell. The best plans are as specific as possible.

"Finally, explanation of a company's differentiation usually focuses on the competition that will be encountered, the barriers to entry for potential competitors, and the sustainable long-term advantage of the business over other competitors. Some other very important components of a plan include market data and description of the management team. It is crucial to understand exactly what skills each member of your team will bring to the business."

Ronald Peterson, president of Three Arrows Capital, thinks that the most important part of your business plan is the very first paragraph. "Often that is the only part that most people will ever read, and of that, the opening sentence is the most important portion," he says. "At Three Arrows Capital, we wrestle with that opening for days, and once we have it right, the rest comes far easier. The competition section is extremely important since not only does it demonstrate and give assurance that you have done your homework, it also alerts you to other business models and solutions in your chosen industry that you need to read and consider."

One Plan Does Not Fit All

Business plans have a lot of elements in common, such as cash-flow projections and marketing plans. And many of them share certain objectives as well, such as raising money or persuading a partner to join the firm. But all business plans are not the same any more than all businesses are.

Depending on your business and what you intend to use your plan for, you may need a very different type of business plan from what another entrepreneur needs. Plans differ widely in their length, detail of their contents, and the varying emphases they place on different aspects of the business.

Differences among Industries

One of the reasons for differences among plans is that industries are different. A retailer isn't much like a manufacturer, and a professional-services firm isn't much like a fast-food restaurant. Each requires certain critical components for success—components that may be irrelevant or even completely absent in the operations of another type of firm.

For instance, inventory is a key concern of both retailers and manufacturers. Expert, innovative management of inventory is a very important part of the success of Walmart, one of the great all-time success stories in retail. Any business plan that purported to describe the important elements of these businesses would have had to devote considerable space to telling how the managers planned to manage inventory.

> "*Sometimes even companies in more closely related industries have significantly different business plans.*"

Contrast that with a professional-services firm, such as a management consultant. A consultant has no inventory whatsoever. Her offerings consist entirely of the management analysis and advice she and her staff can provide. She doesn't have to pay now for goods to be sold later or lay out cash to store products for eventual sale. The management consultant's business plan, therefore, wouldn't have a section on inventory or its management, control, and reduction.

This is just one pretty obvious example of the differences among plans for different industries. Sometimes even companies in more closely related industries have significantly different business plans. For instance, the business plan for a fine French restaurant might need a section detailing how the management intends to attract and retain a distinguished chef. At another restaurant, one catering to the downtown lunchtime crowd, a great deal of plan space might be devoted to the critical concern of location and quick turnaround of diners with very little about the chef.

Presenting Yourself in the Best Light

You want your plan to present yourself and your business in the best, most accurate, light. That's true no matter what you intend to use your plan for, whether it's destined for presentation at a venture capital conference or will never leave your own office or be seen outside internal strategy sessions.

When you select clothing for an important occasion, odds are you try to pick items that will play up your best features. Think about your plan the same way. You want to reveal any positives that your business may have and make sure they receive due consideration.

Types of Plans

Business plans can be divided roughly into four distinct types. There are very short plans, or miniplans, presentation plans or decks, working plans, and what-if plans. They require very different amounts of labor and not always with proportionately different results. That is to say, a more elaborate plan is not guaranteed to be superior to an abbreviated one. Success depends on various factors and whether the right plan is used in the right setting. For example, a new hire may not want to read the same, elaborate version that might be important to a potential investor.

The Miniplan

The miniplan is preferred by many recipients because they can read it or download it quickly to read later on their iPhone or tablet. You include most of the same ingredients that you would in a longer plan, but you cut to the highlights, while telling the same story. For a small-business venture, it's typically all that you need. For a more complex business, you may need the longer version.

The Presentation Plan

The advent of PowerPoint presentations changed the way many, if not most, plans are presented. And while the plan is shorter than its predecessors, it's not necessarily easier to present. Many people lose sleep over an upcoming presentation, especially one that can play a vital role in the future of your business. BUT, presenting your plan as a deck can be very powerful. Readers of a plan can't always capture your passion for the business nor can they ask questions when you finish. In 20 minutes, you can cover all of the key points and tell your story from concept and mission statement through financial forecasts.

Remember to keep your graphics uncluttered and to make comments to accentuate your the ideas rather than simply reading what is in front of your audience.

While a presentation plan is concise, don't be fooled. It takes plenty of planning. The pertinent questions: Who? What? Where? Why? When? and How? need to be answered.

A Guide to Your Deck: The 10-20-30 Plan

Using a deck is a quick, to-the-point means of providing your best selling points, while still sending over your more detailed plan.

The question is: How do you organize and minimize the breadth of a business plan into a PowerPoint presentation? First, it's recommended that you use the 10–20–30 rule, which means 10 slides, 20 minutes, and a minimum of a 30-point font.

1. Your first slide is your title slide, which provides the name of the business, your name and title and contact information, plus a slogan if you have one. You can then read the slide and add, in a sentence, what it is you do.

2. The next slide should introduce a problem that persists and is relatable to your target market. Statistics can help you support your comments, but cite only a couple at best. You want the audience to relate to the problem or certainly understand how it affects others.

3. The third slide should get to your solution. Briefly describe in simple terms how your business has figured out how to alleviate the problem. Make sure the audience understands that you have a unique approach. You might also add a few words to support your overall value proposition.

4. Next you want to explain how you will make money. What are your revenue sources? Who are your customers? What is your pricing structure? Then talk briefly about how you expect to profit.

5. Now present a little more detail on your operating plan. How does it all work? Self -service? Kiosks? Personal service? Give them the short version of how the business operates. From buying the goods to marketing them, to sales and shipping, give a short summary of how it works. Include a little technology—remember, "a little!"

This is where you may need a second, visual slide to show how it all works.

6. Now it's time to present your marketing plan in a few short words. After all, if you're going to create dynamic advertising and promotional campaigns, what better way to start than briefly explaining how you plan to market the business. Give some specifics, rather than saying: "on the internet" or "on TV." Let your listeners know that you have a plan for marketing and can keep it within a reasonable budget.

7. Competition. Mention your key competitors—be nice. Then explain what gives you the competitive edge.

8. Talk about the team. Remember, people invest in other people. This is where you introduce your team, with a few very brief highlights (one line) of each member's background that relates to the business at hand.

9. Financials. This slide should show a clear projection with a three-to-five year forecast. Explain the method you used to arrive at your numbers.

10. And finally, show them where you are at present. What have you done thus far, and how are you looking to move forward sooner rather than later? Present a positive call to action based on what you have accomplished to date and what you will accomplish in the future.

There are many ways to go about putting together your deck. And yes, if you need to go to 12 slides, do so, but try not to go longer.

A few tips:

- Don't talk in jargon; not everyone is deeply embedded in your industry.
- Don't post slides and then read them word for word. Your audience can read. Show something that is easy for them to digest, and use your comments to provide a little deeper explanation. This way you present more information, some printed and some verbally.

> *"The miniplan is preferred by many recipients who can read it or download it quickly to read later on their iPhone."*

■ Take a breath between slides so you don't start motoring along.

■ Do not focus on technology, technology, and more technology even if you are a tech company.

■ Don't overload slides with too much material—people can only read and digest so much.

■ Remember less is more. Don't try to pack too much into a PowerPoint presentation. Your listeners can always read the full plan for more details.

The Working Plan

A working plan is a tool to be used to operate your business. It has to be long on detail but may be short on presentation. As with a miniplan, you probably can afford a somewhat higher degree of candor and informality when preparing a working plan. In a plan you intend to present to a bank loan committee, you might describe a rival as "competing primarily on a price basis." In a working plan, your comment about the same competitor might be, "When is Jones ever going to stop this insane price-cutting?"

A plan intended strictly for internal use may also omit some elements that you need not explain to yourself. Likewise, you probably don't need to include an appendix with resumes of key executives. Nor would a working plan especially benefit from product photos.

Internal policy considerations may guide the decision about whether to include or exclude certain information in a working plan. Many entrepreneurs are sensitive about employees knowing the precise salary the owner takes home from the business. To the extent such information can be left out of a working plan without compromising its utility, you can feel free to protect your privacy.

> "It has to be long on detail but may be short on presentation."

This document is like an old pair of khakis you wear to the office on Saturdays or that one ancient delivery truck that never seems to break down. It's there to be used, not admired.

What-If Plans

When you face unusual circumstances, you need a variant on the working plan. For example, you might want to prepare a contingency plan when you are seeking bank financing. A contingency plan is a plan based on the worst-case scenario that you can imagine your business surviving—loss of market share, heavy price competition, defection of a key member of your management team. A contingency plan can soothe the fears of a banker or investor by demonstrating that you have indeed considered more than a rosy scenario.

> *"In 20 minutes, you can cover all of the key points and tell your story from concept and mission statement through financial forecasts."*

Your business may be considering an acquisition, in which case a pro forma business plan (some call this a what-if plan) can help you understand what the acquisition is worth and how it might affect your core business. What if you raise prices, invest in staff

>> Sliding By

For Tod Loofbourrow, the presentation of his plan was everything—literally. The president and founder of Foundation Technologies, a human resources software company, grew his company to 70 employees without ever having a conventional plan written down on paper.

But that doesn't mean Loofbourrow didn't plan or use his plan wisely. Instead, he confined his planning to creating impressive presentations, primarily in the form of slides created in PowerPoint, that conveyed the mission and promise of Foundation to investors. "We raised $8 million in venture capital with eight PowerPoint slides," he says.

The key task of a plan, he feels, is the ability to convey the company's story economically and convincingly rather than to amass a pile of details.

training, and reduce duplicative efforts? Such what-if planning doesn't have to be as formal as a presentation plan. Perhaps you want to mull over the chances of a major expansion. A what-if plan can help you spot the increased needs for space, equipment, personnel, and other variables so you can make good decisions.

What sets these kinds of plans apart from the working and presentation plans is that they aren't necessarily describing how you will run the business. They are essentially more like an addendum to your actual business plan. If you decide to acquire that competitor or grow dramatically, you will want to incorporate some of the thinking already invested in these special purpose plans into your primary business plan.

Your Presentation Counts

Just as fine dining locales offer finer sensory experiences than coffee shops or fast-food eateries, your presentation will differ from a working plan.

A working plan should be free from major errors, but a presentation plan must be proofread carefully several times by several people so that it is definitely free of grammatical errors or typos. You also may find inconsistencies in a working plan that you need to address as you move forward with your business planning. These must not exist in a plan ready for presentation.

It's also essential that a presentation plan be accurate. A mistake here could be construed as a misrepresentation by an unsympathetic outsider. At best, it will make you look less than careful. If the plan's summary describes a need for $40,000 in financing, but the cash flow projection shows $50,000 in financing coming in during the first year, you might think, "Oops! Forgot to update that summary to show the new numbers." The investor you're asking to pony up the cash, however, is unlikely to be so charitable.

Think Visually

From infographics to YouTube, we are clearly embracing visuals and graphics as never before. Depending on your industry and the software you are using, it may be in your best interest to utilize graphics to enhance the presentation of any business plan. If, for example, you are in the fashion, food, or design industry or you are creating a new product, your

>> Take Precautions

Because most business plans are created and disseminated electronically, it is easier for others to forward your email than it was for them to copy and hand over a hardcopy. You can use a password-protected website to post your plan and then simply give people the web address and the password. Of course, the password can also be distributed to others. By asking people to sign a non-disclosure agreement for a hardcopy or an electronic business plan, you are making it clear that you are trusting them and making them think harder about sharing the plan with others. The reality is, however, that no matter how you disseminate a business plan, if someone wants to show it to anyone else, they'll do so. Therefore, try to send your plan to people you believe are trustworthy.

visual image will certainly be worth a thousand words. The key is to choose the best graphics and insert them appropriately—keep in mind that any visual must fit into the plan. Don't overdo it, but consider the impact visuals are having in marketing where studies show that people are much more likely to remember any type of presentation or advertisement with visuals than those without.

You can also provide plan readers with information and even apps to look at what it is you are proposing. Having everyone in the room on the same page, literally, can allow them to utilize interactive features and help you display any new technology that factors into your business operations.

Why You May Want More than One Plan

So you've looked over the different types of plans. Which one is for you? Odds are that you'll need more than one variety. If you want to get maximum impact from your plan, you'll need to tailor it to address the particular needs of each potential audience.

Target Audiences

The potential readers of a business plan are a varied bunch, ranging from bankers and venture capitalists to employees. Although this is a diverse group, it is a finite one. And each type of reader does have certain typical interests. If you know these interests up front, you can be sure to take them into account when preparing a plan for that particular audience.

Active venture capitalists see hundreds of plans in the course of a year. Most plans probably receive no more than a glance from a given venture capitalist before being rejected; others get just a cursory inspection. Even if your plan excites initial interest, it may receive only a few minutes of attention to begin with. It's essential, when courting these harried investors, that you make the right impression fast. Emphasize a cogent, succinct summary and explanation of the basic business concept, and do not stint on the details about the impressive backgrounds of your management team. That said, make it concise and to the point. Remember, time is of the essence to venture capitalists and other investors.

Bankers tend to be more formal than venture capitalists and more concerned with financial strength than with exciting concepts and impressive resumes. For these readers, you'll want to give extra attention to balance sheets and cash-flow statements. Make sure they're fully detailed and come with notes to explain any anomalies or possible points of confusion.

Angel investors may not insist on seeing a plan at all, but as we pointed out in Chapter 2, your responsibilities as a businessperson require you to show them one anyway. For such an informal investor, prepare a less-formal plan. Rather than going for impressive bulk, seek brevity. An angel investor used to playing her hunches might be put off by an imposing plan rather than impressed with your thoroughness.

fact or fiction

Many entrepreneurs don't write plans, so if you do, that should place you in a select group, right? Actually, it's a pretty big group. Famed venture capitalist Frederick R. Adler estimates he's seen 3,000 plans, but most, he says, "are pretty lousy."

If you were thinking about becoming a partner in a firm, you'd no doubt be very concerned with the responsibilities you would have, the authority you would carry, and the ownership you would receive in the enterprise. Naturally, anyone who is considering partnering with you is going to have similar concerns. So make sure that any plan presented to a potential partner deals comprehensively with the ownership structure and clearly spells out matters of control and accountability.

Customers who are looking at your business plan are probably doing so because they contemplate building a long-term relationship with you. They are certainly going to be more concerned about your relationships with your other customers and, possibly, suppliers, than most of your readers. So deal with these sections of your plan in greater depth, but you can be more concise in other areas. Customers rarely ever read a company's business plan, so you'll probably have your miniplan available for these occasions.

Suppliers have a lot of the same concerns as customers, except they're in the other direction on the supply chain. They'll want, above all, to make sure you can pay your bills, so be sure to include adequate cash flow forecasts and other financial reports. Suppliers, who naturally would like their customers to order more and more, are likely to be quite interested in your growth prospects. In fact, if you can show you're probably going to be growing a lot, you may be in a better position to negotiate terms with your suppliers. Like customers, most suppliers do not take the time to read lengthy business plans, so again, focus on the shorter version for such purposes.

Strategic allies usually come to you for something specific—technology, distribution, complementary customer sets, etc. So any plan you show to a potential ally will stress this aspect of your operation. Sometimes potential strategic partners may also be potential competitors, so you may want to present your plan in stages, saving sensitive information such as financials and marketing strategies for later in the process when trust has been established.

plan pointer

Instead of writing a whole new plan for each audience, construct a modular plan with interchangeable sections. Pull out the resume section for internal use, for example, and plug it back in for presentation to an investor. A modular, mix-and-match plan saves time and effort while preserving flexibility. Many people do this with resumes: They have sections that they include or take out depending on the job for which they are applying.

Managers in your company are using the plan primarily to remind themselves of objectives, to keep strategies clear, and to monitor company performance and market conditions. You'll want to stress such things as corporate mission and vision statements and analyses of current industry and economic factors. The most important part of a plan intended for management consumption is probably in the financials. You'll want to take special care to make it easy for managers to compare sales revenue, profitability, and other key financial measures against planned performance.

There's one caution to the plan-customization exercise. Limit your alterations from one plan to another to modifying the emphasis of the information you present. Don't show one set of numbers to a banker you're trying to borrow money from and another to a partner you're trying to lure on board. It's one thing to stress one aspect of your operation over another for presentation purposes and entirely another to distort the truth.

>> Expert Advice <<

Help When You Are Ready to Create Your Business Plan

"Keep the plan as short as possible and very simple to read," says Scott Simpson, formerly of Battery Associates. "Remember that the plan is a road map and a catalyst for the business. Don't get bogged down on details that don't matter. It isn't going to be helpful to have 30 pages of analysis discussing why revenues five years out will be $100 million vs. $110 million."

Simpson says that companies need to concentrate on the important stuff, like why your business will provide a compelling solution to a big problem, and why your company and not the others will be successful. "There's no need to spend tons of money on the plan. Gimmicks are cool, but at the end of the day, the content must stand on its own," he says.

"Also, don't create your plan in a vacuum. Read analyst reports, attend trade shows, understand your competition, and, most importantly, talk to potential customers. A plan written without knowledge of what problem you're solving for your customer represents a business that will most likely fail. Finally, know your audience. If the business plan is intended to help secure financing for your company, make sure that it covers the most vital information on which investors will focus."

Jim Caruso, founder and chair of Telecom Alley Inc., offers this advice: Clearly determine the audience for your plan, and write the plan for that audience and its interests phrased in its own words. Understand and closely follow any guidelines provided by your venture's backers, such as VCs. Differences may include expected length of executive summary, number of years of financial projections, projected funding sources, and investment horizon and exit strategy. Each audience has its own leaning. Investors' interest often shifts with changes in market conditions, so stay on top of their considerations.

Events in the stock markets can kill your opportunity if your idea falls from favor in financial circles. Pay attention to what is taking place in the economy as you might need to adjust your business plan or hold it until your business better fits the economic environment. This isn't to say that a down economy means you can't start a business. Quite the contrary, many businesses do well in such an economy if they are helping people weather the storm by providing good prices on necessities or offering solutions to problems caused by the economy. If, for example, your consulting firm educates businesses on how to spend less and retain more employees, you may be looking for funding at the right time. If you seek outside investors, understand valuation methods that determine what your venture is worth. Understand dilution of shareholding and how that affects your control of your own fate. Recognize that investors want the opportunity to cash out or exit. Most realistically, a successful exit comes from acquisition, not an IPO. Consider which companies are potential acquirers. This is actually a part of speaking directly to the interests of your audience, the investor.

Stay flexible and silent about what you believe the venture is worth until you are in serious negotiation. It is best to have a VC firm's term sheet without ever stating what you believe the value to be. This avoids leaving money and shares on the table that could be yours. Expect the business plan to be a living document that improves with every tough question asked by a potential investor, business partner, or customer.

Include Investments

If you are already invested in the stock market, bonds, or even more directly in other businesses, you should let this be clearly known in your business plan. This provides readers with

1. an understanding that you are somewhat versed in matters of investing,
2. your level of risk tolerance, based on your investments, and
3. your plans for growth or ability to raise capital depending on your choices of investments.

Investing indicates that you are planning ahead and looking to make profits either through long-term growth or through dividends and other income-producing investment vehicles. Personal investments, and, of course, business investments, are important to readers as they paint a picture of how you will handle financing.

Writing Your Business Plan

Executive Summaries Sell Ideas

The first part of your plan that anybody will see, after the title page and table of contents, is the executive summary. This could be considered an expanded table of contents (in prose form) because it's more than an introduction to the rest of the plan. It's supposed to be a brief look at the key elements of the whole plan—and it's critical.

The actual executive summary should be only a page or two. In it you may include your mission and vision statements, a brief sketch of your plans and goals, a quick look at your company and its organization, an outline of your strategy, and highlights of your financial status and needs. If you've ever read a CliffsNotes version of a classic novel, you get the idea. Your executive summary is the CliffsNotes of your business plan.

Labor over your summary. Polish it. Refine it. Ask friends and colleagues to take a look at it, and then take their suggestions to heart. If your plan isn't getting the response you want when you put it to work, suspect a flaw in the summary. If you get a chance to look at another plan that was used to raise a pile of cash, give special scrutiny to the executive summary.

The summary is the most important part of your whole plan. Even if a plan is relatively short, it's difficult for most people to keep that much information in their minds at once. It's much easier to get your arms around the amount of information—just one or two pages—in an executive summary. Your plan is going to be judged on what you include in the summary and on how well you present it.

A good rule of thumb for writing an effective and efficient business plan is to avoid

>> Super Summary

Jimmy Treybig, the founder of Tandem Computers and later a venture capitalist in Austin, Texas, says the executive summary is the most important part of the plans he reviews. "What I want is 20 sentences that tell me why someone who gives them money is going to get rich," says the veteran businessman.

Treybig's 20 sentences should contain information on how the business will address the market, the product idea, the competitive advantage, the amount of money that is needed, who is on the team, and how it will all come together. Most important of all, he says, the executive summary should convey urgency. Treybig wants to be told, "It's going to explode, and I'd better invest now or I'm going to miss out."

repeating information. Brief is better and clearer, and needless repetition may annoy some readers and confuse others. Take extra care when writing your summary. You'll be glad you did.

Ultimately, you want the executive summary to be as strong as possible because it is also the first thing people read in your plan, and we all know the power of a strong first impression. This is where you want to wow people and make them think. This is like the coming attractions, or trailers, at the movie theater. You want that trailer to be enticing and bring the audience members back to see the film. Likewise, you want your readers to want to read your plan.

Purposes of the Executive Summary

The executive summary has to perform a host of jobs. First and foremost, it should grab the reader's attention. It has to briefly hit the high points of your plan. It should point readers with questions requiring detailed responses to the full-length sections of your plan where they can get answers. It should ease the task of anybody whose job it is to read it, and it should make that task enjoyable by presenting an interesting and compelling account of your company.

The first question any investor has is, "How much?" followed closely by, "When will I recoup my investment?" Perceived risk and exit strategies are supportive information, and these in turn are supported by the quality of the management team and the proposed strategies.

plan pointer

Five minutes. This is how long an average reader will spend with your plan. If you can't convey the basics of your business in that time, your plan is in trouble. So make sure your summary, at least, can be read in that time and that it's as comprehensive as possible within that constraint. If you are using a deck, limit yourself to one slide and one minute of comments.

It doesn't much matter whether you are presenting the plan to a family member, friend, banker, or sophisticated investors such as investment bankers or venture capitalists. They all need the same information. Concealing the amount and terms will only lessen your chances of a successful financing.

>> Points to Include in an Executive Summary

A suggested format for an executive summary:

1. The business idea and why it is necessary. (What problem does it solve?)

2. How much will it cost, and how much financing are you seeking?

3. What will the return be to the investor? Over what length of time?

4. What is the perceived risk level?

5. Where does your idea fit into the marketplace?

6. What is the management team?

7. What are the product and competitive strategies?

8. What is your marketing plan?

9. What is your exit strategy?

If you can address each of these in two or three sentences, you have a 20- to 27-sentence executive summary.

What's the Big Idea?

Let's face it, every new and successful enterprise is the result of someone with an idea. People aren't going to finance you without knowing your idea. Sometimes the idea is so powerful that it generates a tremendous response right off the bat. This is unusual, but it does happen—it's when the reader stops you and says, "You don't have to tell me anymore, I'm sold." More often, you'll need to explain why your idea has merit and how it can solve a common problem by making things easier, faster, or cheaper for the prospective customer(s).

Business ideas that no one has ever thought of are rare. So are new inventions. BUT, new spins on old ideas are plentiful. Some of these are game changers, while others simply give consumers something new that solves a problem or makes some aspect of life easier. Then there are ideas that fall into the "same old, same old" category. No matter how brilliantly crafted, written, and presented your business plan is, it will be difficult to win your investors, and later customers, with an old idea that does NOT have a new twist. Therefore, you want to wow them first with your idea! If they're not interested, no matter what your financials are, they won't help.

How Much Cash?

If you are using your plan as a financing proposal, and you probably are, put this information right up front. Are you seeking a loan, convertible debt, or equity investment? What terms, both in interest and length of loan, are you requesting? If equity, what is the probable exit strategy—and when will the exit strategy be executed?

Some readers will stop right here. That's fine. Other readers will appreciate your frankness. Being coy about amounts and terms will only harm your venture.

Using the Cash

Provide a short explanation of how you'll use any financing you seek. Tell the investor why you need the money. Nobody wants to lend you money if they don't know exactly why you need it. It's not necessary to get into much detail here—just make it clear that you need it for x, y, and z. You don't have to justify every penny and wind up feeling obligated to ask for a loan of $23,558.36 because that's the exact price of everything you need. You should also let the reader know how the investment will help the company grow and/or increase its profits. Why else would you be seeking funding? The best use of somebody else's money is to buy or build something that will make more money, both for you and for that person.

The Goals of Financiers

In your executive summary, consider the following:

- Friends and family want to get their money back someday but are not very interested in timing and returns.
- Bankers look for free cash flow to pay back the principal and interest of their loan. They also look closely at management experience and marketing. They may ask for collateral. By law they have to

be conservative, that is, risk averse, so they are not great candidates for risky financing.

- Angel investors look for moderate rates of return, usually above the prime rate, plus some capital appreciation. They sometimes want to be involved at a hands-on level.
- Venture capitalists seek annual compound rates of return in the area of 35 to 50 percent per annum. They

> *"It's a rare company that doesn't have any investment from the entrepreneur or entrepreneurs who started it."*

seldom want to go longer than three to five years to cash out. They always want to know what the exit strategy is.

You may have special considerations to address in any given plan, depending on its target. For instance, you may know or suspect that one of the conditions of getting a loan from your parents is that you employ your black-sheep cousin. Be sure your summary of management has a slot—Director of Ephemera might work—for that unworthy individual.

Don't forget yourself: It's a rare company that doesn't have any investment from the entrepreneur or entrepreneurs who started it.

Who Will Own What?

When a business starts generating profits and plowing them back into the firm, value can build rapidly. Even if you aren't in an industry likely to purchase buildings or patent valuable technology, the business derives value from the fact that it can generate profits into the future.

Because your business is valuable, spell out who owns what. If you have many equity investors coupled with a pile of creditors, this can get pretty complicated.

plan pointer

Assessing your own strengths and weaknesses is a lot harder than assessing others' good and bad points, right? So when it comes time to select your best features, it's also time to solicit feedback from others. Ask people whose opinions you trust, such as colleagues, associates, and peers, whether your assessment of your idea is off base or on target.

For the summary section of your plan, a basic description such as "Ownership of the company will be divided so that each of the four original partners owns 25 percent" will suffice. If you have to negotiate details of exactly what any equity investors will get, there's time to do that later. For now, you just want to give people an idea of how the ownership will be divided.

Give It a Happy Ending

If you tell a story in the summary, give it a happy ending. Although it's your duty to fully disclose to investors any significant risk factors, you can save that for later. The summary is the place to put your best foot forward, to talk up the upside and downplay the downside.

As always, accentuating the positive doesn't mean exaggeration or lying. If there is a really important, unusual risk factor in your plan—such as that one certain big customer has to make a huge order for the whole plan to work—then you will want to mention that in your summary. But run-of-the-mill risks like unexpected competition or customer reluctance can be ignored here.

Paint a convincing portrait of an opportunity so compelling that only a dullard would not recognize it and desire to take part in it.

Company Description

If your company is complex, you'll need a separate section inside the plan with a heading like "Company Description" to describe its many product lines, locations, services, or whatever else it is that makes it a little too complicated to deal with quickly. In any event, you provide a brief description, no longer than a few sentences, of your company in the executive summary. And for many firms, this

plan pointer

Every business needs a good corporate slogan, and the company description of your plan is a good place to work on one. Keep it short—six words or fewer—and make a specific quality statement or service promise. Top examples: "You're in Good Hands with Allstate," FedEx's "When It Absolutely, Positively Has to Be There Overnight," and Nike's "Just DO It."

>> Raising the Fundraising Roof

Raising money for a business is ordinarily considered a pretty staid line of work. But not when Howard Getson gets involved. The president and cofounder of IntellAgent Control Corporation became famous for his brash but effective requests for money to grow his sales-automation software manufacturing company.

How brash? In 1996, Getson sent a letter to prospective investors with outrageous lines like, "Return this letter now! You may already have invested $10 million!" and "This is the most undervalued financing we've ever agreed to accept."

How effective? Getson raised $6.8 million from 70 investors over two years with similar pitches.

Why does it work? Getson melds his in-your-face style with solid financial acumen. "Really," he explains, "it is the perfect blend of direct-mail schlock and true business sense."

is an adequate basic description of their company. Here are some one- or two-sentence company descriptions:

- John's Handball Hut is the Hamish Valley's leading purveyor of handball equipment and clothing.
- Boxes Boxes Boxes Inc. will provide the people of the metropolitan area with a comprehensive source for packing materials, containers, and other supplies for the do-it-yourself move.
- Salem Segway Witch Tours offers tourists the only Segway tours of the infamous home of the 17th-century witch trials.

Optional Information

The following items are not a necessity in your business plan: mission statement and corporate vision. If you have honed either down to a clear and concise sentence, by all means, use it in your plan.

Mission Statement

A mission statement is a sentence or two describing the company's function, market, competitive advantages, and the business goals and philosophies.

Many mission statements communicate what your business is about and should include a description of what makes you different from everybody else in your field. Mission statements have a place in a plan: They help investors and other interested parties get a grip on what makes your company special. A mission statement should be clearly written. Here are some examples:

- River City Roadsters buys, restores, and resells classic American cars from the 1950s and 1960s to antique-auto buffs throughout Central Missouri.
- Captain Curio is the Jersey Shore's leading antique store, catering to high-quality interior decorators and collectors across the tristate area.
- August Appleton, Esq., provides low-cost legal services to personal-injury, workers' compensation, and age-discrimination plaintiffs in Houston's Fifth Ward.

Corporate Vision

A mission statement describes the goals and objectives you could "reasonably" expect to accomplish. A small software company whose mission statement included the goal of "putting Microsoft out of business" would be looked upon as foolishly naive.

In a vision statement, however, just those sorts of grandiose, galactic-scale images are perfectly appropriate. When you "vision"—to borrow the management consultant's trick of turning nouns into verbs—you imagine the loftiest heights you could scale, not the next step or several steps on the ladder.

Does a vision statement even have a place in a business plan? You could argue that it doesn't, especially because many include personal components such as "to love every minute of my work and always feel I'm doing my best." But many investors deeply respect visionary entrepreneurs.

So if you feel you have a compelling vision, there's no reason not to share it in your plan.

Extract the Essence

The key to the executive summary is to pick out the best aspects of every part of your plan. In other words, you want to extract the essence. Instead of describing everyone in your company, tell only about your key managers. Instead of talking about all your products, mention only the major ones or discuss only product lines instead of individual products. It's a highlight reel, so to speak.

>> Expert Advice <<
Article Tools and Summarizing the Summary

Within the overall outline of the business plan, the executive summary will follow the title page. The summary should tell the reader what you are planning to do. All too often, the business owner's desires are buried and lost when the reader scrolls through. Clearly state what you are planning to do (your ideas) and what you are seeking in the summary.

The statement should be kept short and businesslike, ideally no more than half a page. It could be longer, depending on how complicated the use of funds may be, but the summary of a business plan, like the summary of a loan application, is generally no more than one page. Within that space you'll need to provide a synopsis of the entire business plan. Key elements that should be included are:

1. *Financial requirements.* Clearly states the capital needed to start or expand the business. Detail how the capital will be used, and the equity, if any, that will be provided for funding. If the loan for initial capital will be based on security instead of equity within the company, you should also specify the source of collateral.
2. *Business concept.* Describes the business, its product, and the market it will serve. It should point out just exactly what will be sold, to whom, and why the business will hold a competitive advantage.
3. *Financial features.* Highlights the important financial points of the business including sales, profits, cash flows, and return on investment.

4. *Current business position.* Furnishes relevant information about the company, its legal form of operation, when it was formed, the principal owners, and key personnel.

5. *Major achievements.* Details any developments within the company that are essential to the success of the business. Major achievements include items like patents, prototypes, location of a facility, any crucial contracts that need to be in place for product development, or results from any test marketing that has been conducted.

When writing your statement of purpose, don't waste words. If the executive summary is eight pages, nobody's going to read it because it will be very clear that the business, no matter what its merits, won't be a good investment because the principals are indecisive and don't really know what they want. Make it easy for the reader to realize at first glance both your needs and capabilities.

Management
Makes Money

I n the management section of your plan you describe who will run the company. This may be no more than a simple paragraph noting that you'll be the only executive and describing your background. Or it may be a major section in the plan, consisting of an organizational chart describing interrelationships among every department and manager in the company, plus bios of all key executives.

Time and again, financiers utter some variation of the following statement: "I don't invest in ideas; I invest in people." Although there's some question as to whether this is the whole story—investors certainly prefer capable people with good ideas to inept people with good ideas—there's no doubt that you, and the people who run your company, will receive considerable scrutiny from financiers as well as from customers, suppliers, and

>> Capitalizing on Experience

For entrepreneur Bill Dunnam, his management experience really was the company. The basic idea behind the Pennsylvania-based Hanks Root Beer Co., the company he cofounded nearly 20 years ago, was to compete in a soft-drink industry dominated by Coke and Pepsi—not too promising. But Dunnam's 11 years' experience working for Coca-Cola had the power to convince everybody—well, everybody except former Coke colleagues. "They were like, 'You're nuts, Bill,'" he recalls. Investors didn't agree, and they helped him get Hanks off the ground and up to $2 million in sales the second year. Today, the company's products range from root beer to vanilla cream soda and citrus punch.

anyone else with an interest in your plan. People are, after all, a company's most important asset. Not adequately addressing this issue in a business plan is a serious failing. Luckily, it's one of the easiest parts.

All about You

They say "pay yourself first" when you run a business. It's important when doing a business plan to feature yourself first. After all, you are the person, the entrepreneur, behind the business venture, and it is you who will have to put your neck on the line, answer the hard questions, and take the criticism—as well as the praise and acclaim, should there be some.

Before you can impress people with your management team, it's important to let your readers know who is at the helm and who is selecting the management team. You, therefore, have to let them know your background, including your vision, your credentials, and why you chose the management team you did.

A business follows the lead of the founder, and as such, you need to briefly explain what is expected of this management team and the role you see it, as a group, playing in the future of this business.

Your Managers

Identifying your managers is about presenting what they bring to the table. You can provide this by describing them in terms of the following characteristics:

- *Education.* Impressive educational credentials among company managers provide strong reasons for an investor or other plan reader to feel good about your company. Use your judgment in deciding what educational background to include and how to emphasize it. If you're starting a fine restaurant, for example, and your chef graduated at the top of her class from the Culinary Institute of America, play that front and center. If you're starting a courier service and your partner has an anthropology degree from a little-known school, mention it but don't make a big deal out of it.

- *Employment.* Prior work experience in a related field is something many investors look for. If you've spent ten years in management in the retail men's apparel business before opening a tuxedo outlet, an investor can feel confident that you know what you're doing. Likewise, you'll want to explain the key, appropriate positions of your team members. Describe any relevant jobs in terms of job title, years of experience, names of employers, etc. But remember, this isn't a resume. You can feel free to skim over or omit any irrelevant experience. You do not have to provide exact dates of employment.

- *Skills.* A title is one thing; what you learn while holding it is another. In addition to pointing out that you were a district sales manager for a stereo-equipment wholesaler, you should describe your responsibilities and the skills you honed while fulfilling them. Again, list the skills that your management team has that pertain to this business. A great cook may have incredible accounting skills, but that doesn't matter in the kitchen of the new restaurant.

> *"Prior work experience in a related field is something many investors look for."*

>> Beading the Competition

Jerry Free had no experience as an inventor or manager of a product company when he came up with a better way to put up sheetrock walls. What he did have was vast expertise and understanding of the issues involved in putting up sheetrock developed through years of doing just that kind of work.

So when he went to a large company, U.S. Gypsum, asking for help marketing Speed Bead, an invention that makes corners easier to build in drywall construction jobs, it listened. Impressed by Free's grasp of drywall installation issues and Speed Bead's well-thought-out design, U.S. Gypsum agreed to fund the patenting as well as marketing and distribution of the idea, in exchange for licensing rights.

"My idea was so simple, I couldn't believe it hadn't been done," says Free. "And if it hadn't, then why not?" The simple answer is, nobody else had the idea and the practical experience to make it workable. It also took several thousand dollars in advisors' fees and five years of waiting. But now Free's Speed Bead expertise paid off—he's still installing drywall but does it from a new truck bought with licensing royalties.

Each time you mention skills that you or a member of your management team has spent years acquiring at another company, it will be another reason for an investor to believe you can do it at your own company.

- *Accomplishments.* Dust off your plaques and trot out your calculator for this one. If you or one of your team members has been awarded patents, achieved record sales gains, or once opened an unbelievable number of new stores in the space of a year, now's the time to tell about it.

  Don't brag. Just be factual and

buzzword

Functional organization is a term describing a company or other entity with a structure that divides authority and reporting along functions such as marketing or finance. These functions cross product lines and other boundaries.

remember to quantify. If, for example, you have 12 patents, your sales manager had five years of 30 percent annual sales gains, and you personally oversaw the grand openings of 42 stores in 11 months, this is the stuff investors and others reading your business plan will want to see. Investors are looking to back impressive winners, and quantifiable results speak strongly to business-people of all stripes.

buzzword

Line organization describes an organization divided by product lines, means of production, industries served, etc. Each line may have its own support staff for the various functions.

- *Personal.* Who cares about personal stuff? Isn't this business? Sure, but investors want to know with whom they're dealing in terms of the personal side, too. Personal

>> Whom Else Do You Include in Your Plan?

If you're the only manager, this question is an easy one. But what if you have a pretty well-established organization already? Should you mention everyone down to shop foremen or stop with the people who are on your executive committee? The answer is, probably neither. Instead think about your managers in terms of the important functions of your business.

In deciding the scope of the management section of your plan, consider the following business functions, and make sure you've explained who will handle those that are important to your enterprise:

- Accounting
- Advertising
- Distribution
- Finance
- Human Resources
- Legal
- Training

- Marketing
- Operations
- Production
- Purchasing
- Sales
- Technical Operations

information on each member of your management team may include age, city of residence, notable charitable or community activities, and, last but far from least, personal motivation for joining the company. Investors like to see vigorous, committed, involved people in the companies they back. Mentioning one or two the relevant personal details of your key managers may help investors feel they know what they're getting into, especially in today's increasingly transparent business climate.

Many businesses contain unique functions. For example, only product companies such as software publishers have product-testing departments. List functions that are unique to your company under the "Other" category.

What Does Each Person Do?

There's more to a job than a title. A director in one organization is a high-and-mighty individual, whereas in another company a person bearing the same title is practically nobody. And many industries have unique job titles, such as managing editor, creative director, and junior accountant level II, that have no counterparts in other industries.

In a longer plan, when you give your management team's background and describe their titles, don't stop there. Go on and tell the reader exactly what each member of the management team will be expected to do in the company. This may be especially important in a startup, in which not every position is filled from the start. If your marketing work is going to be handled by the CFO until you get a little further down the road, let readers know this up front. You certainly can't expect them to figure that out on their own.

In a shorter business plan, or miniplan, choose those people most vital to your business. If you are opening a martial arts studio, the instructors, or lead instructor, are significant, as is the software developer in a new software company. While you have room to describe these people in more detail in a longer plan, in the shorter miniplans, just use one defining sentence for your top five people.

Expanding Your Team

If you do have significant holes in your management team, you'll want to describe your plans for filling them. You may say, for example,

"Marketing duties are being handled on a temporary basis by the vice president for finance. Once sales have reached the $500,000 per month level, approximately six months after startup, a dedicated vice president of marketing will be retained to fulfill that function."

In some cases, particularly if you're in a really shaky startup and you need solid talent, you may have to describe in some detail your plans for luring a hotshot industry expert to your fledgling enterprise. Then, briefly describe your ideal candidate. For a miniplan you may write "We plan to hire a marketing VP who excels in reaching our 20–29 target market."

Hiring and Projections

One of the beauties of being an entrepreneur, as opposed to a solo practitioner or freelancer, is that you can leverage the activities and skills of all the people whom you employ. This is one of the secrets to building a personal fortune. And it's one you can use even if you didn't happen to be born with a silver spoon in your mouth or an oil well in your backyard.

To use a simple example of the profit power of people, say you start a public relations firm. You bill clients $60 an hour, plus other office expenses, for services provided by your account executives (AE). You pay your staff $30 an hour, including benefits. Before expenses for rent and other overhead items, then, you clear $30 for every hour one of your AEs bills. If you can grow your AE staff very large (and generate enough business to keep them busy), it can leverage your earnings very rapidly indeed. Of course, you have to train people to work autonomously and take control of their tasks so you do not have to spend time managing their every move—otherwise, you're losing money by using your time in an unproductive manner.

The decision of how many people you want to manage is entirely up to you. It depends on the time commitment that you cannot make for doing other tasks or the need to perform skills that aren't your strengths. Part of hiring other people is to have them handle aspects of the business that you cannot or should not be doing. After all, we have different personalities, interests, and passions. There are very few one-person businesses, unless you are including independent contractors. Businesses are run by teams of people, from two or three to thousands, and team members excel in a

buzzword

Line and staff organizations are hybrids in which staff managers, such as planners and accountants, act as advisors to support line managers, such as the operations vice president.

wide range of areas. You also need to factor in how much you expect to grow. Some entrepreneurs want to retain a small, easy-to-manage business, while others want to build an empire.

Let's say, for example, you wish to add a second shift at your small factory manufacturing smartphone cases. Your day shift employs ten factory floor workers plus a supervisor. Can you just hire 11 people and start running the swing shift? Not necessarily. It may be that two of those workers only work part-time on the production line, spending much of their day helping the shipping department process incoming materials and outgoing orders. Two more may devote several hours to routine maintenance procedures that won't have be done twice a day even when a second shift is added. So your real needs may be for seven production workers and a supervisor—a savings of 20 percent in your projected staffing increase. It's decisions like this that easily can make the difference between a highly profitable operation and one barely scraping by. Figure 7–1 can help here.

Adding and Retaining Key Employees

If you want your business to grow, you'll want to have key employees that share your vision and goals. Sometimes you will find an established individual, like a highly acclimated chef for your restaurant or an art director with years of experience for your company. In other cases, you may not know when you bring someone on board what the future holds, but you believe she has what it takes to become a key employee. These are individuals that you can envision moving up the path of ascension. Either way, you should make it clear in your business plan which key positions you want to fill and how you plan to go about finding the people to fill those roles.

Of course the economy will factor into your decision on whom to hire and how much you can afford to pay them. In a struggling economy, more highly skilled employees will be seeking work, but you may not be

Strategic Hiring Worksheet

To help you in your strategic staffing projections, consider these factors:

1. What are your key business objectives? _____

_____

(*Hint*: These may be things such as increasing sales or reducing costs. The idea is to make sure that your hiring decisions fit your strategy. If, for example, geographically expanding your retail store chain is a primary objective, a staffing plan will have to include managers for each new location.)

2. What skills will your employees need? _____

_____

3. What new skills will current employees need to possess? _____

_____

(*Hint*: You may find you are better off with fewer workers who are more highly trained or have different skill sets.)

4. Which of these skills are central to your business—your core competencies?

_____

(*Hint*: You may want to outsource peripheral functions. Accounting, legal matters, and human resources are frequently outsourced by companies whose main business is elsewhere and who find it doesn't make sense to spend the effort to attract and retain skilled employees in these areas.)

5. List the jobs and job descriptions of the people it will take to provide these skills. _____

_____

(*Hint*: The idea here is to identify the employees whose job titles may mask their actual function in the organization so you can figure out how many people, and what type of people, you really need to include.)

Figure 7-1. Strategic Hiring Worksheet

Strategic Hiring Worksheet

6. Determine how many people you will be hiring and what your budget will be for these positions. Will there be any job sharing? _____

_____

(*Hint*: Make sure your salaries are commensurate with the going rates in your region. If you can pay more, you can attract a higher level of employees. If you pay less, then try to find non-monetary benefits that you can also offer, such as telecommuting, which saves employees time and money on getting to and from work each day.)

Now you should be able to make an accurate projection of not only how many but what kind of people you need to achieve your long-term objectives.

Figure 7-.1. Strategic Hiring Worksheet, continued

in a position to risk high salaries. In such instances you may opt for trial periods before committing to full-time salaries. You may also look for independent contractors for key positions. Remember, it is much easier to find skilled people in various aspects of business than it is to learn everything yourself. When the economy is going well, however, you will have to up the ante to bring on key employees because there is more competition. Then there is your plan to hold onto key employees, which is important to include in your business plan.

The things that make employees want to come to work for you and stay vary. For employees, choosing whom to work for is a highly personal decision. That's why it's crucial to understand the individual needs of your key employees so that you can give them exactly what they want. If you offer only a higher salary to an employee whose most

plan pointer

An organizational chart graphically sorts your company into its major functional departments— finance, administration, marketing, production, etc. It's the quickest, clearest way to say who is in charge of what and who reports to whom.

important concern is that she work at a job offering flexible hours so she can care for an elderly parent, then you probably won't retain that employee.

Here are some common concerns that drive employment decisions:

- *Benefits*. Paid holidays and sick leave, health insurance, and retirement plans such as 401(k)s are among the benefits listed as most desirable by employees.
- *Compensation*. Salary, bonuses, stock options, profit sharing, and auto mileage allowances are among the most important compensation issues to employees.
- *Miscellaneous*. On-site child care, flexible schedules, telecommuting, paid memberships to business groups, and health perks such as yoga classes or free medical screenings are also important to employees.

buzzword

Outsourcing is a key strategy for startups. If you've ever fired your bookkeeper and started sending payroll to a service, you've outsourced. Basically, you are using a service instead of your own employee(s) to do a specific task. Outsourcing can save time and money for support staff jobs and add flexibility in production staffing. Again, it shows that you are watching the bottom line closely and not hiring people full time for part-time duties.

Your business plan should consider the above issues and describe the inducements you will offer key employees to encourage them to stay.

plan of action

The Perfect Hire (Entrepreneur Press), by Katherine Graham-Leviss, quickly, economically, and precisely advises you on finding, hiring, and keeping the best employees.

Especially in a small company, an investor is likely to be very leery of a plan that appears to be based on the capabilities of a handful of employees unless the business owner has clearly given a lot of thought to keeping these important people on board.

The above list is by no means comprehensive, however. Employee needs are as complex as humanity. One person may stay because she likes the view out her window on a high floor; somebody in an identical office may leave because heights make him nervous. One of the most important needs, especially for highly motivated employees, is maintaining a constant atmosphere of learning, challenge, and advancement. If you can find a way to let your employees grow as your company does, and feel a sense of ownership and inclusion, they're likely to be more conscientious and motivated.

Board of Directors or Advisors

A board of directors gives you access to expertise, provided you choose them wisely, but at the cost of giving up control of the business to them. Technically, the officers of a corporation report to the board of directors, who bear the ultimate responsibility for the proper management of the company. Most boards will have financial, marketing, and organizational experts. Such a board lends great credibility to a company. Board members can provide more than oversight and sounding board skills; they provide a wealth of contacts and referrals.

A board of advisors is a less-formal entity. You can have the same kind of people on an advisory board but you don't report to them nor do they have the same power as a board of directors. Beware of creating a rubber-stamp board. You need the variety and breadth of experience and skills a board (of directors or advisors) brings to the table. Running a business is hard enough without adding an echo chamber. Your board should be able to challenge your thinking, help you solve knotty problems, and even change management if necessary.

>> Seek Consistent Outside Advice

Jim Caruso, founder of Telecom Alley Inc., suggests having a board of advisors. "You may create a board of advisors for your venture, offering each advisor a nominal shareholding in exchange for a couple of hours of good advice each month. The first advice would be reading and commenting on the business plan. These advisors should come from current or expected customers, business partners, or others that are CEOs or industry experts that approached and won a similar prospective customer."

Your board members, and their reasons for being included, should be a brief part of your longer business plan, not the miniplan.

Outside Professionals

Some of the most important people who'll do work for you won't work for you. Your attorney, your accountant, and your insurance broker are all crucial members of your team. A good professional in one of these slots can go a long way toward helping you succeed. The same may be true, to a lesser extent, for real estate brokers, management consultants, benefits consultants, computer consultants, trainers, and both creative and IT help.

plan pointer

Keep in mind that there are many consultants out there, some of whom are invaluable and others who take in information and regurgitate it back to you in some other form. Choose wisely.

Your business plan should reassure readers that you have your bases covered in these important professional positions. Readers don't necessarily want to see an attorney on staff. It's fine that you merely state that you retain the services of an attorney in private practice on an as-needed basis. In fact, often it's more prudent to show that you are not spending money on full-timers that you don't need.

You don't even need to name the firm you're retaining, although a prestigious name here may generate some reflected respect for you. For instance, if your firm is audited by a prominent firm instead of a local one-man accounting shop, then by all means play it up. Few things are more comforting to an investor than the knowledge that this investment's disbursement will be monitored regularly and carefully by an expert.

> *"Your business plan should reassure readers that you have your bases covered in important professional positions."*

Investors want profit. They don't just give money to people they like or admire. But it's also true that if they don't like, admire, or at least respect the people

>> Checking It Twice

Here are some common licenses and certifications you may need. Check this list to see if there's anything you may have forgotten:

- Business license
- DBA (doing business as) or fictitious name statement
- Federal Employer ID Number
- Local tax forms
- Sales tax permit or seller's permit
- Health inspection certificate
- Fire inspection certificate
- Patent filings
- Trademark registration
- Zoning variance

Many of these forms and certificates will take days, weeks, months, or longer to arrive after you request them from the appropriate parties. So don't wait until the last minute to do so. Nothing is more frustrating than sitting in a ready-to-open store, with employees on the clock and interest charges on inventory and fixtures ticking away as well, but unable to serve customers because you don't have your sales tax permit.

running your company, they're likely to look elsewhere. The management section of your plan is where you tell them about the human side of the equation. You can't control your readers' responses to that, but you owe it to them and to yourself to provide the information.

Licenses and Certifications

Some paperwork is just paperwork, and some paperwork is essential. Every business must file tax returns, and most businesses need certain licenses and certifications to do business. Your plan should take notice, however briefly, of the fact that you have received or applied for any necessary licenses and certificates. If you don't mention the subject, some plan readers will assume all is hunky-dory. Others, however, may suspect the omission means you haven't thought about it or are having trouble getting the paperwork in order. Addressing those concerns now is a worthwhile idea.

Aside from the usual business licenses and tax forms, there are any number of certificates and notices you may require, depending on circumstances. Owners of buildings must have their elevators inspected regularly and, in some cities, post the safety inspection record in public. Plumbers must be licensed in many states. Even New York City hot dog vendors must be licensed by the city before they can unfurl their carts' colorful umbrellas.

> *"Every business must file tax returns, and most businesses have to have certain licenses and certifications to do business."*

For some businesses, their certification or occupational license is essentially what they sell. Think of a CPA. A lot of people sell accounting services. When you go to a CPA, you're paying for the probity and skill represented by the CPA designation, not just another accountant. You're basically buying those initials. FYI: Patents, trademarks, and other signs of creativity and resourcefulness that are registered or licensed can be impressive.

>> Expert Advice <<

Alex W. Thomson, Esq., is the director of the Corporate Practice group at the Pittsburgh law firm, Houston Harbaugh. He offers this advice concerning other legal issues when putting together your business plan.

As you begin to create a business plan for your company, sound legal advice is important. Attorneys are an integral part of strategic business planning because they offer the guidance necessary to ensure short- and long-term stability. Proper planning and organization in the beginning will lessen the likelihood of problems arising as your business develops.

Prior to creating a business plan, five issues should be reviewed with your attorney:

1. What type of entity will the business use?
2. How will you raise money to fund the business endeavors?
3. How will you staff the business, and what compensation and benefits will you provide to your employees?
4. Does the business have important intellectual property or proprietary information, and if so, how will it be protected?
5. How will doing business abroad be handled?

Attention to detail in each of these areas is imperative in creating a successful strategic business plan.

In establishing your company's legal entity, consider the advantages and disadvantages of each type—sole proprietorship, partnership, C corporation, S corporation, and limited liability company (LLC). Choosing the right business entity is imperative in a successful business venture because there are many tax and nontax implications. A good lawyer can help you determine which entity would be best for your particular company and situation.

Financing a business requires knowledge of the laws governing the ways in which companies may raise money. For instance, when taking on investors, whether they are family and friends, angel investors, or venture capital investors, there are securities law issues that may inhibit the way in which money may be accepted.

An important question to ask is, "How do I raise money and not violate the law?" Legal professionals can guide you in your planning process to ensure that your company will not violate the laws regarding financing.

Determining staffing needs is yet another necessary component of a strong business plan. A lawyer can develop contracts and other detailed documents important in the hiring process. Salary issues need to be determined, too—for example, will your employees be paid hourly or will they be salaried? Other considerations include incentive plans and employee benefits, such as health insurance, retirement plans, and stock options. An employee handbook can also be a useful tool to set up a foundation for employee policies and procedures. All issues regarding employees typically require a lawyer's involvement to avoid the specific liabilities that your company may face. In fact, your corporate attorney may not be the right person for labor law, so you may need to discuss hiring issues, including handbooks and even employee forms, with a labor lawyer.

Intellectual property and proprietary information can provide a company with a needed competitive advantage. Therefore, because of the potential importance of intellectual property and proprietary information, an attorney should be consulted to ensure that it is properly protected. Ensuring all employees sign proprietary information and invention agreements is one step in protecting your company's intellectual property and proprietary information. Obtaining patents or federal registration of the company's trademarks is also critical to proper protection.

Another aspect of the business plan should include how relationships with customers and suppliers will be established and what the terms of the legal relationship will be with them. The necessary question to ask and answer is whether standard terms and conditions will apply or whether each relationship will be contracted individually. In addition is the need to decide whether any of the Uniform Commercial Code (UCC) provisions will be overridden. Certain UCC provisions, such as implied warranties, will govern unless specifically disclaimed.

To find a competent attorney for your company, seek referrals from other business managers. It's important to meet with more than one firm to determine which one is best for your particular company. Look for experience in your industry, as well as chemistry between you and the firm. Keep in mind that you may need more than one attorney to cover all the different bases. A good law firm, housing lawyers with different specialties, such as contracts, labor, taxes, etc., may be beneficial to your needs.

Don't be afraid to talk about fees. It is important to know what you're paying for to determine if you're getting your money's worth.

Successful businesses deal with a variety of laws and regulations on a daily basis, so it is important to hire an attorney who specializes in your business and can help facilitate growth of your company. Consulting an attorney before drafting your business plan will result in a more well-thought-out and better drafted business plan. This will lessen the likelihood of problems as the company grows, saving both time and money. Through knowledge and experience, a good lawyer can efficiently aid in the creation of a successful business plan.

What You Are Really Selling

Every business has something to sell, and the product section is where you tell readers what it is you're selling. (For simplicity's sake, the term "product" is used to refer to both products and services unless otherwise indicated.) This is clearly a very important section of your plan. Even if you have assembled a brilliant managerial team, or have strong financial underpinnings, unless you have something to sell or at least plans to develop something new, you don't really have a business at all. Business is about providing people with something they need. Your business should solve a problem, make life easier, expedite a process, or even simply entertain, but you need to be selling something to have a business.

Although many businesses are founded to develop new, never-before-seen products, they're still built around a product, even

>> They Sold the Bottle Before the Drink

When Dan DaDalt went after investors to back his idea for a new red-colored rum liquor, he and his partner didn't bother mixing up any booze. They spent $1,000 on a Lucite mockup of the dramatic red bottle and showed that. Investors liked the flavor—to the tune of $800,000 for the two entrepreneurs. Such preselling is becoming more common today in certain industries, such as e-book publishing, where authors test the market and even start promoting their new book online, often through blogs, before selling it. Other businesses do this with mock-ups. They test the waters online and get an idea of how many pre-orders they could get before completing the product. The power of the internet and social media makes it possible to see if your impending product has value.

though it may not exist at the moment. And even for these development-stage enterprises, it's just as important to describe the planned-for product and make a presentation that illustrates what people can expect.

What Is Your Product or Service?

It's easy to talk eloquently about a product you believe in. Some highly marketing-oriented businesses, in fact, are built as much on the ability to wax rhapsodic about a product as they are on the ability to buy or source compelling products to begin with. Think of J. Peterman, the catalog operation that became famous—and highly successful—by selling prosaic products with the help of romantic, overblown advertising copy, prior to going bankrupt in 1999.

It's important in your plan to be able to build a convincing case for the product or service upon which your business will be built. The product description section is where you do that. In this section, describe your product in terms of several characteristics, including cost, features, distribution, target market, competition, and production concerns. Figure 8–1 can help you define your product.

Here are a few sample product descriptions:

Product Description Worksheet

Features describe the make, shape, form, or appearance of a product, the characteristics that you use to describe products. These features convey benefits to the customer. Benefits (perceived benefits) are the emotional or other end results that your product or service provides that customer, the satisfaction or fulfillment of needs that a customer receives from your products or services. In the famous phrase "My factories make cosmetics, we sell hope," cosmetics are the products, hope is the benefit.

Product Description	Features	Benefit Conveyed	Importance for My Product
Physical characteristics:	Shape		
	Color		
	Size		
	Weight		
	Fresh		
Specified characteristics:	Made by . . .		
	Imported from . . .		
	Price		
	New! Improved!		
	Location		
	Delivery		
Follow-up service	Availability		
	Durability		
	Reliability		
	Service		
	Ease of use		
	Tech support		
	Used by		

Figure 8-1. Product Description Worksheet

- *Street Beat* is a new type of portable electronic rhythm machine used to create musical backgrounds for street dances, fairs, concerts, picnics, sporting events, and other outdoor productions. The product is less costly than a live rhythm section and offers better sound quality than competing systems. Its combination of features will appeal to sports promoters, fair organizers, and charitable and youth organizations.

- *Troubleshooting Times* is the only monthly magazine for the nation's 6,000 owners of electronics repair shops. It provides timely news of industry trends, service product reviews, and consumer product service tips written in a language service shop owners can understand.

- *HOBO, the Home Business Organization,* provides business-consulting services to entrepreneurs who work out of their homes. The group connects home-business owners with experts who have extensive experience counseling home-business owners in management, finance, marketing, and lifestyle issues. Unlike entrepreneurial peer groups, which charge members for attending sessions whether or not they receive useful advice, HOBO will guarantee its services, asking home-business owners to pay only if they derive solid benefit from the service.

> ### plan pointer
>
> No ideas to differentiate your product? Steal someone else's. That is, combine your product with another to create something new. Dry cleaners do this when they offer coupons for the neighborhood pizza parlor—which gives out cleaning coupons with each pie. It's called cooperative marketing.

A business plan product description has to be less image-conscious than an advertising brochure but more appealing than a simple spec sheet. You don't want to give the appearance of trying to dazzle readers with a glitzy product sales pitch filled with a lot of hype. On the other hand, you want to give them a sampling of how you are going to position and promote the product.

A business plan product description is not only concerned with consumer appeal. Issues of manufacturability are of paramount concern to plan readers, who may have seen any number of plans describing exciting products that, in the end, proved impossible to design and build economically.

If your product or service has special features that will make it easy to build and distribute, say so. For instance, the portable rhythm machine maker should point out in the business plan that the devices will be constructed using new special-purpose integrated circuits derived from military applications, which will vastly increase durability and quality while reducing costs. Figure 8–2 on page 140 shows potential unique selling propositions that any product or service may be able to provide. Look at the list and ask yourself what your product has to offer buyers in each category.

buzzword

Unique selling proposition is a term for whatever it is that makes you different from and better than the competition in the eyes of your customers. It's why they buy from you instead of from someone else.

What Makes It Worthwhile?

A product description is more than a mere listing of product features. You have to highlight your product's most compelling characteristics, such as low cost or uniquely high quality, that will make it stand out in the marketplace and attract buyers willing to pay your price. Even the simplest product has a number of unique potential selling strengths.

Many of the common unique selling strengths are seemingly contradictory. How can both mass popularity and exclusive distribution be strengths? The explanation is that it depends on your market and what its buyers want.

- *Features.* If your product is faster, bigger, or smaller, or comes in more colors, sizes, and configurations than others on the market, you have a powerful selling strength. In fact, if you can't offer some combination of features that sets you apart, you'll have difficulty writing a convincing plan.
- *Price.* Everybody wants to pay less for a product. If you can position yourself as the low-cost provider (and make money at

Unique Selling Proposition Worksheet

When you've explained the selling propositions associated with your product in each of these categories, give each one a score from 1 to 10 based on your evaluation of how convincing a case you can make for that being a unique selling proposition. The one or two strengths with the highest scores will be your candidates for inclusion in business plan product description.

Features
For products:
Price
Time saving
Ease of transport (mobility)
Availability
Cutting edge / new
Training and support
Financing
Other
For the service providers:
Customer service
Reputation
Knowledge
Experience
Fast delivery
Endorsements
Other

Figure 8-2. Unique Selling Proposition Worksheet

these rock-bottom prices), you have a powerful selling advantage. Conversely, high-priced products may appeal to many markets for their better-quality, high-end value. People with discerning tastes want quality and do not buy based solely on price points, so saving money is not always the issue. Price is also dependent on other issues such as service. People will pay more for good customer service.

- *Time Savings.* People buy products to help them expedite a process. If yours is faster and can help them get out of the office and on their way home more quickly, they want it. Today, everyone is looking to save time, so products and services that help people do that are valuable.

- *Ease of Transport.* The mobile world has taken over. People are using their mobile phones to go online as much if not more than their laptops. How mobile is your product? Today's consumers like to take things with them—they want apps and gadgets that are portable.

- *Availability.* Typically, the more easily accessible your products are the better it is for business. In most cases, you want to have products and services that people can get quickly. Today, thanks to the internet, you no longer need brick-and-mortar locations in many communities. Scarcity, however, can also generate a higher demand, so you may have a marketing plan to release products at intervals and let the demand—and the desire—build. Scarcity doesn't mean that you will be running out anytime soon. For service providers, availability means a good location or locations that are easy to get to.

plan pitfall

Don't count on getting your product into a major retailer on its own merits. The glut of tens of thousands of new products introduced annually, combined with the existing plethora of more than 30,000 products stocked by a typical supermarket, puts retailers in the driver's seat. They demand— and get from almost all new product makers—slotting fees, which are simply payments for the right to be on store shelves. The same goes for big online retailers like Amazon.

- *Cutting Edge/New.* If you have something to offer that is not on the market, this is a major selling point or competitive edge. Get out there and patent it, market it, and sell it before someone comes along and steals your thunder. You can also utilize technology to build upon products or services you already provide, such as an app.

- *Training and Support.* These are components of service that have become increasingly important, particularly for high-technology products. For many sophisticated software products and electronic devices, a seller who can't provide tech support to buyers will have no chance of success.

- *Financing.* Whether you "tote the note" and guarantee credit to anyone, offer innovative leasing, do buybacks, or have other financing alternatives, you'll find that giving people different, more convenient ways to pay can lend your product a convincing strength.

- *Customer Service.* Excellent service is perhaps the most important thing you can add to any product or service today. In a world where word travels fast through social media, you want to provide top-notch customer service. The shoe giant Zappos has built its reputation by providing excellent customer service. Make this a top priority.

- *Reputation.* Why do people pay $10,000 for a Rolex? The Rolex reputation is the reason. At its most extreme, reputation can liter-

plan pointer

Tell people about what you sell. Your website, your packaging, and your marketing campaign should let people know what to expect when they purchase your products. Social media and Facebook pages should also have a lot written about your company and your product. And in case you receive social media comments that are not always favorable, you can address such negative comments in a polite manner. Savvy shoppers are reading more and more about what they intend on buying—so give them something positive to talk about.

ally keep you in business, as is the case with many companies, such as IBM and Walmart, whose well-developed reputations have tided them over in hard times.

fact or fiction

Don't make assumptions when you're looking at a new product or service idea. For instance, you might think that horse-shoers are an endangered breed in the automobile era. But actually the leisure and sport horse industry is thriving, and there are more farriers active today than when horses were the main mode of transport. Just because something seems out of fashion doesn't mean you're out of luck.

- *Knowledge.* Your knowledge and the means you have of imparting that to customers is an important part of your total offering. Retailers of auto parts, home improvement supplies, and all sorts of other goods have found that simply having knowledgeable salespeople who know how to replace the water pump in a '95 Chevy will lure customers in and encourage them to buy.

- *Experience.* "We've been there. We've done thousands of installations like yours, and there's no doubt we can make this one work as well." Nothing could be more soothing to a skeptical sales prospect than to learn that the seller has vast experience at what he's doing. If you have ample experience, make it part of your selling proposition.

- *Fast Delivery.* Nobody wants to wait for anything anymore. If you can offer overnight shipping, on-site service, or 24/7 availability, it can turn an otherwise unremarkable product or service into a very attractive one.

- *Endorsements.* There's a reason Peyton Manning makes millions of dollars a year from endorsements. People want to relate to Peyton and share his aura, if only obliquely.

- *Other Factors.* There are many wild cards unique to particular products, or perhaps simply little used in particular industries, with which you can make your product stand out. For instance, consider a service agreement guarantee. When consumers know they can get a product repaired under a service guarantee or return a faulty

>> High Flier

Today you can be a frequent shopper, frequent diner, and frequent just-about-anything-else in addition to being the consumer that started it all, the frequent flier. The innovation that revolutionized airline marketing and marketing of many other types of products and services is credited to Robert Crandall, former CEO of American Airlines.

In the early 1980s, Crandall faced a difficult situation. He and other airlines flew the same passengers on the same planes over the same routes and, because they were subject to the same economics, at about the same price. How to make travelers choose American over United, Delta, and other rivals?

Crandall's solution was the now-ubiquitous frequent flier club. Passengers who chose American would accumulate points for each trip. When they had enough, they could redeem the points for free or discounted travel and, later, other awards.

The idea neatly solved the problem of how to differentiate nearly identical transportation services and also encouraged American passengers to become fiercely loyal to the airline.

product for a refund, they're often more likely to buy it over otherwise superior competitors offering less powerful warranties.

Liability Concerns

To a typical consumer who's purchased her share of shoddy products from uncooperative manufacturers, it's encouraging to hear about a multimillion-dollar settlement of a consumer's claim against some manufacturer. It provides proof that the high and mighty can be humbled and that some poor schmuck can be struck by lightning and receive a big fat check.

To manufacturers and distributors of products, however, the picture looks entirely different. Liability lawsuits have changed the landscape of a number of industries, from toy manufacturers to children's furniture retailers. If you visit public swimming pools these days, for instance, you don't see the diving boards that used to grace the deep ends of almost all such recreational facilities. The reason is that fear of lawsuits from injured divers, along with the allied increase in liability insurance premiums, have made these boards no longer financially feasible.

If you're going to come out with a diving board or offer diving-board maintenance services, you need to be prepared for this legal issue. Dealing with it may be as simple as merely including a statement to the effect that you foresee no significant liability issues arising from your sale of this product or service. If there is a liability issue, real or apparent, acknowledge it and describe how you will deal with it in your plan. For instance, you may want to take note of the fact that, like all marketers of children's bedroom furniture, you

> *"If there is a liability issue, real or apparent, acknowledge it and describe how you will deal with it in your plan."*

attach warning labels and disclaimers to all your products and also carry a liability insurance policy. In fact, warning labels may seem ridiculous, but in a litigation-crazed society, you will actually see labels such as the one on a portable stroller that read, "Please remove child before folding." Really? Funny as it may sound, let it be known that you will take all necessary steps to protect your business, your products, and yourself from litigation.

You must have an attorney's advice on almost anything you plan to market. A layman's opinion on whether a product is more or less likely to generate lawsuits is not worth including in a plan.

On the subject of liability, here is a good place to deal with the question of whether you are already being sued for a product's perceived failings and, if so, how you plan to deal with it. If you can't find an answer, you may wind up like private aircraft manufacturers, many of which were forced out of the business by increases in lawsuits following crashes.

It's often difficult to get an attorney to commit himself on paper about the prospects for winning or losing a lawsuit. Many times plans handle this with a sentence saying something along the lines of, "Our legal counsel advises us the plaintiff's claims are without merit."

>> **Expert Advice** <<

The following are some key points about products.

> *Product knowledge is important, but you need more.* Sure, you have to know the products and services you sell in detail. But product knowledge alone is useless, and that is where many marketing plans run afoul of the first law of marketing: Put the Customer First. Customers don't buy products or services. They buy solutions to problems, relief from an itch, satisfaction of a felt need. In short, they buy benefits.

> *Benefits are not features.* Features are characteristics of products or services that are independent of the buyer's perceptions. A tractor lawn mower may have a 3 hp gas motor, be green with a natty yellow design, have a warranty good for two years and cost $1,695, payable in 12 easy monthly installments. Those are all features.

> The benefits to the buyer include confidence (3 hp is plenty powerful for a suburban lawn and will carry its owner in comfort up and down gentle slopes), prestige (John Deere knows how to make its buyers feel good), and convenience and economy (price and terms). Benefits perceived will differ from one customer to the next—another buyer might buy the same lawn mower because his son-in-law is the dealer, or because his neighbor says it's a great machine, or just because it caught his eye.

> The key point is that benefits are dependent on the perceptions of the market, whereas features are dependent on the product or service.

> *The perceptions of the market are determined only by research.* Armchair research does not count. If you know your market and study your demographics, you will know what your customers perceive to be value. Then and only then can you safely match your products or services to their demands. You get to know what your markets want by asking them, by knowing them, by researching their buying behaviors. Some of this is almost subliminal—but what sets the big winners apart is that they take the extra time to do this research.

Riding
Industry Trends

> "It doesn't matter how hard you row. What matters is
> what boat you're in."
>
> —Peter Worrell, Investment Banker

Peter's point is that it isn't enough to just work hard or work harder. If you are in the wrong industry at the wrong time, making your business grow is going to be difficult. Not impossible, just difficult. The investment community tends to believe that any business can be buoyed by an industry on the rise and that the opposite is true in an industry whose tide is ebbing. This means it's important for you to include an industry analysis in your business plan.

Readers of your business plan may want to see an industry on a fast-growth track with few established competitors and great potential. Or they may be more interested in a big, if somewhat slower-growing, market with competitors who have lost touch with the market, leaving the door open for rivals.

> *"One of the things you will try to do with your plan is present a case for your industry being, if not the next big thing, at least an excellent opportunity."*

Whatever the facts are, you'll need to support them with a snapshot analysis of the state of your industry and any trends taking place. This can't be mere off-the-cuff thinking. You need to support your opinions with market research that identifies specific competitors and outlines their weaknesses and strengths and any barriers to entry into the market. Finally, and perhaps most important, you'll have to convincingly describe what makes you better and destined to succeed.

Convincing doesn't necessarily mean you need to be more complex. Peter van Stolk, founder of Urban Juice & Soda, fulfilled all desired functions of an industry description by merely pointing visitors to his bookcases full of the hundreds of new beverages that he had been asked to distribute in his many years in business. Most are long gone, proving his main point: "The beverage industry is competitive, but there aren't a lot of smarts."

>> Local Is Profitable

Over 90 percent of all businesses are local. Unless your business is set up to market to regional or larger markets, focus on customers in your immediate geographic location. You can use your knowledge of the conditions and trends in the local economy to advantage. You can identify and study direct and indirect competitors in the local market far more thoroughly than in a wider area. The better you know your market area, the better you will be able to serve it—and make a profit.

The State of Your Industry

In the early 1980s, all an entrepreneur needed was the word "energy" in the title of his company to draw the attention of financial backers. At other times, fields such as biotechnology, computer software, or internet commerce have been seen as veins of gold waiting to be mined by gleeful investors. In recent years the term "solution," was big in the tech world, even if nobody was completely sure what the problem was for which your solution would apply. Today, the mobile technology field will quickly generate attention, but you'd better have something new and interesting to offer because it is quickly becoming saturated with apps for almost everything you can think of. One of the things you will try to do with your plan is present a case in support of your industry—why it is valuable and how it will continue to be important.

When preparing the state of the industry section, you'll need to lift your eyes from your own company and your own issues and focus them on the outside world. Instead of looking at your business as a self-contained system, you'll describe the whole industry in which you operate and point to your position in that universe. You can then start to zero in on your country, your state, and your local community, deepening on how far your business stretches.

This part of your plan may take a little more legwork than other sections because you'll be drawing together information from a number of outside sources. You may also be reporting on or even conducting your own original research into industry affairs. See Figure 9–1 on page 150.

buzzword

Psychographics is the attempt to accurately measure lifestyle by classifying customers according to their activities, interests, and opinions. Although not perfect, a psychographic analysis of your marketplace can yield important marketing insights.

Market Research

Successful entrepreneurs are renowned for being able to feel a market's pulse intuitively, to project trends before anyone else detects them, and to identify needs that even customers are hardly yet aware of. After you are famous, perhaps you can claim a similar

Industry Analysis Worksheet

To start preparing your industry analysis and outlook, dig up the following facts about your field:

1. What is your total industry-wide sales volume? In dollars? In units?

   _____

2. What are the trends in sales volumes within your industry? _____

   _____

3. Who are the major players and your key competitors? What are they like? _____

   _____

4. What does it take to compete? What are the barriers to entry? _____

   _____

5. What technological trends affect your industry? _____

   _____

6. What are the main modes of marketing? _____

   _____

7. How does government regulation affect the industry? _____

   _____

8. In what ways are changing consumer tastes affecting your industry?

   _____

9. Identify recent demographic trends affecting the industry. _____

   _____

10. How sensitive is the industry to seasons and economic cycles?

    _____

11. What are key financial measures in your industry (average profit margins, sales commissions, etc.)?

    _____

Figure 9-1. Industry Analysis Worksheet

> *"Market research aims to understand the reasons consumers will buy your product."*

psychic connection to the market. But for now, you'll need to reinforce your claims to market insight by presenting solid research in your plan.

Market research aims to understand the reasons consumers will buy your product. It studies such things as consumer behavior, including how cultural, societal, and personal factors influence that behavior. For instance, market research aiming to understand consumers who buy in-line skates might study the cultural importance of fitness, the societal acceptability of marketing directed toward children and teens, and the effect of personal influences such as age, occupation, and lifestyle in directing a skate purchase.

Market research is further split into two varieties: primary and secondary. Primary research studies customers directly, whereas secondary research studies information that others have gathered about customers. Primary research might be telephone interviews or online polls with randomly selected members of the target group. You can also study your own sales records to gather primary research. Secondary research might come from reports found on the websites of various other organizations or blogs written about the industry. For your plan, you can use either type of research or a combination of both. See Figure 9.2 for some basic market research questions.

The basic questions you'll try to answer with your market research include:

- *Who are your customers?* Describe them in terms of age, occupation, income, lifestyle, educational attainment, etc.

plan pointer

You can tell investors where you are in your industry with a good descriptive company name. Experts say to avoid the vague and generic in favor of the explicit and unique. So General Duplication is bad, while Xerox—a unique word that echoes "xerography," which is the technical name for the process of plain-paper copying—is perfect.

Market Research Questions

About your buyers

Age_____

Annual income range _____

Gender_____

Ethnicity_____

Occupation _____

Homeowner _____

Preferred media _____

Keep in mind the more you ask, the fewer answers you will get—people stop answering when you ask for too much information. Keep it short and sweet, and provide some small incentive if you are asking people to fill out surveys.

About your competition

Market share _____

Advertising plans _____

Distribution _____

Product features _____

Time in business _____

About their products

Why purchased _____

Price _____

Service _____

Packaging _____

Figure 9-2. Market Research Questions

Market Research Questions

How used _____

How frequently purchased_____

What to improve _____

It's hard to get primary research on your competitors without hiring a spy. Therefore, you will need to do your due diligence and research them online, in business libraries, through their media presence, and so on.

Figure 9-2. Market Research Questions, continued

- *What do they buy now?* Describe their buying habits relating to your product or service, including how much they buy, their favored suppliers, the most popular features, and the predominant price points.
- *Why do they buy?* This is the tricky one, attempting as it does to delve into consumers' heads. Answers will depend on the product and its uses. Cookware buyers may buy the products that offer the most effective nonstick surfaces, or those that give the most pans in a package for a given amount of money, or those that come in the most decorative colors.
- *What will make them buy from you?* Although some of these questions may seem difficult, you'd be surprised at the detailed information about markets, sales figures, and consumer buying motivations that is available, especially if you are patient while searching the web. Tapping these information sources to provide the answers to as many questions as you can will make your plan more convincing and your odds of success higher. Also, the business plan software programs have detailed research included and online research available. Utilize this functionality if you are using such software and add additional data you find elsewhere. The reason to add some of your own unique material is that everyone using the software program is tapping into the same database, and you want

your business plan to differ from that of the last entrepreneur in your field.

There is also an industry selling market research, and it's a big, booming one. You can find companies that will sell you everything from industry studies to credit reports on individual companies. Market research is not cheap. It requires significant amounts of expertise, manpower, and technology to develop solid research. Large companies routinely spend tens of thousands of dollars researching things they ultimately decide they're not interested in. Smaller firms can't afford to do that too often.

For companies of all sizes, the best market research is the research you do on your own. In-house market research might take the form of original telephone interviews with consumers, customized crunching of numbers from published sources, or perhaps competitive intelligence you've gathered on your rivals through the social media. You can gather detailed research on customers, including their likes, dislikes, and preferences through Facebook and use Google Analytics to sort out the numbers as they pertain to your web visitors. People are researching and making their opinions felt through their actions on the web, so you can gain a lot of marketing insight by looking closely at what is going on electronically.

Another likely source of in-house market research is information that comes from data you already have. This information will come from analyzing sales records, gathering warranty cards containing the addresses and other information about purchasers, studying product-return rates and customer complaints, and so on. All of this data should be updated and maintained on a regular basis.

You can get in-house market research data from your own files, so it's cheaper than buying it. It's also likely to be a lot fresher than third-party market research, which may be dated or biased.

Of course, if you are starting out, your own customer records will not yet exist, meaning you will need to do your due diligence within your industry. When looking at comparable businesses (and their data), find a close match. For comparative purposes, consider:

1. companies of relative size.

2. companies serving the same geographic area, which could be global if you are planning to be a web-based business.

3. companies with a similar ownership structure. If you are two partners, look for businesses run by a couple of partners rather than an advisory board of 12.

4. companies that are relatively new. While you can learn from long-standing businesses, they may be successful today because of their 25-year business history and reputation.

You will want to use the data you have gathered not only to determine how much business you could possibly do but also to figure out how you will fit into and adapt to the marketplace.

One limitation of in-house market information is that it may not include exactly what you're looking for. For instance, if you'd like to consider offering consumers financing for their purchases, it's hard to tell how they'd like it since you don't already offer it. You can get around this limitation by conducting original research—interviewing customers who enter your store, for example, or counting cars that pass the intersection where you plan to open a new location—and combining it with existing data. Follow these steps to spending your market research dollars wisely:

1. Determine what you need to know about your market. The more focused the research, the more valuable it will be.

2. Prioritize the results of the first step. You can't research everything, so concentrate on the information that will give you the best (or quickest) payback.

3. Review less-expensive research alternatives. Small Business Development Centers and the Small Business Administration can help you develop customer surveys. Your trade association will have good secondary research. Be creative.

4. Estimate the cost of performing the research yourself. Keep in mind that with the internet you should not have to spend a ton of money. If you're considering hiring a consultant or a researcher, remember this is your dream, these are your goals, and this is your business. Don't pay for what you don't need.

Trends

Timing, in business as in other areas of life, is everything. Marc Andreessen, founder of Netscape Communications, had the good fortune to develop software for browsing the web just as the internet, which had been around for 20 years, was coming to widespread popular attention. The timing of his move made him hundreds of millions of dollars, but some of those who came later fell by the wayside.

The best time to address a trend is before it is even beginning and certainly before it is widely recognized. If you can prepare a business that satisfies a soon-to-be popular need, you can generate growth that is practically off the scale. (This is, by the way, the combination that venture capitalists favor most.) The problem, of course, is spotting the trends first and acting quickly before others jump in line ahead of you.

There are a couple of different techniques you can use to identify trends and to present your identifications in your plan. A trend is basically a series of occurrences that indicates a pattern. Some trend analysts look at past events (usually trends themselves) and project them forward. For example, trend analysts in recent years have looked at the huge numbers of baby boomers, the surge of people born in the years between 1946 and 1964. They then projected forward to see that these baby boomers would be retiring in the near future and saw a defined market for that segment of the population.

plan pointer

Become a trend spotter. Look at the latest popular inventions, new technology, and products in your potential industry. If you're in fashion, for example, you want to be at every fashion expo you can attend. Every industry has conferences, expos, and other places in which the latest ideas are on display. But, these are not the trends you are looking for—they are already happening. Your job is to look at what you would like to see as the next logical outgrowth of these trends. This is how the cell phone became the smartphone and how silent movies became talkies, and years later motion pictures became 3-D motion pictures. What is missing or what could improve upon the latest trends you are seeing? That's how you use trends to create the next trend or be prepared for it.

>> Soaking the Rich

Sometimes you don't need fancy market research to spot a customer need. Lonnie Johnson, an engineer at NASA's Jet Propulsion Laboratory, was tinkering with a heat-pump design when he attached a nozzle to a piece of tubing and stuck it on his bathroom faucet. It made a lousy heat pump, he noticed, but a great water pistol.

Johnson made a portable prototype for his daughter, who promptly soaked every kid in the neighborhood. Faced with mounting demands for defensive armament, Johnson took his prototype to the offices of a toy maker called Larami Corporation. When he squirted a jet of water across the meeting room, the executives were hooked.

Johnson's informal market research—and his dramatic presentation of his invention—led Larami to offer him a licensing agreement for the Super Soaker line of water pistols. The deal produces millions annually in licensing fees for Johnson, who has since started his own research and development company (www.johnsonrd.com). There's no word on how he does his market research nowadays.

Another good way to forecast trends is by test marketing. You try to sell something in a single store and see how it does before you roll it out in your whole chain. The key to this technique is trying it in a well-selected test market, one that closely resembles the market you'll try to sell to later on.

Focus groups and surveys try to catch hold of trends by asking people what's hot. You can ask open-ended questions: What type of apps or new mobile phone features would you like to see? Or show them product samples and see how they react. This is also tricky because you are dealing with a small group of, you hope, representative people and extrapolating to a larger group. If your group isn't representative, your results may be misleading.

Some other ways you can try to nail a trend in advance: Talk to salespeople who are in touch with customer needs, quiz executives whose

plan pointer

Forecast Pro is a software program that lets nonstat-isticians produce sophisti-cated business forecasts. Engineered for lay users, it automatically selects the best forecasting technique for the job you're doing. For more information on Forecast Pro, go to its parent company, Adaptive Insights at www.adaptive insights.com where you can get a free demo.

jobs are watching the big picture, read a wide variety of periodicals and try to spot connections, or hire think tanks of experts to brainstorm over what the future might hold.

In most of these trend-forecasting techniques, statistics play a big role. Mathe-maticians assign numerical values to variables such as loyalty to existing brands, then build a model that can indicate trends that are invisible to intuitive analysis. Providing some statistics in the trends section of your plan can make it more convincing.

Barriers to Entry

If you want to become a semiconductor manufacturer, you'll need a billion-dollar factory or two. If you want to have a TV network, you'll need programming and cable carriage in the major markets. These problems are called barriers to entry, and they exist to some extent in all industries. The barriers may be monetary, technological, distribution, or market-related, or they may simply be a matter of ownership of prime real estate. (This last is frequently cited as the real competitive advantage of McDonald's. "Whenever you see a good site, you find out McDonald's already owns it," groused one fast-food competitor.)

An important part of analyzing your market is determining what the barriers to entry are and how high they stretch. If the barriers are high, as is the case with automobile manufacturing, you can be assured new competitors are likely to be slow in springing up. If the barriers are low, such as opening a nail salon, which does not have a huge overhead, you have more opportunity to get into the game.

Be alert for innovative competitors when writing the section of your plan in which you analyze barriers to entry. Clearly some markets are also more saturated than others, and today some are dominated by the McDonald's of their industry. For example, it's hard to open a bookstore today with Amazon changing the way people buy books. In that industry, you need to be creative and explore entry into specialty books, mystery books, or another niche within the larger market. Exploring entry points in the marketplace carefully will save you from a disastrous error and will certainly demonstrate to investors that you've thought your plan through and are not jumping to conclusions.

Identifying Competitors

You're not alone, even if you have a one-person, homebased business. You also have your competition to worry about. And your backers will worry about competition, too. Even if you truly are in the rare position of addressing a brand-new market where no competition exists, most experienced people reading your plan will have questions about companies they suspect may be competitors. For these reasons, you should devote a special section of your plan to identifying competitors.

If you had to name two competitors in the athletic shoe market, you'd quickly come up with Nike and Reebok. But these by far aren't the only competitors in the sneaker business. They're just two of the main ones, and depending on the business you're in, the other ones may be more important. If you sell soccer shoes, for instance, Adidas is a bigger player than either of the two American firms. And smaller firms such as Etonic, New Balance, and Saucony also have niches where they are comparatively powerful.

You can develop a list of competitors by talking to customers and suppliers, checking with industry groups, and reading trade journals. But it's not enough to simply name your competitors. You need to know their manner of operation, how they compete.

Does a competitor stress a selective, low-volume, high-margin business, or does she emphasize sales growth at any cost, taking

plan pitfall

Think twice before deciding barriers to entry are high for all potential competitors. For instance, you need billions of dollars to start a semiconductor company—but not if you contract out fabrication of the silicon chips to a manufacturer. Several years back, many semiconductor startups did exactly that, providing serious competition for rivals who assumed the barrier was too high to allow many new entries.

every job that comes along, whether or not it fits any coherent scheme or offers an attractive profit? Knowing this kind of information about competitors can help you identify their weaknesses as well as their names.

What Makes You Better?

This is one of the most important sections of your plan. You need to convince anyone thinking of joining with your company, as an investor or in another way, that you offer something obviously different and better than what is already available. Typically, this is called your competitive advantage, but it's not an overstatement to call it your company's reason for being.

>> Where the Elite Meet to Eat

The Elite Café in Waco, Texas, serves as a good case study of competitive edge. The Elite has been near the campus of Baylor University, serving home-style cooking for decades under the same ownership. Why do people stop there to eat instead of at one of the dozens of other restaurants along Interstate 35, many of them national chains with instantly recognizable names?

- *Convenience.* The Elite Café is near an exit ramp from both directions, and getting back onto the highway is easy.
- *Visibility.* The Elite has a big sign that is easy to spot in plenty of time to get off the highway.
- *Customer base.* After decades in the same spot, the Elite is a familiar dining place for thousands of Central Texas residents and travelers.
- *Geography.* The main reason, however, is probably related to the fact that the Elite is located very near the midpoint of the drive between Dallas and Austin, the state capital. Anybody making that drive is likely to decide to stop halfway through to ease the job, and when they do, there will be the Elite Café.

Your competitive edge may lie in any of the product features discussed in the last chapter, including cost, features, service, quality, distribution, and so forth. Or it could be something totally different. The success of a retail convenience store located on an interstate highway, for instance, might depend almost entirely on how close it is to an exit ramp. Compare what you have to offer to that of your competitors, including your online competitors. Look for your competitive edge without knocking or denigrating your competition—your goal is not to say they aren't good but that you are a better choice—and explain why.

To figure out your competitive advantage, start by asking yourself:

plan pitfall

To prepare convincing industry studies, name all competitors, not just the biggies. Start with the primary ones. Then keep going to the secondary ones, trying to identify virtually every company that's a significant player in your field. Only when you have a comprehensive list of competitors can you truly understand what you're up against.

1. *Why do people buy from me instead of my competitors?* Think about this question in terms of product characteristics. Ask your customers why they buy from you. Ask noncustomers why they don't. Ask suppliers, colleagues, and anybody you can find.

   Use online surveys, read reviews on places like Yelp or Angie's List, and get a feel for what people like and don't like about the places that do what you do . . . or are planning to do.

2. *What makes me different and, I hope, better?* Your competitive advantage is not quite as important if your company operates in the beginning stages of a new industry. When interest and sales in a new field are growing fast, you can survive and prosper even if you aren't clearly better than the rest. If, however, you plan to take market share away from established competitors in a mature industry, then competitive edge is all-important. Without a convincing case for being very different and much better than the rest, your business plan will have a hard time swaying anybody.

>> **Expert Advice** <<

Centurion Consulting Group develops all types of plans for new and ongoing national and international companies, including strategic, business, marketing, growth, financial, feasibility, and operations plans. Barbara Lewis, president of the company, also believes that a business plan is critical to the success of a company. "Just like you wouldn't build a house without a blueprint, you shouldn't build a business without a plan," she says. "The company's 'big picture' is the strategic portion of the plan, which includes the mission, vision, strengths, weaknesses, opportunities, and threats. Other essential elements of the plan include the marketing analysis and strategy and the operations and financial analysis and strategy."

One of the basic problems that she sees in plans is the market analysis. "Most plans don't define the market size, identify market characteristics, or have a realistic assessment of competitors," she says. "Yet the company's marketplace is one of the most important issues. Understanding the market goes a long way toward developing a cogent strategy and comprehensive tactical plan."

Marketing
The Plan within Your Plan

What are you selling? How are you selling it? Why would anybody want to buy from you? Where can they find your product or services? After all, even the greatest invention will not launch a successful business if people do not know where to find it.

Once upon a time the most important aspect of marketing for a brick-and-mortar business was location, location, location—indeed, to a large extent it still is. But today, in the virtual world that is the internet, location may be replaced by Facebook, Facebook, Facebook.

Your marketing plan is all about knowing your target market and making sure those customers know where they can find you. However, before you can start reaching out to your public, you need to have a marketing strategy that defines what you are selling, at what price(s), from where, and how you are going to spread the word. To simplify, you can use the four Ps of marketing: product, price, place, and promotion.

Defining Your Product

Product, the first of the four Ps, refers to the features and benefits of what you have to sell (as usual, we're using the term as shorthand for products and services). Many modern marketers have a problem with this "P" because it doesn't refer to customer service, which is an important part of the bundle of features and benefits you offer to customers. However, it's pretty easy to update product by simply redefining it to include whatever services are offered.

There are a number of issues you need to address in your product section. You need to first break out the core product from the actual product. What does this mean? The core product is the nominal product.

buzzword

A branding strategy is a marketing plan that calls for the creation of a name, symbol, or design that identifies and differentiates a product or company from other products and/or companies. Levi Strauss followed a branding strategy when it devised the Dockers brand for a new line of men's casual pants. A company like Nike has a worldwide recognizable symbol—the swoosh—that lets you know you are looking at Nike products.

Say you're selling snow cones. A snow cone is your core product. But your actual product includes napkins, an air-conditioned seating area, parking spaces for customers, and so forth. Similarly, an electronics store nominally sells computers, tablets, and devices, but it also provides expert advice from salespeople, a service department for customers, opportunities to comparison shop, software, and so on.

It's important to understand that the core product isn't the end of the story. Sometimes the things added to it are more valuable than the core product itself. That's not necessarily bad, but failing to understand this is likely to lead to trouble.

Defining Your Customer

Marketing great toys for five-year-olds to teenagers isn't going to work nor will selling single's cruises to married couples or milkshakes to people who are lactose intolerant. While you may not be able to define everyone who is a likely customer, you need to know your target audience and know it well.

You need to talk about your ideal customer as if he or she is someone you know very well. For example, she or he is 25 to 29 years of age, earning x amount of money, has no children yet, and earned a college degree.

A new Italian restaurant might say it's going for families eating out on a budget who live within a five-mile radius of its location. It might quote Census Bureau figures showing there are 12,385 such families in its service area. Even better, it would cite National Restaurant Association statistics about how many families it takes to support a new Italian restaurant.

A bicycle seat manufacturer might have identified its market as casual middle-aged cyclists who find traditional bike seats uncomfortable. It may cite American College of Sports Medicine surveys, saying that sore buttocks due to uncomfortable seats is the chief complaint of recreational bicyclists.

It is important to quantify your market's size if possible. If you can point out that there are more than six million insulin-dependent diabetics in the United States, it will bolster your case for the new easy-to-use injection syringe your company has developed.

In addition to fully defining your product, you need to address other issues in your marketing plan. For instance, you may have to describe the process you're using for product development. Tell how you come up with ideas, screen them, test them, produce prototypes, and so on.

You may need to discuss the life cycle of the product you're selling. This may be crucial in the case of quickly consumed products such as corn chips and in longer-lasting items like household appliances. You can market steadily to corn-chip buyers in the hopes they'll purchase from you frequently, but it makes less sense to bombard people with offers on refrigerators when they need one only every 10 or 20 years. Understanding the product's life cycle has a powerful effect on your marketing plan, as does knowing logical buying habits. For example, one popular department store was offering a buy-one-get-one-at-half-price deal on fine jewelry. The deal was not generating a strong response because most people do not shop for expensive jewelry in "bulk" quantities but instead take a personalized

>> The Universally Wrong Assumption

It's always easy to market something by saying, "Everyone will love it!" But that's the kiss of death in marketing. No matter how wonderful a product or service may appear, nothing will please "everyone." Therefore, each product or service must have a defined market if you are serious about your business succeeding. Narrow your demographic group by positioning your product appropriately. That may include more than one place, such as bicycles might go under bikes or sporting goods, but not "everywhere" or for "everyone."

> *"Your marketing plan should be able to stand alone if taken out of the context of your business plan."*

approach. In fact, such a promotion was cheapening the products.

Other aspects of the product section may include a branding strategy, a plan for follow-up products, or line extensions. Keeping these various angles on products in mind while writing this section will help you describe your product fully and persuasively.

Setting Prices

One of the most important decisions you have to make in a business plan is what price to charge for what you're selling. Pricing determines many things, from your profit margin per unit to your overall sales volume. It influences decisions in other areas, such as what level of service you will provide and how much you will spend on marketing. Pricing has to be a process you conduct concurrently with other jobs, including estimating sales volume, determining market trends, and calculating costs. There are two basic methods you can use for selecting a price.

One way is to figure out what it costs you altogether to produce or obtain your product or service, then add in a suitable profit margin. This markup method is easy and straightforward, and assuming you can sell sufficient units at the suggested price, it guarantees a profitable operation. It's widely used by retailers. To use it effectively, you'll need to know all of your costs as well as standard markups applied by others in your industry.

The other way, competitive pricing, is more concerned with the competition and the customer than with your own internal processes. The competitive pricing approach looks at what your rivals in the marketplace charge, plus what customers are likely to be willing to pay, and sets prices accordingly. The second step of this process is tougher— now you have to adjust your own costs to yield a profit. Competitive pricing is effective at maintaining your market appeal and ensuring your enterprise's long life, assuming you can sell your goods at a profit. See Figure 10–1 on page 168 to determine your pricing objectives.

Pricing is inherently strategic. You can use prices to attack competitors, position your

plan pointer

Product beauty may be only skin deep. Packaging, far from merely containing goods, is an important part of your product. Attractive packaging lures looks. Sturdy packaging ensures goods arrive intact. Environmental conscious- ness means recycled or organic packaging may be more important than the product inside. So attend to outer as well as inner product beauty.

business, test a new market, and/or defend a niche. The only hard-and-fast rule to follow in setting prices is: Set prices carefully, deliberately, knowledgeably, and with long-range goals in mind. All the rest are footnotes. See Figure 10–2 on page 169 for help in determining your pricing strategy.

Further Pricing Thoughts

Why is setting price so tough? Perhaps because nobody really understands it. Pricing is as much art as science. Price too low and lose money. Price too high and lose customers. Price in the middle and lose position. It seems like a no-win situation for most small-business owners. There is no mechanical way to grind out the right price. There is no shortcut. It's a matter of doing your research, and then it often comes down to some trial and error.

> "Small businesses simply cannot afford to compete on price."

Setting Pricing Objectives

Before you can select a pricing approach, you need to know your pricing objectives. Following are questions to ask yourself about your pricing goals:

1. Which is more important: higher sales or higher profits? _____

   _____

2. Am I more interested in short-term results or long-term performance?

   _____

3. Am I trying to stabilize market prices or discourage price-cutting?

   _____

4. Do I want to discourage new competitors or encourage existing ones to get out of the market? _____

   _____

5. Am I trying to quickly establish a market position, or am I willing to build slowly? _____

   _____

6. Do I have other concerns, such as boosting cash flow or recovering product development costs? _____

   _____

7. What will the impact of my price decision be on my image in the market? How does that fit the image I want? _____

   _____

8. What reputation do I want, "sells low and beats prices" or "provides higher-quality goods and/or more personalized service?" _____

   _____

Answer these questions first, then prioritize them to decide how each objective will weigh in setting your pricing strategy. That way, when you present your price objectives in your business plan, it will make sense and be supported by reasonable arguments integrated with your overall business goals.

Figure 10-1. Setting Pricing Objectives

Price Range Worksheet

Pricing is always considered in a competitive context. Part of your pricing strategy involves providing answers to the questions implicit in this worksheet.

Item: Price range: $ _____ (low) to $ _____ (high).

Establish a price floor

Mark-on (gross margin) is _____% of retail price.

Manufacturer's suggested price is $ _____.

Fixed costs are $ _____.

Variable costs are $ _____.

Break-even point is $ _____.

Special considerations for this product or service price:

Level of service: _____

Status:_____

Comparative quality:_____

Loss leader: _____

Demand:_____

Product life: _____

Overhead:_____

Market penetration costs: _____

Turnover rate is _____ times per year.

Industry average is $_____.

Going rate is $_____.

I estimate that _____ units will be sold.

Top price (what the market will bear) based on the customers' perceptions of value: $_____.

Figure 10-2. Price Range Worksheet

Small businesses simply cannot afford to compete on price. Low-balling drives small businesses out of business, cheapens their image, and costs them the opportunity to upgrade their customer base. It's a race to the bottom and simply does not work.

There's always someone willing to sell on price alone. Sometimes the price competition comes from a giant like Walmart, which buys in such huge quantities that suppliers cave in and pare their margins to the bone. (Walmart has revolutionized inventory management and distribution, which allows them to make vast profits on thin margins. They aren't just competing on price.) Sometimes the competitor is a newcomer who thinks—erroneously—that the best way to enter a market is to buy market share with loss-leader pricing.

The two main ways to deal with price competition are to meet the price (cave in and watch your margins evaporate) or to reposition yourself so the price competition is indirect (repositioning).

Filling in the Price/Quality grid in Figure 10–3 for your products is a useful exercise. Fill in the grid with autos or computers or whatever it is you are selling. Knowing where your business operates best makes a big difference in your promotional plans.

Other useful grids are price/service, price/convenience, and so on. You can also use these grids to spot a market gap. Remember, your competitive edge can support your prices. For example, you can charge a little more if you can ship faster than your competitors or if your product is much longer lasting.

fact or fiction

The best plan describes a business selling something everybody needs and yet has no competition, right? Not quite. Business plan readers see so many plans making such claims that they are highly skeptical. If you really are in such a position, you'll have to document it thoroughly. Being the first to come up with a brilliant idea sounds wonderful, but you need to determine why no one has thought of it before. Perhaps it is cost ineffective or not practical. Business plan readers are aware that when something sounds too good to be true, often it is. You may be truly innovative or you may just be another person with an idea that hasn't worked in the past.

Price/Quality Grids

Use this grid to locate market gaps, areas where there may be an opportunity for your business to grow. Suppose there is no direct competitor in the high price/high quality sector, while the other areas are overserved. (Usually the low price range is jammed. Check it out.) That may open a market for you to fill. It's always interesting to note that high price and high quality do not necessarily go together, nor do low price and low quality.

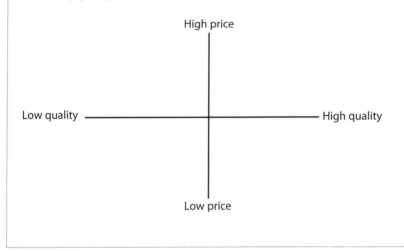

Figure 10-3. Price/Quality Grid

Place

Place refers to channels of distribution, or the means you will use to put your product where people can buy it. This can be very simple: Retailers and many service businesses (restaurants, personal services, business services) rely primarily on location. For manufacturers, conventional distribution systems have three steps: producer, wholesaler, and retailer. You may occupy or sell to members of any one of these steps. Some companies with vertically integrated distribution, such as Dell, occupy all the steps themselves. Others, like franchisors, are parts of systems that orchestrate the activities among all channels. Still others, such as independent retailers, operate in one channel only.

Location Considerations

For retailers, the big place question involves real estate. Location commonly determines success or failure for many retailers. That doesn't necessarily mean the same location will work for all retailers. A low-rent but high-traffic space near low-income housing may be a poor choice for a retailer stocking those Armani suits but will work fine for a fast-food restaurant or convenience store. Your location decision needs to be tied to your market, your product, and your price.

Two of the most common tools for picking location are census data and traffic surveys. Retailers relying on walk-in traffic want to get a location that has a lot of people walking or driving past. You can usually get traffic data from local economic development agencies or by simply sitting down with a clipboard and pencil and counting people or cars yourself. Census data describing the number, income levels, and other information about households in the nearby neighborhoods can be obtained from the same sources. An animal clinic, for example, wants to locate in an area with a lot of pet-owning households. This is the type of information you can get from census surveys. The census website, census.gov, is a great place to start searching for data. You can also learn a lot about marketing research by going to the Marketing Research Association at marketingresearch.org/.

Site Sensitivity

Manufacturers require certain basic conditions for their sites, but retailers and some service firms are exquisitely sensitive to a wide variety of location factors. In some cases, a few feet can make the difference between a location that is viable and one that is not.

Site selection plans for retailers should include traffic data, demographics of nearby populations, estimated sales per square foot, rental rates, and other important economic indicators. Service firms such as restaurants will want many of the same things. Service firms such as pest control services and bookkeeping businesses will want to provide information about local income levels, housing, and business activity.

Store design also must be addressed. Retailing can be as much about entertaining shoppers as it is about displaying goods. So store design becomes very important, especially for high-fashion retailers or well-known tech companies such as Apple. Floor plans are probably not enough here. Retailers may want to include photos or illustrations of striking displays, in-store boutiques, and the like.

Then there is the internet and e-commerce, where physical location gives way to driving traffic to the site. This is where you need a Facebook page, Twitter handle, YouTube channel, Pinterest for photos, and so forth. Social media is where etailers can make themselves known but only by using the accepted methods of the genre. Social-media marketing is a different animal, and that means getting to know your prospective customers online without being sales hungry or pushy. The hard sales push turns off the social media crowd. It is more about engaging effectively and building community.

To get started, however, you need a Facebook page that draws attention and a presence on social media, which can take time to build. Followers on social media serve two very important purposes:

1. They can become regular customers if you keep providing them with products they like to buy.
2. They can spread the word to their social-media followers. Word-of-mouth marketing is huge and cost-free to you once you've set the wheels in motion.

The power of the internet is such that it can reach millions of people without your having to pay to reach them. It is light years ahead of direct mailing, which can work in smaller business circles but does not make sense at a national or global level.

You need to be able to plan a social-media campaign, which means adapting to the rules of the road and using any social media platform correctly. It means putting forth your message in a creative and interesting way. This also holds true for blogs. There are tons of bloggers out there, but those who have interesting content get far more readers than those that do not.

In the social media, you want to

- pose interesting questions.
- answer the questions of others to demonstrate your expertise.
- be transparent and honest.

■ be consistent and **NOT** say different things on different platforms.

■ make friends and build relationships with people rather than sell-ing, selling, selling. (Social media is "social." Just as you wouldn't start a sales pitch at a party or social engagement, so, too, you wouldn't do it on social media either.)

■ stay on top of what is going on—don't launch into old news and retreaded themes.

■ maintain an ongoing presence—participate often and update your web presence.

Setting Up Your Online Presence

Every successful business today has at least a website (and some have more than one) as well as a presence on Facebook and other social-media sites. Just as you set up a retail store to best position your products, you want to set up your site to do the same. Your social media helps lead customers to your site and your business. It all ties together.

Your website is also influenced by what type of business you are running. For a brick-and-mortar business, it can be an adjunct means of marketing you and your goods.

For a business selling through its locations and on the internet, it is a means of taking local shopping worldwide. Many etailers have found that they may carry items that do marginally well in their local stores but have an audience thousands of miles away. That's the beauty of the internet. Of course, this means factoring such shipping into your operations.

For businesses that are strictly web driven, you'll need to show how the site works and all that is set up behind the site for taking orders, shipping them, and handling customer service, which is important for all businesses today, but especially so for online businesses where buyers cannot walk in and return an item face to face.

Along with the reasoning behind your site, you'll also want to have a website designed to suit your type of business and demographics. Therefore, a high-end jeweler and kid-friendly fast-food restaurant will look quite different from one another on the web.

You'll also want to keep it simple. Try not to overwhelm the viewers. Some white space isn't a bad thing. It's also important that you have a

>> 20 Keys to Having an Excellent Website That Enhances Your Marketing Plan

1. Update it regularly– nobody wants old news or information.

2. Use content that interests your visitors—make it about them, not all about you.

3. Avoid too many bells and whistles that slow down the site.

4. Make it navigation friendly—people who get lost will leave.

5. Make it interactive with polls and surveys .

6. Provide an "about us" page so visitors (including current customers) know who you are.

7. Use colors that don't glare or make it hard to read.

8. Check out how the pages look on various computers and mobile devices.

9. Double-check to make sure all links work.

10. Maintain control—even if someone else designs it, learn how to make your own changes.

11. Link only to businesses you know are reliable.

12. Keep it original—you can borrow ideas, but don't use content from other sources, at least not without the permission of the other site owner or manager.

13. Include a blog—if you don't write very well, hire a blogger.

14. Use visuals—photos are worth thousands of words.

15. Link to your social-media sites—Facebook, Twitter, LinkedIn, YouTube, Pinterest, etc. You need not be on all of them—look at their demographics.

16. Make it clear how people can find you if you have brick-and-mortar location(s).

17. Make it clear how they can pay you—and make sure the process is simple— if you are selling on the internet.

18. Include a site map.

19. Use keywords in the site for SEO purposes to be found by search.

20. Have easy-to-find contact information on every page.

consistent message (for all marketing). If you're the high-end jeweler, then everything should have the same high-end appeal, photos, and wording. If you're the kid-friendly fast-food place, then everything should be about families and kids. Be consistent.

One of the best ways to determine what you want, whether you end up using site-building software or hire someone to build your site, is to look at other sites and write down what you like.

Many companies devote great time and effort to their web and social-media presence. They look at the statistics provided and plan carefully how and when to post their messages.

The more your business is dependent on the internet, the more you will discuss it in your plan of operations. But, you should definitely include it in your marketing plans. A business today without any mention of using the internet is suspicious.

Distribution Concerns

There are three main issues in deciding on a placement strategy: coverage, control, and cost. Cost, it goes almost without saying, is an important part of any business decision, including distribution concerns. The other two issues, however, are unique to distribution and are trickier.

Coverage refers to the need to cover a large or a small market. If you're selling laundry soap, you may feel the need to offer it to virtually every household in America. This will steer you toward a conventional distribution scheme running from your soap factory to a group of wholesalers serving particular regions or industries, to retailers such as grocery stores, and finally to the consumer. It can also be accomplished by selling online, saving you the need for numerous warehouses.

> *"If you need control over your distribution, it will powerfully influence placement decisions."*

What if you are reaching out to only a small group, such as chief information officers of Fortune 500 companies? In this case, the conventional, rather lengthy distribution scheme is clearly inappropriate. You're likely to do better by selling directly to the CIOs through a company sales staff, sales reps, or perhaps an agreement with another company that already has sales access to the CIOs. In both these cases, coverage has a lot of say in the design of your distribution system.

fact or fiction

Ever feel you're going to have to cut prices to stay in business? Don't trust that feeling! Studies show 16 out of 17 businesses that lower prices to compete eventually go out of business.

Control is important for many products. Ever see any Armani suits at Target? The reason you haven't is that Armani works hard to control its distribution, keeping the costly apparel in high-end stores where its lofty prices can be sustained. Armani's need for control means that it deals only with distributors who sell to designer boutiques. Many manufacturers want similar control for reasons of pricing, after-sale service, image, and so forth. If you need control over your distribution, it will powerfully influence placement decisions.

The distribution scheme is of critical importance to manufacturers. Say you make a mass-market consumer good such as a toy. Whether you plan effectively to get your product onto shelves in the major grocery,

>> Scarcity and Urgency Work

One popular approach to marketing is to make products more valuable via scarcity and present a sense of urgency through limited-time offers. From highly touted sales to special sales for preferred customers, a sense of "act now" works in your marketing plans. People also see value in a limited edition or an item that is not always easy to get. Don't make up false scarcity or customers may see through it—but think about what you may run out of and let people know they should order while it's still available. The home shopping channels made a fortune by having a clock ticking away so that people would run to their phones to purchase an item before it disappeared (until tomorrow). Disney offers its classic films for sale through television commercials that ask you to buy now before the film goes back into the vault for years to come.

drug, and discount store chains may make all the difference between success and failure.

If you're selling an informational product to a narrow market, such as political consulting services to candidates for elected office, physical distribution is of less importance. However, for just about all companies, an effective placement strategy is a big determinant of success.

Promotion

Promotion is virtually everything you do to bring your company and your product in front of consumers. Promotional activities include picking your company name, going to trade shows, buying advertisements, making telemarketing calls, using billboards, arranging co-op marketing, offering free giveaways, building and maintaining your online presence, and more. Not all promotions are suitable for all products, of course, so your plan should select the ones that will work best for you, explain why they were chosen, and tell how you're going to use them. Figure 10–4 will help you see where your needs are.

> **buzzword**
>
> Co-op promotions are arrangements between two businesses to cross-promote their enterprises. When a soft drink can carries a coupon good for a discount on the price of entry to an amusement park, that's a co-op. Countless variations exist.

Promotion aims to inform, persuade, and remind customers to buy your products. It uses a mix that includes four elements: advertising, personal selling, sales promotion, and publicity or public relations.

Advertising Concerns

Advertising is a large part of marketing and promotion for most businesses. Television is still leading the way, while online advertising is surging past print advertising. In 2011, for example U.S. advertising saw $32 billion spent in online advertising, $36 billion in print advertising, and $60.7 billion in TV advertising. In 2014 the numbers have changed, with online advertising up to $52.8 billion, print down slightly to $33.1 billion, and television up slightly to $67.8 billion. Yes, online ads are gaining quickly, but television is still on top when it comes to advertising.

Advertising Budget Worksheet

Select the advertising and promotional expenses you anticipate from the following list. Briefly describe the goal, such as "new leads" or "10 percent sales gain." Then estimate how frequently you'll insert an ad, run a spot, meet with a consultant, and so forth. Finally, determine how much this will cost. The bottom line is the starting figure for your marketing budget.

Medium	Purpose/Goal	How Often?	Annual Budget
Ad agencies			
Brochures			
Consultants			
Designers			
Direct mail			
Displays			
Internet			
Magazines			
Newspapers			
Outdoor ads			
Public relations			
Radio			
Sales calls			
Samples			
Specialties			
Telemarketing			
Television			
Trade journals			
Trade shows			
Yellow pages			
Total			

Figure 10-4. Advertising Budget Worksheet

plan of action

You can get mounds of economic and demographic marketing information— much of it free—from the U.S. Census Bureau. To learn more, contact the following office: Economic and Demographic Statistics, Bureau of the Census, U.S. Department of Commerce, Data User Service Division, Customer Service, Washington, DC 20233, www.census.gov, or call (301) 763-4100.

Because most businesses cannot afford television ads, except in local markets, the choices come down to (primarily) print and the internet.

But, while the web is the place to be, print still offers some perks. For example, newspapers, magazines, and other forms of print are tangible and stay in people's view somewhere in the house—even on the rare occasion when the computer is turned off. Brand recognition is still easy to spot on the page or on a sign or billboard. Consumers tend to look longer at a print ad and skim less frequently than when they are looking at ads online, and because there are fewer print ads than in the past, your ad can stand out more. Of course. before you can advertise, you need to figure out why you are advertising: What are your goals?

You may be advertising to raise your corporate profile, to improve a tarnished image, or simply to generate foot traffic. Whatever you're after, it's important to set specific goals in terms of such things as revenue increase, unit volume growth for new business, inquiries, and so forth. Without specific objectives, it's hard to tell what you can afford to do and whether the campaign is living up to expectations.

Also, keep in mind that promotional plans, such as giveaways and freebies—caps, pens, T-shirts, etc.— should also be part of your plan to market your business.

Other Kinds of Promotion

Sales promotion is kind of a grab bag of promotional activities that don't fit elsewhere. If you offer free hot dogs to the first 100 people who come to your store on Saturday morning, that's a sales promotion. This category also includes in-store displays, trade shows, off-site demonstrations, and just about anything else that could increase sales and isn't included in the other categories.

Publicity is the darling of small businesses because it lets them get major exposure at minimal cost. If you volunteer to write a gardening column for your local newspaper or a blog for a gardening website, it can generate significant public awareness of your plant nursery and position you as a leading expert in the field, all for the price of a few hours a week spent jotting down some thoughts on a subject you already know very well. To buy comparable exposure might cost thousands of dollars. Press releases announcing favorable news about your company are one tool of publicity; similar releases downplaying bad news, if necessary, are the flip side.

> *"The key to effective personal selling is recruiting and training excellent salespeople."*

Public relations is a somewhat broader term that refers to the image you present to the public at large, government entities, shareholders, and

>> One Man's Pursuit of Excellence

Three decades ago, in his book *In Praise of Excellence,* author and business expert Tom Peters wrote about an entrepreneur who was way ahead of his time when it came to putting together a publicity and marketing plan. Stew Leonard was an entrepreneur who owns a store in Norwalk, Connecticut, that he calls "the world's largest dairy." Leonard has gone on to combine the genius of Walt Disney and Dale Carnegie to deliver a message to his customers: "Have fun!" Today, there are several Stew Leonard's throughout Connecticut and the New York area, and the business is hugely successful. Customers will drive miles and miles out of their way to go there and enjoy the hoopla he has put together. From kids' culinary classes to Easter egg hunts, he has learned how to make the customers' shopping experience fun, and that is part of what keeps those customers coming back. Customer service is priority one with Stew Leonard. There is a three-ton granite boulder that sits at the entrance to his store, and it features the store's two cardinal rules. "Rule Number 1: The customer is always right. Rule Number 2: If the Customer is ever wrong, go back and reread Rule Number 1."

employees. You may work at public relations through such tools as your website, company newsletters, e-newsletters, legislative lobbying efforts, your annual report, and the like.

Whatever you do, don't neglect public relations and publicity. There is no cheaper or more powerful tool for promotion.

Follow-Up Plan

Customers may ask, "What have you done for me lately?" Investors and others reading your business plan want to know, "What are you going to do for me tomorrow?" Any serious business plan has to take note of the fact that every product has a life cycle, that pricing pressures change over time, that promotions need to stay fresh, and that new distribution opportunities are opening up all the time. So the portion of your plan where you describe how you'll continue your success is a vital one.

The annals of business are full of companies that turned out to be one-trick ponies that introduced a product or service that zoomed to stardom but failed to follow it up with another winner. In the best cases, these companies survive but fade back into obscurity. In the worst, they fail to negotiate the switch from booming sales to declining sales and disappear completely.

Diversifying into more than one product is another good way to reduce the risk. It's a good idea to divert part of any boost in revenues to studying market trends and developing new products.

Investors looking at a plan, especially those contemplating long-term involvement, are alert to the risk of backing a one-trick entrepreneur. Showing competitive barriers you've erected and systems for developing new products is an important part of calming their fears.

There's one caveat when it comes to learning new tricks, however. Very simple concepts are the easiest to communicate, and extremely focused companies usually show the fastest growth—although not always over the long term. So you don't want to appear, in the process of reducing risk, that you've lost sight of the answers to the key questions: What are you selling? How are you selling it? And why would anybody want to buy from you?

>> **Expert Advice** <<
Clever Marketing

"I believe that generally the most important part of the plan is the marketing section," says Paul Hall from the Mason Entrepreneurship Center in Virginia. "As a general observation, business plans are essential for financing and desirable if the plan is used only to manage the business. We find that a startup with a business plan is much more likely to succeed than one without. The larger and more complex the venture, the more important it is to have a plan written out."

"It is critical to know the market size and makeup (demographics and psychographics), the competition, the niche where you have a competitive advantage, and your projected market share. Next would be the economics of the business: gross and operating margins, profit potential, fixed and variable costs, break-even, months to profitable cash flow. As business philosopher Peter Drucker once said, 'The modern company has only two key elements, innovation and marketing.'"

How Does Your Business Work?

The marketing section of your plan addresses a major part of operations: how you identify and attract customers. Operations is concerned with how you buy, build, and prepare your product or service for sale. That covers a lot of ground, including sourcing raw materials, hiring labor, acquiring facilities and equipment, and shipping the finished goods. And it's different ground depending on whether you're a manufacturer, a retailer, or a service firm.

Not surprisingly, investors and other plan readers pay careful attention to the part of your plan describing your operations. Most entrepreneurs are highly expert, interested in operations, and love to talk about it—in fact, one risk is that you'll go into too much detail here and wind up with what amounts to a technical treatise in which the essential marketing element seems lost.

> *"The simplest way to treat operations is to think of it as a linear process that can be broken down into a sequence of tasks."*

David Wheeler recognized that risk when seeking investors for his software startup called InfoGlide Inc. So one of his first hires was someone to take on the job of CEO, to interface directly with investors and high-profile prospects, so Wheeler could get back to the operations he loved. "That's what I like," he says, "working with database code, not doing product demos."

The basic rule for your operations section is to cover just the major areas—labor, materials, facilities, equipment, and processes—and provide the major details—things that are critical to operations or that give you competitive advantage. If you do that, you'll answer investors' questions about operations without overwhelming them.

The simplest way to treat operations is to think of it as a linear process that can be broken down into a sequence of tasks. Although several tasks may be performed simultaneously, leave the scheduling to a later part of the operations section. In Figure 11–1, each task is broken down into smaller elements, and as you run your business, you will naturally do so. For your business plan, make sure that the broad outlines of your operations are covered.

Once the initial task listing is complete, turn your attention to who is needed to do which tasks. Keep this very simple. You don't have to look at minor tasks (who opens the door? who fetches the mail?), but you do have to concentrate on major tasks such as producing a product or delivering a service. Use your judgment. Then fill out the form in Figure 11–2 for each major task.

Operations for Retail and Service Firms

Service firms have different operations requirements from manufacturers. Companies that maintain or repair things, sell consulting, or provide health care or other services generally have higher labor content and lower investments in plants and equipment.

What Has to Be Done: Task Listing

Task	Daily	Weekly	Monthly	Other (specify)
1.				
2.				
3.				
4.				
5.				
6.				
7.				
8.				
9.				
10.				

Figure 11-1. What Has to Be Done: Task Listing

Tasks Requiring More Than One Person

Name of task	
People needed	
Elements of the task	
Timing (when they do it)	
Time allotted	
Total time, including support	
Comments	

Figure 11-2. Tasks Requiring More Than One Person

> *"Companies that maintain or repair things, sell consulting, or provide health care or other services generally have higher labor content and lower investments in plants and equipment."*

Another important difference is that service and retail firms tend to have much simpler operational plans than manufacturers. In the process of turning raw materials into finished goods, manufacturers may employ sophisticated techniques in a complex series of operations. By comparison, it's pretty simple for a retailer to buy something, ship it to his store, and sell it to a customer who walks in.

That's not to say operations are any less important for retailers and service firms. But most people already understand the basics of processes such as buying and reselling merchandise or giving haircuts or preparing tax returns. So you don't have to do as much explaining as, say, someone who's manufacturing microprocessors.

The Importance of People

For service and retail firms, people are the main engines of production. The cost of providing a service is largely driven by the cost of the labor it entails. And retail employees' skills and service attitudes drive their employers' productivity and market acceptance to a great degree.

A service-firm plan, then, has to devote considerable attention to staffing. Regional educational attainment data will help readers understand why you think you can hire sufficient semi- and high-skilled workers for a service or repair operation. You'll want to include background information and, if possible, describe employment contracts for key employees such as designers, marketing experts, buyers, and the like.

You'll want to walk the reader through the important tasks of these employees at

buzzword

Ecommerce is short for electronic commerce and basically refers to selling things through sites on the internet.

>> Service Operations Checklist

- ❑ Staffing completed (or staffing plan completed)
- ❑ Organization chart completed
- ❑ Marketing implemented
- ❑ Sales policies
- ❑ Customer relations policies
- ❑ Service delivery policies
- ❑ Administering monitoring and control policies
- ❑ Follow-up procedures

Note that staffing and organizational issues precede marketing, sales, and delivery of the service. Service operations are people-intensive, and careful management goes a long way to making sure that your quality controls are effective.

all levels so they can best understand how your business works and what the customer experience is like.

Buying

The ability to obtain reliable, timely, and reasonably priced supplies of easily salable merchandise is perhaps the prime skill of any retailer. Buying is both art and science. Knowing what the economical ordering quantities are for a given product is mechanical, but knowing which items to stock requires knowledge of customer desires and demand. Buying is based on your marketing plan. Without clear knowledge of the marketing environment, you cannot make wise purchasing decisions.

fact or fiction

Is success a matter of buying low or selling high? Retailers say that, contrary to popular opinion, they really make their money when they buy, not sell, goods. The trick, mastered by successful retailers like Walmart and Toys "R" Us, is to buy goods for a price low enough that you can sell them at a profit while still attracting customers and discouraging competitors.

>> Retail Operations Checklist

❑ Marketing (include sales projections, location, promotional efforts, advertising, and online marketing efforts.

❑ Staffing

❑ Training sales staff

❑ Buying procedures (include delivery times, freight-in, reorder points)

❑ Inventory control

❑ In-store sales tools

❑ Sales policies

❑ Customer service policies and procedures

❑ Service delivery policies

❑ Administering monitoring and control policies

❑ Follow-up procedures

❑ Back room operations staffed

Note the importance of training sales staff and customer service representatives. Many retailers omit this to their economic loss. The major reason consumers give for not returning to a store is discourteous or unhelpful sales staff. Point out that you will train your sales staff so that they will act as a powerful resource for your company.

If you have what consumers want when few of your competitors do, you're almost guaranteed to have strong sales. If you run out of a hot item, on the other hand, disappointed consumers may leave your store, never to return.

Operations plans for retailers, therefore, devote considerable attention to sourcing desirable products. They may describe the background and accomplishments of key buyers. They may detail long-term supply agreements with manufacturers of in-demand branded merchandise. They may even discuss techniques for obtaining, on the gray market, desirable products from manufacturers who try to restrict the flow of goods to their stores.

Weekly Time Plan

Name:	Week Ending:		
Problems/Objectives	**Schedule**		
	Monday		
	Tuesday		
	Wednesday		
	Thursday		
	Friday		
	Saturday		
	Sunday		

Figure 11-3. Weekly Time Plan

As the owner, you have to juggle dozens of details and, in the press of daily business, run the risk of not performing some essential step. Figure 11–3 can be used to plan your week before you get caught up in the chaos. Use it to focus your efforts on the most important items on your to-do list.

Operations for Manufacturers

Companies that make things have certain characteristics in common that set them apart from others, including retailers and service firms. They take raw materials and labor and transform them into sellable products. Although they may also distribute the products and sell direct to customers (thus involving the retail and service aspects of operations), most manufacturers

"Product development, marketing, and distribution all play important roles, but it's the production process that sets manufacturers apart from all other enterprises."

buzzword

Kaizen, a Japanese term for continuous improvement, swept the world of business operations in the 1980s and early 1990s. The idea is to constantly obtain small gains in productivity and quality over a long period.

concentrate on the production end and farm out the retail and service to other firms.

Process Points

The lead actor in manufacturing is the process of production. Product development, marketing, and distribution all play important roles, but it's the production process that sets manufacturers apart from all other enterprises. And the better your production process, the better a manufacturer you will be. It's the star that leads to your company's success.

A manufacturing production process consists of several components. One step is usually fabrication, or the making of products from raw materials. There is also assembly of components, testing, and inspection of finished goods.

Manufacturing processes can become extremely detailed, as is the case with the many parts found in mobile technology. If you're an operations-minded entrepreneur, you may revel in these details. But control your enthusiasm for such detail when it comes to writing a business plan. Stick to the important processes, those essential to your production or that give you a special competitive advantage.

Personnel and Materials

Manufacturers combine labor and materials to produce products. Problems with either one of these critical inputs spell trouble for your business and for its backers. Business plan readers look for strong systems in place to make sure that personnel and materials are appropriately abundant.

plan pointer

How much detail should you include about the technology you employ? We're living in a highly technical environment. That means you should explain some of the key technology that comes into play during your operations—in lay terms. You need to go into greater detail only if your business relies heavily on technology, sells technology, or utilizes some unique technology that is uncommon in your industry.

>> Manufacturing Company Checklist

- ❑ Marketing plan completed
- ❑ Staffing completed (or staffing plan completed)
- ❑ Organization chart completed
- ❑ Product plan completed
- ❑ Basic manufacturing operations listed in sequence
- ❑ Raw materials purchased
- ❑ Equipment obtained
- ❑ Labor skills available and assigned
- ❑ Time lines and deadlines assigned
- ❑ Potential roadblocks identified
- ❑ Managerial controls in place
- ❑ Sales policies reviewed
- ❑ Customer relations policies outlined
- ❑ Service delivery policies developed
- ❑ Administering monitoring and control policies
- ❑ Follow-up procedures checked

Manufacturing is complex. Your checklist will most likely differ from the one given in this sidebar. A small contractor, for example, makes things but is less complex, so might have a checklist like this:

- ❑ Develop work schedule
- ❑ Hire labor
- ❑ Set up equipment
- ❑ Acquire necessary materials
- ❑ Monitor work schedule

The key point: Identify the major pieces or aspects of your operation in your business plan.

plan pitfall

Stay up on technology if you're in the software industry and be careful. There are numerous ways unscrupulous folks can tap into intellectual property, such as recorded music or films. It is harder than ever to catch those who pirate—or steal—such protected properties. But, if you are caught, you can get in real trouble. So be careful not to inadvertently use other people's music, images, etc. Conversely, protect intellectual properties, and if you see your original material showing up elsewhere, contact an attorney.

You should show in your plan that you have adequate, reliable sources of supply for the materials you need to build your products. If you are working with suppliers in other parts of the world, show that they are reliable and that you have established a system that will make such international production run smoothly. A global marketplace means that you have more opportunities to find the materials or products you need and to find new markets for sales. This can be impressive to your readers. However, you need to define and provide the details of how your business will benefit from being a part of the global marketplace. Even if you are not planning to actively pursue global partnerships or buy from vendors around the globe or market to customers in other countries, if you are selling via your website, you need to address the possibility of international sales.

Estimate your needs for materials and describe the agreements with suppliers, including their length and terms that you have arranged to fulfill those needs. You may also give the backgrounds of your major suppliers and show that you have backup sources available should problems develop.

It's an interesting spectacle, every now and then, to watch an industrial giant such as an auto maker or railroad paralyzed by a labor strike. It illustrates the importance of ensuring a reliable supply of adequately trained people to run your processes. It also illustrates the need for a backup plan.

You'll first need to estimate the number and type of people you will require to run your plan. Startups can do this by looking at competitors' plants or by relying on the founders' prior experience at other companies. Existing firms can extrapolate what they'll need to expand from current

>> The Making of a Baron

The person most famous for building an empire based on ownership of capital equipment is Andrew Carnegie. In the 19th century, this Scottish immigrant to America rose from beginnings as a textile-plant worker to become a baron of steel and oil.

Carnegie was always a hard worker—as a teenage delivery boy he was his family's primary source of income. But it was his savvy in acquiring capital equipment that made him a business legend.

At the age of 21, Carnegie borrowed to buy shares in a new railroad being built near his Pennsylvania home. A few years later, he acquired oil field assets in Titusville, Pennsylvania. In railroad car manufacturing, bridge building, and, finally, iron and steel mills, Carnegie followed the same strategy: Control the means of production.

Shortly after 1900, Carnegie sold out to J.P. Morgan. Those holdings became U.S. Steel.

operations. Then show that you can reasonably expect to be able to hire what you need. Look at local labor pools, unemployment rates, and wage levels using information from chambers of commerce or similar entities. If you plan to import sizable numbers of workers, check out housing availability, and build an expense for moving costs into your budget.

Getting Equipped

Manufacturing a product naturally requires equipment. A manufacturer is likely to need all sorts of equipment such as cars, trucks, computers, telecom systems, and, of course, machinery of every description for bending metal, milling wood, forming plastic, or otherwise making a product out of raw materials.

Much of this equipment is very expensive and hard to move or sell once purchased. Naturally, investors are very interested in your plans for purchasing equipment. Many plans devote a separate section to describing the ovens, drill presses, forklifts, printing presses, and other equipment they'll require.

This part of your plan doesn't have to be long, but it does have to be complete. Make a list of every sizable piece of equipment you anticipate needing. Include a description of its features, its functions, and, of course, its cost.

Be ready to defend the need to own the more expensive items. Bankers and other investors are loath to plunk down money for capital equipment that can be resold only for far less than its purchase price. Also consider leasing what you need if you are starting out. Once you show that you are responsible at paying your bills and sales look good, you can apply for a small-business loan or a line of credit with greater success.

The Facilities Section

Everybody has to be somewhere. Unless you're a globe-trotting consultant whose office is his suitcase, your plan will need to describe the facilities in which your business will be housed. Even home-based business owners now describe their home offices, as the trend continues to grow rapidly, thanks largely to mobile communications.

Land and buildings are often the largest capital items on any company's balance sheet. So it makes sense to go into detail about what you have and what you need. Decide first how much space you require in square feet. Don't forget to include room for expansion if you anticipate growth. Now consider the location. You may need to be close to a labor force and materials suppliers. Transportation needs, such as proximity to rail, interstate highways, or airports, can also be important. Next ask whether there is any specific layout that you need. Draw up a floor plan to see if your factory floor can fit into the space you have in mind. Manufacturers today do most of their ordering and communications online, so you need to make sure that wherever you are located has excellent connectivity.

> "To figure the cost of facilities, you'll first have to decide whether you will lease or buy space and what your rent or mortgage payments will be for the chosen option."

To figure the cost of facilities, you'll first have to decide whether you will lease or buy space and what your rent or mortgage payments will be for the chosen option. Don't forget to include brokerage fees, moving costs, and the cost of any leasehold improvements you'll need. Finally, take a look at operating costs. Utilities including phone, electric, gas, water, and trash pickup are concerns; also consider such costs as your computer connections, possibly satellite connections, as well as maintenance and general upkeep. See Figure 11–4 on page 198 to analyze your requirements.

>> Scaling Success by the Century

Would you like to create a company that will last 150 years? The solid foundation provided by a secure, broad-based patent could be just what you need. Take the case of Fairbanks Scales.

More than 150 years ago, a Vermont entrepreneur named Thaddeus Fairbanks grew dissatisfied with the scales available to weigh hemp processed by a company he'd started with his brother. Fairbanks had already invented a couple of modestly successful contraptions, including a stove and an iron plow, and he felt he could improve on the inaccurate and ponderous steelyard scales then in wide use.

After a spell in his invention shop, Thaddeus emerged with a new type of scale that used a system of levers and could be buried in the ground, allowing wagonloads of hemp and other materials to be easily, quickly, and accurately weighed. He obtained a patent on the invention and then, backed with $4,000, he and brothers Joseph and Erastus formed Fairbanks Platform Scale in 1830.

From that humble beginning, with the help of Thaddeus's patented scale technology, Fairbanks Scales would dominate the business of weighing everything from postal letters to canal barges for the next century. After a merger with its largest distributor in 1916, the company became known as Fairbanks Morse. In 1988, Fairbanks Scales was purchased back from Fairbanks Morse and is now the oldest continuing operating manufacturing company in America.

Facilities Worksheet

Use this worksheet to analyze your facilities requirements. Fill out the sections, then test available facilities against your requirements.

Space Requirements

Initial space _____

Expansion space _____

Total space _____

Location Requirements

Technology requirements including connectivity _____

Proximity to labor pool_____

Proximity to suppliers_____

Transportation availability _____

Layout Requirements: _____

_____

Cost Requirements (Dollar Amounts of Estimated Expenses)

Purchase/lease costs_____

Brokerage costs _____

Moving costs_____

Improvements costs _____

Operating costs_____

Total Cost _____

Figure 11-4. Facilities Worksheet

These aren't the only operations concerns of manufacturers. You should also consider your need to acquire or protect such valuable operations assets as proprietary processes and patented technologies. For many businesses—Coca-Cola with its secret soft drink formula comes to mind—intellectual property is more valuable than their sizable accumulations of plants and equipment. Investors should be warned if they're going to have to pay to acquire intellectual property. If you already have it, they will be happy to learn they'll be purchasing an interest in a valuable, and protected, technology.

buzzword

Logistics is the science of moving objects from one location to another. For manufacturers and retailers, the logistics of supplies and products is crucial. For service firms, often the logistics of moving employees around is more important.

Information Technology and Operations

Whatever business you are in, technology most likely plays a key role. Retailers place their orders faster and more accurately using computers and track their inventory while other business owners make international deals thanks to computers and communication technology.

Other key technology that fits into your operations, such as that of a medical-equipment manufacturer, should be included in the business plan. Explain how this technology is significant to your business and how it can separate you from your competitors.

>> Expert Advice <<

Many businesses succeed or fail on the basis of things that only employees notice. Walmart didn't become the world's largest retailer because it snagged the best locations or hired the best ad agencies. It beat out Sears, Montgomery Ward, and the rest because of its extremely efficient systems for stocking and distributing the most profitable products in the most profitable manner. It's likely that your business is based in large part on some aspect of its operations—manufacturing, logistics, customer service—that business plan readers will want to know about.

Expressing Your Ideas in Financial Terms

Financial data is always at the back of the business plan, but that doesn't mean it's any less important than up-front material such as the description of the business concept and the management team. Astute investors look carefully at the charts, tables, formulas, and spreadsheets in the financial section because they know that this information is like the pulse, respiration rate, and blood pressure in a human being. It shows the condition of the patient. In fact, you'll find many potential investors taking a quick peak at the numbers before reading the plan.

Financial statements come in threes: income statement, balance sheet, and cash flow statement. Taken together they provide an accurate picture of a company's current value, plus its ability to pay its bills today and earn a profit going forward. This information is very important to business plan readers.

You can typically gather information and use an Excel or other financial program to make your spreadsheets. You will also find them available in the business plan software that we discussed at the start of the book. These programs also do the calculations.

Income Statement

An income statement shows whether you are making any money. It adds up all your revenue from sales and other sources, subtracts all your costs, and comes up with the net income figure, also known as the bottom line.

buzzword

Income statements answer the question, "Am I making or losing money?"

Income statements are called various names—profit and loss statement (P&L) and earnings statement are two common alternatives. They can get pretty complicated in their attempt to capture sources of income, such as interest, and expenses, such as depreciation. But the basic idea is pretty simple: If you subtract costs from income, what you have left is profit.

>> Keep Spreadsheets Simple

Robert Crowley, former president of Massachusetts Technology Development Corporation, once described it as "this horrible disease . . . called spreadsheet-itis. It's the most common ailment in business plans today." Crowley says spreadsheet software allows business plan writers to easily crank out many pages and many varieties of financial documents. But this is a case of the more, the less merry. As a rule, stick with the big three: income, balance sheet, and cash flow statements.

These three statements are interlinked, with changes in one necessarily altering the others, but they measure quite different aspects of a company's financial health. It's hard to say that one of these is more important than another. But of the three, the income statement may be the best place to start.

To figure your income statement, you need to gather a bunch of numbers, most of which are easily obtainable. They include your gross revenue, which is made up of sales and any income from interest or sales of assets; your sales, general, and administrative (SG&A) expenses; what you paid out in interest and dividends, if anything; and your corporate tax rate. If you have those, you're ready to go.

Sales and Revenue

Revenue is all the income you receive from selling your products or services as well as from other sources such as interest income and sales of assets.

plan pitfall

Don't confuse sales with receipts. Your sales figure represents sales booked during the period, not necessarily money received. If your customers buy now and pay later, there may be a significant difference between sales and cash receipts.

Gross Sales

Your sales figure is the income you receive from selling your product or service. Gross sales equal total sales minus returns. It doesn't include interest or income from sales of assets.

plan pitfall

Profit and loss statements rightly get lots of attention. Without long-term profits, the future is questionable. But long-term profits aren't the whole answer. You need balance sheets to know your financial position and cash flow statements to see how that position has changed.

Interest and Dividends

Most businesses have a little reserve fund they keep in an interest-bearing bank or money market account. Income from this fund, as well as from any other interest-paying or dividend-paying securities they own, shows up on the income statement just below the sales figure.

Other Income

If you finally decide that the branch office out on County Line Road isn't ever going to turn a decent profit, and you sell the land, building, and fixtures, the income from that

buzzword

What sounds like Elmer Fudd is actually a common acronym used on many financial statements. EBIT stands for earnings before interest and taxes. It is an indicator of a company's profitability, calculated as revenue minus expenses, excluding tax and interest.

sale will show up on your income statement as "other income." Other income may include sales of unused or obsolete equipment or any income-generating activity that's not part of your main line of business.

Costs

Costs come in all varieties—that's no secret. You'll record variable costs, such as the cost of goods sold, as well as fixed costs—rent, insurance, maintenance, and so forth. You'll also record costs that are a little trickier, the prime example being depreciation.

Cost of Goods Sold

Cost of goods sold, or COGS, includes expenses associated directly with generating the product or service you're selling. If you buy smartphone components and assemble them, your COGS will include the price of the chips, screen, and other parts, as well as the wages of those doing the assembly. You'll also include supervisor salaries and utilities for your factory. If you're a solo professional service provider, on the other hand, your COGS may amount to little more than whatever salary you pay yourself and whatever technology you may use for your business.

Sales, General, and Administrative Costs

You have some expenses that aren't closely tied to sales volume, including salaries for office personnel, salespeople compensation, rent, insurance, and the like. These are split out from the sales-sensitive COGS figure and included on a separate line.

Depreciation

Depreciation is one of the most baffling pieces of accounting wizard work. It's a paper loss, a way of subtracting over time the cost of a piece of equipment or a building that lasts many years even though it may get paid for immediately.

Depreciation isn't an expense that involves cash coming out of your pocket. Yet it's a real expense in an accounting sense, and most income statements will have an entry for depreciation coming off the top of pretax earnings. It refers to an ongoing decrease in asset value.

If you have capital items that you are depreciating, such as an office in your home or a large piece of machinery, your accountant will be able to set up a schedule for depreciation. Each year, you'll take a portion of the purchase price of that item off your earnings statement. Although it hurts profits, depreciation can reduce future taxes.

In Figure 12–1 on page 206, the income statement for NetKnowledge Internet Training Center, total receipts from tuition charged to students came to $23,568. The company got an extra $115 from interest on bank accounts.

plan pitfall

Acronyms are handy for those who know what they mean. But they can easily get out of hand in the financial data section of a business plan. SG&A, for "sales, general, and administrative expense," and COGS, for "cost of goods sold," are commonly understood. But when you start throwing around NOPAT (net operating profit after taxes) and other obscure terms, you're likely to confuse rather than clarify. Limit acronyms to those that are very familiar.

Interest

Paying the interest on loans is another expense that gets a line all to itself and comes out of earnings just before taxes are subtracted. This line doesn't include payments against principal. Because these payments result in a reduction of liabilities—which we'll talk about in a few pages in connection with your balance sheet—they're not regarded as expenses on the income statement.

Taxes

The best thing about taxes is that they're figured last, on the profits that are left after every other thing has been taken out. Tax rates vary widely according to where your company is located, how and whether state and local taxes are figured, and your special tax situation. Use previous years as a guidepost for future returns. If you are just opening your business, work carefully with your accountant to set up a system whereby you can pay the necessary taxes at regular intervals.

Sample Income Statement

Sales Receipts	$23,568
Interest Income	115
COGS	12,615
Gross Margin	11,068
Expenses	4,835
Depreciation	1,125
Operating Earnings	5,108
Interest Expense	1,410
Pretax Earnings	3,698
Income Tax	1,109
Net Income	$2,589

Cost of goods sold amounted to $12,615. Subtracting COGS from sales gives the gross margin of $11,068. Subtracting expenses and depreciation from that returns a figure of $5,108 for operating earnings.

NetKnowledge racked up interest charges of $1,410. When this is removed from operating earnings, the resulting net income before taxes is $3,698. With income taxes calculated at $1,109, that leaves a net income of $2,589.

Figure 12-1. Sample Income Statement

Balance Sheet

If the income sheet shows what you're earning, the balance sheet shows what you're worth. A balance sheet can help an investor see that a company owns valuable assets that don't show up on the income statement or that it may be profitable but is heavily in debt. It adds up everything your business owns, subtracts everything the business owes, and shows the difference as the net worth of the business.

plan pitfall

Almost anything can lose value, but for accounting purposes, land doesn't. As a rule, you never depreciate land, although you may depreciate buildings as well as other long-lived purchases.

Actually, accountants put it differently and, of course, use different names. The things you own are called assets. The things you owe money on are called liabilities. And net worth is referred to as equity.

A balance sheet shows your condition on a given date, usually the end of your fiscal year. Sometimes balance sheets are compared. That is, next to the figures for the end of the most recent year, you place the entries for the end of the prior period. This gives you a snapshot of how and where your financial position has changed.

A balance sheet also places a value on the owner's equity in the business. When you subtract liabilities from assets, what's left is the value of the equity in the business owned by you and any partners. Tracking changes in this number will tell you whether you're getting richer or poorer.

Assets

An asset is basically anything you own of value. It gets a little more complicated in practice, but that's the working definition.

Assets come in two main varieties: current assets and fixed assets. Current assets are anything that is easily liquidated or turned into cash. They include cash, accounts receivables, inventory, marketable securities, and the like.

Fixed assets include stuff that is harder to turn into cash. Examples are land, buildings, improvements, equipment, furniture, and vehicles.

fact or fiction

You always want to maximize profits, right? Savvy entrepreneurs know that managing reported profits can save on taxes. Part of the trick is balancing salaries, dividends, and retained earnings. Tax regulations treat each differently, and you can't exactly do whatever you want. Get good advice, and be ready to sacrifice reported profits for real savings. But, do not play games when it comes to the IRS—they even caught Al Capone when the FBI could not. Stay within the legal parameters with your tax strategies.

plan pointer

The two sides of a balance sheet—assets and liabilities—can be presented side by side or one on top of the other. The first is called columnar format; the second, report format. There's no rule about which is best. Do whatever looks or feels natural.

The fixed asset part of the balance sheet sometimes includes a negative value—that is, a number you subtract from the other fixed asset values. This number is depreciation, and it's an accountant's way of slowly deducting the cost of a long-lived asset such as a building or a piece of machinery from your fixed asset value.

Intellectual properties, such as patents and copyrights, also fall into the asset category. For some companies, a recipe, a formula, or a new invention may actually be their most valuable asset. Of course, the actual value is often very hard to determine. Patents, trademarks, copyrights, exclusive distributorships, protected franchise agreements, and the like do have somewhat more accessible value.

You'll also have intangibles such as your reputation, your standing in the community, and "goodwill," which are difficult to put a value on. Probably the best way to think of goodwill is like this: If you sell your company, the IRS says the part of the sales price that exceeds the value of the assets is goodwill. As a result of its slipperiness, some planners never include an entry for goodwill, although its value may in fact be substantial.

Liabilities

Liabilities are the debts your business owes. They come in two classes: short-term and long-term.

Short-term liabilities are also called current liabilities. Any debt that is going to be paid off within 12 months is considered current. That includes accounts payable you owe suppliers, short-term bank loans

plan pointer

Legendary investor Warren Buffett reads thousands of financial statements describing businesses every year. He says that in most cases, the first thing he goes to is the balance sheet to check a company's strength. So if you'd like to attract an investor of Buffett's stature, spend time on the balance sheet.

(shown as notes payable), and accrued liabilities you have built up for such things as wages, taxes, and interest.

Any debt that you won't pay off in a year is long-term. Mortgages and bank loans with more than a one-year term are considered in this class. Figure 12–2 shows a typical balance sheet.

Cash Flow Statement

The cash flow statement monitors the flow of cash over a period of time (a year, a

plan pointer

One of the key characteristics of a balance sheet is that it balances. The bottom lines of both sides of the balance sheet, assets on one half and liabilities in the other, should always equal, or be balanced.

Sample Balance Sheet

December 31, 20XX

Assets		Liabilities	
Cash	$4,387	Notes Payable	$11,388
Accounts Receivable	12,385	Accounts Payable	2,379
Inventory	1,254	Interest Payable	1,125
Prepaid Expenses	3,548	Taxes Payable	3,684
Other Current Assets	986	Other Current Liabilities	986
Total Current Assets	22,560	Total Current Liabilities	19,562
Fixed Assets	27,358	Long-Term Debt	4,896
Intangibles	500	Other Noncurrent Liabilities	1,156
Other Noncurrent Assets	0	Total Liabilities	$25,614
		Net Worth	24,804
Total Assets	**$50,418**	**Total Liabilities & Net Worth**	**$50,418**

Figure 12-2. Sample Balance Sheet

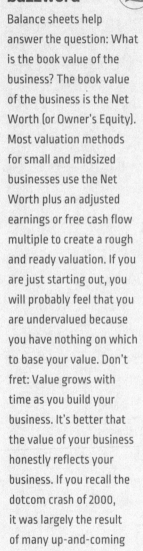

buzzword

Balance sheets help answer the question: What is the book value of the business? The book value of the business is the Net Worth (or Owner's Equity). Most valuation methods for small and midsized businesses use the Net Worth plus an adjusted earnings or free cash flow multiple to create a rough and ready valuation. If you are just starting out, you will probably feel that you are undervalued because you have nothing on which to base your value. Don't fret: Value grows with time as you build your business. It's better that the value of your business honestly reflects your business. If you recall the dotcom crash of 2000, it was largely the result of many up-and-coming dotcoms being greatly overvalued.

quarter, a month) and shows you how much cash you have on hand at the moment.

The cash flow statement, also called the statement of changes in financial position, probes and analyzes changes that have occurred on the balance sheet. It's different from the income statement, which describes sales and profits but doesn't necessarily tell you where your cash came from or how it's being used.

A cash flow statement consists of two parts. One follows the flow of cash into and out of the company. The other shows how the funds were spent. The two parts are called, respectively, sources of funds and uses of funds. At the bottom is, naturally, the bottom line, called net changes in cash position. It shows whether you improved your cash position and by how much during the period.

Sources of Funds

Sources of funds usually have two main sections in it. The first shows cash from sales or other operations. In the cash flow statement, this figure represents all the money you collected from accounts during this period. It may include all the sales you booked during the period, plus some collections on sales that actually closed earlier.

The other category of sources of funds includes interest income, if any, plus the proceeds from any loans, line of credit drawdowns, or capital received from investors during the period. Again, these figures represent money actually received during the period. If you arranged for a $100,000 line of credit but only used $10,000 during this period, your sources of funds would show $10,000.

>> Penny's Lack of Pennies

When Penny McConnell's dreams came true, her cash flow fell short. The owner of an eight-person cookie bakery, McConnell had been making a living selling low volumes of fresh Penny's Pastries brand cookies to local stores. Then a buyer from Southwest Airlines called and said the airline wanted to serve her new cookies on all its flights. It would be a year's worth of sales—every month.

Inexperienced at planning for such volume, McConnell made crucial mistakes. She cut prices to meet Southwest's budget, which reduced profits. Then she borrowed heavily to buy equipment, order supplies, hire employees, and rent a new facility, increasing expenses sharply.

When costs rose after a technical problem cropped up, profits vanished completely. Then losses mounted. Within six months Penny's Pastries filed for bankruptcy. What happened? Too much spending, too much discounting, and too little planning doomed her from the start. Now in business with another venture, McConnell says a well-thought-out plan might have confirmed what her instincts suggested. "It was such a tremendous increase in volume," she says, "that I had a gut feeling from the beginning it wasn't going to work."

Uses of Funds

The sources of funds section often has only a few entries, although some cash statements break out sources of funds by businesses and product lines. But even simple statements show several uses of funds. A cash flow statement will normally show uses such as cost of goods sold; sales, general, and administrative expense (SG&A); and any equipment purchases, interest payments, payments on principal amounts of loans, and dividends or draws taken by the owners.

Net Change in Cash

Few things feel better for a startup businessperson than having plenty of cash in the bank. And few things offer better picture of what's going on

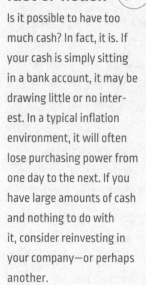

with cash on hand than the net change in cash line on your business plan. Net change in cash equals the difference between total funds in and total funds out. If you bring in $1 million and send out $900,000, your net change in cash is $100,000. Ideally, you want this number to be positive and, if possible, showing an upward trend.

Other Financial Information

If you're seeking investors for your company, you'll probably need to provide quite a bit more financial information than what is in the income statement, balance sheet and cash flow statements. For instance, a personal finance statement may be needed if you're guaranteeing loans yourself. Applying business data to other ratios and formulas will yield important information on what your profit margin is and what level of sales it will take for you to reach profitability. Still other figures, such as the various ratios, will help predict whether you'll be able to pay your bills for long. These bits of information are helpful to you as well as to investors, it should be noted. Understanding and, if possible, mastering them, will help you run your business more smoothly.

Figure 12–3, Sample One-Month Cash Flow Statement for NetKnowledge Internet Training Centers, reflects $23,568 in sales receipts. That includes sales booked and collected during the period and accounts receivable that were collected. The interest entry reflects interest received on NetKnowledge's cash reserves account at the bank. The $10,000 was an injection of capital by one of the firm's partners.

Personal Financial Statement

Investors and lenders like to see business plans with substantial investments by the entrepreneur or with an entrepreneur who is personally guaranteeing any loans and has the personal financial strength to back those guarantees.

Sample Cash Flow Statement

Sources of Cash	
Sales	$23,568
Other Sources	0
Interest	115
Invested Capital	10,000
Total Cash In	$33,683
Uses of Cash	
COGS	$12,615
SG&A	4,835
Interest	1,410
Taxes	1,109
Equipment Purchase	8,354
Debt Principal Payments	2,000
Dividends	0
Total Cash Out	**$30,323**
NET CHANGE IN CASH	**$3,360**
Beginning Cash on Hand	**$4,387**
Ending Cash on Hand	**$7,747**

COGS stands for cost of goods sold and includes primarily salaries paid to NetKnowledge's educators and staff. Sales, general, and administrative (SG&A) expenses include the base salary for NetKnowledge's single salesperson. The interest outlay is for interest on NetKnowledge's line of credit. The $8,354 entry is for a new computerized presentation projector. NetKnowledge paid its credit line down by $2,000 during the same period, and the owners took no draw out of the business.

The net result, equal to total cash in minus total cash out, comes to $3,360, and that is NetKnowledge's net cash flow for the month.

The bottom two entries sum up NetKnowledge's current cash position. You add the amount of cash on hand from the prior period's cash flow statement to the net cash flow figure on this statement.

Figure 12-3. Sample Cash Flow Statement

Your personal financial statement is where you show plan readers how you stack up financially as an individual.

The personal financial statement comes in two parts. One is similar to a company balance sheet and lists your liabilities and assets. A net worth figure at the bottom, like the net worth figure on a company balance sheet, equals total assets minus total liabilities.

A second statement covers your personal income. It is similar to a company profit and loss statement, listing all your personal expenses, such as rent or mortgage payments, utilities, food, clothing, and entertainment. It also shows your sources of income, including earnings from a job, income from another business you own, child support or alimony, interest and dividends, and the like.

The figure at the bottom is your net income; it equals total income minus total expenses. If you've ever had to fill out a personal financial statement to borrow money for a car loan or home mortgage, you've had experience with a personal financial statement. You should be able to simply update figures from a previous personal financial statement.

Because this is important only to investors or lenders, you want to be careful to include this only when necessary. For a small business looking for a small amount of funding, you may be able to draft something with your accountant verifying your net worth and/or previous year's income.

Financial Ratios

Everything in business is relative. The numbers for your profits, sales, and net worth need to be compared with other components of your business for them to make sense. For instance, a $1 million net profit sounds great. But what if it took sales of $500 million to achieve those profits? That would be a modest performance indeed.

To help understand the relative significance of your financial numbers, analysts use financial ratios. These ratios compare various elements of your financial reports to see if the relationships between the numbers make sense based on prior experience in your industry.

Some of the common ratios and other calculations analysts perform include your company's break-even point, current ratio, debt-to-equity ratio, return on investment, and return on equity. You may not need to calculate all these. Depending on your industry, you may also find it useful to calculate various others, such as inventory turnover, a useful figure for many manufacturers and retailers. But ratios are highly useful tools for managing, and most are quick and easy to figure. Becoming familiar with them and presenting the relevant ones in your plan will help you manage your company better and convince investors you are on the right track.

Break-Even Point

One of the most important calculations you can make is figuring your break-even point. This is the point at which revenue equals costs. Another way to figure it is to say it's the level of sales you need to get to for gross margin or gross profit to cover all your fixed expenses. Knowing your break-even point is important because when your sales are over

plan of action

Wondering how good your credit is? You can get a copy of your credit report from any one of the three major credit bureaus:

- Experian at experian.com
- Equifax at equifax.com
- TransUnion at transunion.com

It is vital for bank loans and other business loans that you are more than aware of your credit score. You should do everything you can to maintain a high score.

this point, they begin to produce profits. When your sales are under this point, you're still losing money. This information is handy for all kinds of things, from deciding how to price your product or service to figuring whether a new marketing campaign is worth the investment.

The process of figuring your break-even point is called break-even analysis. It may sound complicated, and if you were to watch an accountant figure your break-even point, it would seem like a lot of mumbo-jumbo. Accountants calculate figures with all sorts of arcane-sounding labels, such as variable cost percentage and semi-fixed expenses. These numbers may be strictly accurate, but given all the uncertainty there is with projecting your break-even point, there's some question as to whether extra accuracy is worth all that much.

There is, however, a quicker if somewhat dirtier method of figuring break-even. It is described in Figure 12–4. Although this approach may not be up to accounting-school standards, it is highly useful for entrepreneurs,

Break-Even Analysis Worksheet

To determine your break-even point, start by collecting these two pieces of information:

1. *Fixed costs.* These are inflexible expenses you'll have to make independently of sales volume. Add up your rent, insurance, administrative expenses, interest, office supply costs, maintenance fees, etc. to get this number. Put your fixed costs here: _____.

2. *Average gross profit margin.* This will be the average estimated gross profit margin, expressed as a percentage, you generate from sales of your products and services. Put your average gross profit margin here: _____.

Now divide the costs by profit margin, and you have your break-even point. Here's the formula:

$$\frac{\text{Fixed costs}}{\text{Profit margin}} = \text{Break-even point}$$

If, for instance, your fixed costs were $10,000 a month and your average gross profit margin 60 percent, the formula would look like this:

$$\frac{\$10,000}{0.6} = \$16,667$$

So in this case, your break-even point is $16,667. When sales are running at $16,667 a month, your gross profits are covering expenses. Fill your own numbers into the following template to figure your break-even point:

$$\frac{\$_____}{_____} = \$_____$$

Figure 12-4. Break-Even Analysis Worksheet

and more important, it can be done quickly, easily, and frequently, as conditions change.

Once you get comfortable with working break-even figures in a simple fashion, you can get more complicated. You may want to figure break-even points for individual products and services. Or you may apply break-even analysis to help you decide whether an advertising campaign is likely to pay any dividends. Perform break-even analyses regularly and often, especially as circumstances change. Hiring more people, changing your product mix, or becoming more efficient all change your break-even point.

Current Ratio

The current ratio is an important measure of your company's short-term liquidity. It's

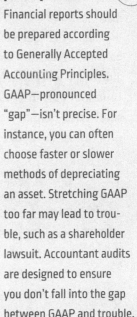

plan pitfall

Financial reports should be prepared according to Generally Accepted Accounting Principles. GAAP—pronounced "gap"—isn't precise. For instance, you can often choose faster or slower methods of depreciating an asset. Stretching GAAP too far may lead to trouble, such as a shareholder lawsuit. Accountant audits are designed to ensure you don't fall into the gap between GAAP and trouble.

>> The $50 Cookie, or Know All Your Costs

Before calculating your break-even point, you need to factor all your costs into your equation. A funny story that clarifies the break-even point comes from a business in New York City that primarily helps rejuvenate underserved communities in the Bronx. In an effort to generate funding, it decided to sell cookies. The cookies cost it $3 in ingredients and sold for $5 each, or a $2 profit. It believed the break-even point was $3 because that's what it cost to make each cookie. If only it were that easy. When it added in the use of the kitchen, which was typically leased from local businesses, along with the labor involved, the packaging, the shipping, and the marketing, it calculated that it was making cookies costing $50 each. Needing to make $50 a cookie just to break even, it made a smart move. It decided to stop making cookies.

probably the first ratio anyone looking at your business will compute because it shows the likelihood that you'll be able to make it through the next 12 months.

Figuring your current ratio is simple. You divide current assets by current liabilities. Current assets consist of cash, receivables, inventory, and other assets likely to be sold for cash in a year. Current liabilities consist of bills that will have to be paid before 12 months pass, including short-term notes, trade accounts payable, and the portion of long-term debt due in a year or less. Here's the formula:

$$\frac{\text{Current assets}}{\text{Current liabilities}} = \text{Current ratio}$$

For example, say you have $50,000 in current assets and $20,000 in current liabilities. Your current ratio would be:

$$\frac{\$50,000}{\$20,000} = 2.5$$

>> Accounting through the Ages

If you don't understand accounting as well as you should, you can't blame it on recent innovations. Double-entry accounting dates at least from 1340, and the first book on accounting, by a monk named Luca Pacioli, was published in 1494.

Surprisingly, a medieval accountant would feel quite comfortable with much of what goes on today in an accounting department. But accountants haven't been sitting back and relaxing during the intervening centuries. They've thought up all kinds of ways to measure the health and wealth of businesses (and businesspeople).

There are more ratios, analyses, and calculations than you can shake a green eye shade at. And wary investors are prone to using a wide variety of those tests to make sure they're not investing in something that went out of style around the time Columbus set sail. So although accounting may not be your favorite subject, it's a good idea to learn what you can. Otherwise, you're likely to be seen as not much more advanced than a 15th-century monk.

The current ratio is expressed as a ratio; that is, the example in Figure 12–4 shows a current ratio of 2.5 to 1 or 2.5:1. That's an acceptable current ratio for many businesses. Anything less than 2:1 is likely to raise questions.

buzzword

Liquidity measures your company's ability to convert its non-cash assets, such as inventory and accounts receivable, into cash. Essentially, it measures your ability to pay your bills.

Quick Ratio

This ratio has the best name—it's also called the acid-test ratio. The quick ratio is a more conservative version of the current ratio. It works the same way but leaves out inventory and any other current assets that may be a little harder to turn into cash. You'll normally get a lower number with this one than with the current ratio—1:1 is acceptable in many industries.

Sales/Receivables Ratio

This ratio shows how long it takes you to get the money owed you. It's also called the average collection period and receivables cycle, among other names. Like most of these ratios, there are various ways of calculating your sales/receivables cycle, but the simplest is to divide your average accounts receivable by your annual sales figure and multiply it by 360, which is considered to be the number of days in the year for many business purposes. Like this:

$$\frac{\text{Receivables}}{\text{Sales}} \times 360$$

If your one-person consulting business had an average of $10,000 in outstanding receivables and was doing about $120,000 a year in sales, here's how you'd calculate your receivables cycle:

$$\frac{\$10,000}{\$120,000} = 1/12$$

$$1/12 \times 360 = 30$$

If you divide 1 by 12 on a calculator, you'll get .08333, which gives you the same answer, accounting for rounding. Either way, your average collection period is 30 days. This will tell you how long, on average, you'll have to wait to get the check after sending out your invoice. Receivables will vary by customer, of course. You should also check the receivables cycle number against the terms under which you sell. If you sell on 30-day terms and your average collection period is 40 days, there may be a problem that you need to attend to, such as customer dissatisfaction, poor industry conditions, or simply lax collection efforts on your part.

Inventory Turnover

Retailers and manufacturers need to hold inventory, but they don't want to hold any more than they have to because interest, taxes, obsolescence, and other costs eat up profits relentlessly. To find out how good they are at turning inventory into sales, they look at inventory turnovers.

The inventory-turnover ratio takes the cost of goods sold and divides it by inventory. The COGS figure is a total for a set period, usually a year. The inventory is also an average for the year; it represents what that inventory costs you to obtain, whether by building it or by buying it.

$$\frac{\text{Average COGS}}{\text{Average inventory}} = \text{Inventory turnover}$$

An example:

$$\frac{\$500,000}{\$125,000} = 4$$

In this example, the company turns over inventory four times a year. You can divide that number into 360 to find out how many days it takes you to turn over inventory. In this case, it would be every 90 days.

It's hard to say what is considered to be a good inventory-turnover figure. A low figure suggests you may have too much money sitting around in the form of inventory. You may have slow-moving inventory that should be marked down and sold. A high number for inventory turnover is generally better.

Debt-to-Equity Ratio

This ratio is one that investors will scrutinize carefully. It shows how heavily in debt you are compared with your total assets. It's figured by dividing total debt, both long- and short-term liabilities, by total assets.

$$\frac{\text{Total debt}}{\text{Total assets}} = \text{Debt-to-equity ratio}$$

Here's a sample calculation:

$$\frac{\$50,000}{\$100,000} = 1{:}2$$

You want this number to be low to impress investors, especially lenders. A debt-to-equity ratio of 1:2 would be comforting for most lenders. One way to raise your debt-to-equity ratio is by investing more of your own cash in the venture.

Profit on Sales

This is your ground-level profitability indicator. Take your net profit before taxes figure and divide it by sales.

$$\frac{\text{Profit}}{\text{Sales}} = \text{Return on sales}$$

For example, if your restaurant earned $100,000 last year on sales of $750,000, this is how your POS calculation would look:

$$\frac{\$100,000}{\$750,000} = 0.133$$

Is 0.133 good? That depends. Like most of these ratios, a good number in one industry may be lousy in another. You need to compare POS figures for other restaurants to see how you did.

Return on Equity

Return on equity, often abbreviated as ROE, shows you how much you're getting out of the company as its owner. You figure it by dividing net profit from your income statement by the owner's equity figure—the net worth figure if you're the only owner—from your balance sheet.

$$\frac{\text{Net profit}}{\text{Net worth}} = \text{Return on equity}$$

Take a look at the ROE for NetKnowledge, the company whose sample income statement and balance sheet was used earlier in the chapter.

$$\frac{\$2,589}{\$21,403} = 12\%$$

NetKnowledge's owners are getting a 12 percent return on their equity. To decide whether this is acceptable, compare it with what you could earn elsewhere, such as in a bank certificate of deposit, stock, mutual fund, or the like, as well as with other companies in your industry.

Return on Investment

Your investors are interested in the return on investment, or ROI, that your company generates. This number, figured by dividing net profit by total assets, shows how much profit the company is returning based on the total investment in it.

$$\frac{\text{Net profit}}{\text{Total assets}} = \text{Return on investment}$$

For NetKnowledge, this would be:

$$\frac{\$2,589}{\$47,017} = 5.5\%$$

Notice that the ROE, which reflects the return on the owners' equity alone, is a lot higher than the ROI. This is because NetKnowledge's leverage—the fact that it has borrowed against its assets—increases the ROE.

Forecasts

Business plans and financing proposals are based on projections. Past financial data can only support your projections, However, financial projections in your business plan express in common financial terms and

>> EVA Sigh of Relief

EVA is an acronym standing for economic value added, and it's one of the most interesting financial management tools available to business owners. The aim of EVA is to find out whether you're doing better with the money you have than you could by, say, investing in U.S. Treasury bills.

EVA has been pioneered by consulting firm Stern Stewart, which has counseled hundreds of companies on how to apply EVA. And experts say that entrepreneurs in particular already understand EVA on a gut level. In any event, the basic concept is fairly simple—you measure EVA by taking net operating earnings before taxes and subtracting a reasonable cost of capital, say 12 percent.

In practice, however, it's complicated. Stern Stewart has identified more than 160 adjustments a company may potentially need to make to accounting procedures before EVA can be effectively implemented. Check them out at sternstewart.com.

formats how you expect the immediate future to play out the scenarios you created in the body of the plan. You can forecast financial statements such as balance sheets, income statements, and cash flow statements to project where you'll be at some point in the future.

Forecasts are necessities for startups, which have no past history to report on. Existing businesses find them useful for planning purposes. Forecasts help firms foresee trouble, such as a cash flow shortfall, that is likely to occur several months down the road, as well as give them benchmarks to which they can compare actual performance.

It's always advisable to be somewhat conservative in your forecasts.

> *"Forecasts are necessities for startups, which have no past history to report on."*

Projected Income Statement

Business planning starts with sales projections. No sales, no business. It's that simple. Even if

plan pointer

There are four kinds of financial ratios: liquidity ratios like the current ratio, asset management ratios like the sales/receivable cycle, debt-management ratios like the debt-to-equity ratio, and profitability ratios like return on investment.

you're in a long-range development project that won't produce a marketable product for years, you have to be able to look ahead and figure out how much you'll be able to sell before you can do any planning that makes sense.

Now that the pressure's on, making a sales projection and the associated income projection may look a little tricky. So let's do it step by step.

First pick a period for which you want to make a projection. You should start with a projection for the first year. To do so, you want to come up with some baseline figures. If you're an existing business, look at last year's sales and the sales of prior years. What's the trend? You may then be able to simply project out the 10 percent annual sales increase that you've averaged the past three years for the next three years.

If you're a startup and don't have any prior years' figures to look at, look for statistics about other businesses within your industry. The most important question to ask is: What has been the experience of similar companies? If you know that car dealers across the nation have averaged 12 percent annual sales gains, that's a good starting point for figuring your company's projections.

You'll also need to do your due diligence to get an idea of how much volume you can expect and what factors will have a positive or negative impact upon your ability to sell.

For example, how many people can your restaurant expect to serve in a given day? Statistics of other restaurants may be hard to find, so you may have to do some research by simply watching customers enter and leave a similar type of restaurant for a couple of days during the breakfast, lunch, and dinner hours. Once you get a feel for how many people it is drawing on average, you can begin to estimate how many you may draw. Take into consideration your location vs. its location and the fact that it has regular customers who are familiar with the menu.

Statistics you can look at include how many people are within a few miles and what percentage meet your demographics. For example, a family-friendly restaurant wants to know how many families are living nearby, while a fine-dining establishment wants to get statistics on how many people with a higher income are living within a few miles of the establishment.

For retailers, the difficult part is determining how much market share you can expect. You need to factor in the need for your product in a given community, which can range from local neighborhoods to worldwide if you are selling on the web. Volume will be the toughest thing to estimate. Try to remain conservative in your estimates, knowing that you may not be selling a lot of products or services right off the bat.

Forecasting expenses is your next step, and it's much easier. You can often take your prior year's cost of goods sold, adjust it either up or down based on trends in costs, and go with that. The same goes for rent, wages, and other expenses. Even startups can often find good numbers on which to forecast expenses because they can just go to the suppliers they plan to deal with and ask for current price quotes plus anticipated price increases.

Projected Balance Sheet

Balance sheets can also be projected into the future, and the projections can serve as targets to aim for or benchmarks to compare against actual results. Balance sheets are affected by sales, too. If your accounts receivable go up or inventory increases, your balance sheet reflects this. And, of course, increases in cash show up on the balance sheet. So it's important to look ahead to see how your balance sheet will appear given your sales forecast.

When you sit down to prepare a projected balance sheet, it will be helpful to take a look at past years' balance sheets and figure out the relationship of certain assets and liabilities that vary according to sales. These include cash, receivables, inventory, payables, and tax liabilities.

If you have any operating history, you can calculate the average percentages of sales for each of these figures for the past few years and use that for your balance sheet projection. You can simply take last year's figures, if you don't think they'll change that much. Or you can adjust the percentage to fit some special knowledge you have about the coming year—you're changing your credit terms, for instance, so you expect receivables to shrink, or you're taking out a loan for an expensive new piece of equipment. Firms without operating history can look at one of the books describing industry norms referred to earlier to get guidance about what's typical for their type of company.

Figure 12–5, the Projected Income Statement for Small Bites, a catering service specializing in children's birthday parties, shows that the planner expects year 2017 revenues to follow the steady trend of 25 percent increases annually; it also shows the effect of opening a second operation in a nearby city.

The expenses section generally tracks expense trends as well, with many costs showing sharp jumps associated with opening the new location. The result is that depressed earnings are projected for the first year of the expanded operation, despite higher revenues.

Cash Flow Pro Forma

Businesses are very sensitive to cash. Even if your operation is profitable and you have plenty of capital assets, you can go broke if you run out of cash and can't pay your taxes, wages, rent, utilities, and other essentials.

plan pitfall

Pro forma and projected financial statements are based on the future and, as such, are imprecise. You need to make them as realistic and reasonable as possible but not believe in them too explicitly. Be extra-sure not to overstate revenue or understate expenses.

Similarly, a strong flow of cash covers up a multitude of other sins, including a short-term lack of profitability. A cash flow pro forma (or cash budget) is your attempt to spot future cash shortfalls in time to take action.

A cash budget differs from a cash flow statement in that it's generally broken down into periods of less than a year. This is especially true during startup, when the company is especially sensitive to cash shortages, and management is still fine-tuning its controls. Startups, highly seasonal businesses, and others whose sales may fluctuate widely should do monthly cash flow projections for a

Sample Projected Income Statement

INCOME PROJECTION				
	2014	**2015**	**2016**	**2017** (projected)
INCOME				
Net Sales	**$138,899**	**$173,624**	**$217,030**	**$271,287**
Cost of sales	69,450	83,339	99,834	135,644
Gross profit	$69,449	$90,285	$117,196	$135,643
OPERATING EXPENSES				
General and Administrative Expenses				
Salaries and wages	$13,890	$17,362	$21,703	$27,129
Sales commissions	6,945	8,681	10,851	13,564
Rent	5,400	5,670	5,954	11,252
Maintenance	1,389	1,458	1,531	2,89
Equipment rental	2,452	2,575	2,703	5,109
Furniture and equipment purchase	3,232	3,394	3,563	6,735
Insurance	1,207	1,267	1,331	1,99
Interest expenses	3,008	3,158	3,316	6,268
Utilities	1,250	1,563	1,953	3,692
Office supplies	776	750	899	977
Marketing and advertising	6,256	6,805	7,150	9,204
Travel	550	750	1,000	1,000
Entertainment	323	301	426	555
Bad debt	139	174	217	323
Depreciation and amortization	1,800	2,700	4,050	6,075
Total Operating Expenses	**$48,617**	**$56,608**	**$66,647**	**$96,776**
Net income before taxes	20,832	33,677	50,549	38,867
Provision for taxes on income	3,125	5,051	7,582	5,830
Net Income after Taxes	**$17,707**	**$28,626**	**$42,967**	**$33,037**

Figure 12-5. Sample Projected Income Statement

>> The Most Important Financial Statement

If you have only one financial statement to manage your business by—and to use in your business plan—let it be the cash flow pro forma. Only the cash flow pro forma can tell you how much capital you will need in a startup (add the startup costs, project the cash flow, then make the cash flow positive by providing capital in the indicated amount). Only the cash flow pro forma will tell you when you will need to borrow money—and how much you will need to borrow. Only the cash flow pro forma will tell you when it is time to pull the plug and bail out before you create negative value in your business.

Used as a budget, your cash flow pro forma will keep you from making spontaneous purchases, help evaluate the cost (in cash flow) of growth, hiring new people, adding facilities or equipment, or taking on more debt.

No business can prosper without a cash flow pro forma.

year ahead, or even two. Any business would do well to project quarterly cash flow for three years ahead.

In Figure 12–6 the balance sheet projects variable expenses and liabilities by taking each item's percentage of the previous year's sales and multiplying that by the estimated sales for the coming year. This generates numbers for all but long-term debt, which the owner knows will rise slightly, and other noncurrent debt, consisting of a note to the owner.

The added detail makes monthly cash flow forecasts somewhat more complicated than figuring annual cash flow because revenues and expenses should be recorded when cash actually changes hands. Sales and cost of goods sold should be allotted to the months in which they can be expected to actually occur. Other variable expenses can be allocated as

plan pointer

When making forecasts, it's useful to change dollar amounts into percentages. So if you figure sales will rise 20 percent next year, you'll enter 120 percent on the top line of the projection. Using percentages helps highlight overly optimistic sales projections and suggest areas, especially in costs, for improvement.

Sample Projected Balance Sheet

	2014	% Sales	2015 (projected)
Sales	$87,740		$110,000
ASSETS			
Cash	$4,387	5.0%	$5,500
Accounts Receivable	12,385	14.1%	15,510
Inventory	1,254	1.4%	1,540
Other Current Assets	986	1.1%	1,210
Total Current Assets	$19,012	21.7%	$23,870
Fixed Assets	27,358	31.2%	34,320
Intangibles	500	0.6%	660
Other Noncurrent Assets	0	0.0%	0
Total Assets	**$46,870**		**$58,850**
LIABILITIES			
Notes Payable	$11,388	13.0%	$14,300
Accounts Payable	2,379	2.7%	2,970
Interest Payable	1,125	1.3%	1,430
Taxes Payable	3,684	4.2%	4,620
Other Current Liabilities	986	1.1%	1,210
Total Current Liabilities	$19,562		$24,530
Long-Term Debt	4,896		5,200
Other Noncurrent Liabilities	1,156		1,156
Total Liabilities	**$25,614**		**$30,866**
Net Worth	$21,256		$27,984
Total Liabilities & Net Worth	**$46,870**		**$58,850**

Figure 12-6. Sample Projected Balance Sheet

percentages of sales for the month. Expenses paid other than monthly, such as insurance and estimated taxes, are recorded when they occur.

As with the balance sheet projection, one way to project cash flow is to figure out what percentage of sales historically occurs in each month. Then you can use your overall sales forecast for the year to generate monthly estimates. If you don't have prior history, you'll need to produce estimates of such things as profit margins, expenses, and financing activities, using your best guesses of how things will turn out.

The cash flow pro forma also takes into account sources of cash other than sales, such as proceeds from loans and investments by owners.

Figure 12–7 is a cash flow pro forma for The Boardroom, a sailboard rental shop. The forecast begins by calculating what percentage of sales occurs in each month. Note that the percentages do not add up to exactly 100 because of rounding. This is still adequately accurate for your

Sample Cash Flow Pro Forma
Monthly Sales Percentages

Month	% of Sales
January	5.0%
February	6.1%
March	7.5%
April	10.5%
May	11.9%
June	13.8%
July	12.2%
August	9.0%
September	7.6%
October	5.5%
November	4.8%
December	6.2%

Figure 12-7. Sample Cash Flow Pro Forma: Monthly Sales Percentages

>> Finding Free Cash Flow Apps

They say there's an app for everything. You can now find cash-flow-projection templates in popular business applications. They may not be highly sophisticated, but they do provide the templates for several key spreadsheets. Google Docs, Intuit's QuickBooks, Pulse, and PlanGuru are all among the places to look for cash-flow templates. They can make setting it all up a lot easier.

purposes. The sales by month portray a tolerably seasonal business, with close to half the annual sales occurring in the late spring and summer months. All the sales are for cash.

Translating these monthly percentages of sales to the cash flow projection provides you with beginning figures. The rest of the figures, for the most part, flow from these sales forecasts, as in Figure 12–8 on page 232.

Notice that there are two nonsales sources of cash: $7,500 in proceeds from a bank loan and $10,000 in a loan from the owner. At the end of the year, after steady payments of interest on the bank loan, the principal is paid in a balloon payment. The loan proceeds are used at the beginning of the year to purchase a new mobile surfboard display stand. Additional personnel are trained during this period to be ready when the busy season starts up. Another equipment purchase occurs just as the busy season gets under way.

The forecast for The Boardroom shows a company that will wind the year up in a strong cash position. It will probably be able to not only pay its bills but also to finance further growth internally. The financial vital signs in the cash flow statement show a patient that is alive and well.

>> **Expert Advice** <<

Some key points about cash flow:

Positive cash flow = Survival

Cash flow buys time (if necessary), builds assets and profits, and keeps suppliers, bankers, creditors, and investors smiling. Without positive cash flow, survival becomes questionable. Negative or feebly positive cash flow

Sample Cash Flow Forecast

Projected Cash Flow: 2015

	Jan.	Feb.	Mar.	Apr.	May	Jun.	Jul.	Aug.	Sep.	Oct.	Nov.	Dec.	TOTAL
CASH RECEIPTS													
Income from Sales													
Cash Sales	$6,550	$7,991	$9,825	$13,755	$15,589	$18,078	$15,982	$11,790	$9,956	$7,205	$6,288	$8,122	$131,131
Total Cash from Sales	6,550	7,991	9,825	13,755	15,589	18,078	15,982	11,790	9,956	7,205	6,288	8,122	$131,131
Income from Financing													
Loan Proceeds	5,000	0	0	2,500	0	0	0	0	0	0	0	0	$7,500
Other Cash Receipts	10,000	0	0	0	0	0	0	0	0	0	0	0	$10,000
Total Cash Receipts	21,550	7,991	9,825	16,255	15,589	18,078	15,982	11,790	9,956	7,205	6,288	8,122	148,631
CASH DISBURSEMENTS													
Expenses													
COGS	2,948	3,596	4,421	6,190	7,015	8,135	7,192	5,306	4,480	3,242	2,830	3,655	$59,010
SG&A	11,555	2,507	3,083	4,316	4,891	5,672	5,014	3,699	3,124	2,261	1,973	2,548	$50,643
Interest	0	80	80	80	80	80	80	80	80	80	80	80	$880
Taxes	0	0	0	1,500	0	1,500	0	0	1,500	0	0	0	$4,500
Equipment Purchase	5,000	0	0	5,000	0	0	0	0	0	0	0	0	$10,000
Debt Principal Payments	0	0	0	0	0	0	0	0	0	0	0	7,500	$7,500
Dividends	0	0	0	0	0	0	0	0	0	0	0	0	$0
Total Cash Disbursements	19,503	6,183	7,584	17,086	11,986	15,387	12,286	9,085	9,184	5,583	4,883	13,783	$132,533
Net Cash Flow	2,047	1,808	2,241	-831	3,603	2,691	3,696	2,705	772	1,622	1,405	-5,661	$16,098
Opening Cash Balance	0	2,047	3,855	6,096	5,265	8,868	11,559	15,255	17,960	18,732	20,354	21,759	$0
Cash Receipts	21,550	7,991	9,825	16,255	15,589	18,078	15,982	11,790	9,956	7,205	6,288	8,122	$148,631
Cash Disbursements	-19,503	-6,183	-7,584	-17,086	-11,986	-15,387	-12,286	-9,085	-9,184	-5,583	-4,883	-13,783	($132,533)
Ending Cash Balance	$2,047	$3,855	$6,096	$5,265	$8,868	$11,559	$15,255	$17,960	$18,732	$20,354	$21,759	$16,098	

Figure 12-8. Sample Cash Flow Forecast

is painful, and unless corrected will either kill a business or damage it so seriously that it never lives up to its potential. Although short periods of negative cash flow occur in almost every business, cash flows have to be positive at least on an annual basis. Some farmers do very well indeed with cash flows that are strongly negative for 11 months of the year. So do some manufacturers (especially in the garment trade). The key is that they know what their cash flow patterns are—and take steps to finance the negative periods, offsetting that cost against the occasional strong positive cash influx from operations.

Unfortunately, the smaller and more thinly capitalized the company, the less able it is to survive extended negative cash flows. This is one reason why so many startups fail. The business idea may be terrific, but sales always come much more slowly than expected while cash goes out twice as fast. And the initial investment is rarely enough to tide the business along until cash flow turns and stays positive.

How can a small business attain positive cash flow? Discipline. A cash flow budget is an unbeatable tool if followed carefully. If there is to be just one financial statement, make sure it's the cash flow pro forma. It acts at once as a cash flow budget and as a benchmark for sales.

Some people have trouble differentiating the cash flow pro forma from the projected P&L. The concept "profit" is so pervasive that it poses a barrier to understanding that positive cash flow does not equal profit (or vice versa). The example of a profitable growing company with negative cash flow succumbing to illiquidity and tumbling into Chapter 11 bankruptcy is commonly cited to disprove the identity. If the sales don't turn to cash soon enough, the company goes broke. Revenues are up, receivables are up, expenses are up, even profits are up. Yet the company runs out of cash, can't pay its bills, and becomes another cash flow victim.

Another conceptual problem is equating P&L losses with negative cash flow. A loss on the P&L can reflect a negative cash flow, but it doesn't have to. For example, publishing companies enjoy some accounting foibles such as deferred income (which suppresses sales by deferring revenues to a later period). The cash comes in December, but because the revenue is not earned until the following year, the company can show a nice loss for tax purposes, while enjoying strongly positive cash flow.

Some ways to understand cash flow (as distinct from P&L categories) include:

> *Students are adept at managing skinny cash flows.* They postpone bill paying, share space to lower costs, use secondhand books whenever possible (if they have to pay the bill, that is), minimize food costs, and so forth. Few of them think of this as cash flow management, but it is—and of a very high order. If they want a ticket to a concert or ball game, they find a way to scrape up the cash. Very few companies are as carefully managed.

> *Emphasize timing.* Timing is everything for cash flow—the transfers of cash, even the dates that bills fall due or when discounts can or cannot be taken. Although timing is always important in business, it is especially important in managing cash flow. A P&L can stand a bit of looseness—it doesn't matter whether a bill is received January 31 or February 10. That ten days can make a big difference in cash flow if the bill falls due before you have the cash in hand to pay it.

> *Compare cash flow to a checking account.* Cash is deposited (cash inflow). Checks are written (cash outflow). The aim is to always have some cash on hand (positive cash flow).

> *For the literate, recall Charles Dickens's character Micawber and his definition of happiness:* "Income of £20.00.00, expenses of £19.19.19. Result: happiness. Expenses of £20.00.01. Result: misery." Micawber, was right; he understood cash flow. Cash flow deals with the ebb and flow of cash. If the flow is positive, it is good. If negative, do something to change it.

The cash flow pro forma is the most important single financial statement in the business plan. Every business needs an annotated cash flow pro forma (by month for the first year, by quarter thereafter) reflecting its business idea.

Enhancing Your Business Plan

Enlightening Extras
Appendices

A business plan is a story, the narrative of your enterprise, and you want to maintain a certain amount of flow as you lead readers from concept to management, through marketing, and on to financials. Some material that you'd probably like to fit into your plan somewhere just doesn't fit well into any of those sections. For instance, you may want to include resumes of some of your management team, product samples, product photos, advertising samples, press clippings, facility photos, or site plans. Some of these, or all of these, can be individual attachments, in a zip file, or on a separate website (or password page of your own website) that you set up and link to. In cases where people are reticent about opening attachments, having your own site set up might be the best option. Keep in mind that people will open only some of a myriad of material, so keep it to a few key items.

For these and other items that the plan writer wants in the plan but that don't seem to belong anywhere, many plans include appendices and attachments. This is material that is optional and that many plan readers may not need to refer to. However, for those readers who want to delve deeper into the workings of the company, appendices provide additional answers.

Key Employee Resumes

The management section of your business plan will contain a listing and brief descriptions of the senior managers and other key employees on your team. However, many investors and lenders are going to want to know more about you and your important associates than you give them in this section. For that purpose, you can include full resumes in an appendix. Since resumes are usually boring, you may, in most cases, opt instead for a short bio highlighting the key areas of an individual's background that are most appropriate for the current endeavor.

Product Samples

If your products are portable enough, you may be able to include samples in your appendix. Some examples of products that are suitable for inclusion in a plan are fabric swatches, stationery samples, printing samples, software screenshots, or even an app on your smartphone. Opening a pastry shop and coming in with something outstanding to present as a sample can also wow your potential backers. Broadway shows often generate backers from readings in which the show, without costumes and scenery, is read and sung by members of the cast. Had the Wright Brothers, back in 1903, needed a backer or investor, rather than having a written plan about flying an airplane, a demonstration flight would have wowed investors more than anything on paper. It's important not to overdo it with product samples. Investors tend to regard many entrepreneurs as being somewhat more product-focused than operations- or marketing-minded. By all means, provide samples if it's feasible and helpful. But don't expect appealing samples to overcome deficiencies in the concept, management, marketing, operations, or financing schemes presented in your plan. No matter how good it tastes, you will not win over backers with the $50 cookie.

>> Make No Mistake

Here are five resume mistakes (and exceptions):

1. *Too long*. Most resumes should be one page. After ten years, go to two pages. Exception: Health care, academic, and scientific curricula vitae may run many pages and cover virtually every paper published or seminar attended by the subject.

2. *Too individualistic*. A resume is generally conservative in tone, appearance, and content. You don't want to use a wild typeface or an odd format or include highly personal information such as the fact that you had no date to the senior prom. Exception: People in creative fields such as advertising or entertainment can let it all hang out.

3. *Too boring*. A resume should be more than a leaden list of job titles and dates of employment. You should stress what you learned while working at each position (or, in the case of serial entrepreneurs, each prior company you founded). Exception: If you organize your resume with a separate section where you detail all your skills and accomplishments, it's appropriate to briefly list jobs below.

4. *Inconsistent or error-filled*. If you say you have experience with software marketing but then fail to describe a prior position with that responsibility, it's going to look odd. The same holds true if you misspell a former employer's company name or make an obvious error in dates of employment. Exception: None.

5. *Too detailed*. Overly technical jargon, complicated descriptions of responsibilities in prior jobs, and irrelevant information—such as the street address of a prior employer—are only going to throw resume readers off the track you want them on. Limit the information to what's relevant, and don't try to impress anyone with your mastery of minutiae. Exception: If you're in a highly technical field, judicious use of insider expressions can help convince a skeptic that you are as knowledgeable as you claim to be.

>> **Make No Mistake,** continued

An additional mistake, albeit often not unintentional, is lying. A business writer was once asked if he had ever written fiction. To this, he replied, "Only my resume, sir." Sure people may embellish a little, but if you really want someone to invest in your company, lend you money, or take a strong interest in your business proposition, honesty is an important factor. Make sure your own resume and those of your key players are as accurate as possible.

Product Photos

Photos can fit into your business plan and certainly in your deck. Appendices are also good places to include photographs of products whose appearances are important or whose features are difficult to explain in words. It's normal and acceptable to include line drawings of products in the main sections of your plan. But again, most investors are more interested in such items as your balance sheet, management experience, and cash flow projections than they are in glossy product photos. Nonetheless, product photos (by a professional photographer—not taken on your cell phone) can help them visualize what you are talking about, especially if the concept is new and innovative. Photos can serve a purpose . . . but you also need to have all of the numbers in place.

plan pointer

Don't draw the line at two dimensions when considering illustrations of products and other key features of your plan. Three-dimensional models, mock-ups, and prototypes let investors get a hands-on feel for what you're proposing. If you've prepared a 3-D sample or model, you can use it to give your plan a high degree of physical reality.

Advertising Samples

It may be advisable to include examples of the advertising or marketing campaign you intend to use to market your products or services. For many companies, innovative and persuasive advertising approaches are essential

>> Presentation Preparation

If you are going to demonstrate what your product or service can do, here are some tips:

- Be well rehearsed in advance.

- Have backups of anything that could halt your demonstration—extra batteries, an Ethernet connection in case wifi doesn't work, etc. Leave no stone unturned.

- Keep it brief.

- Don't build to a great climax, start by flying the plane, giving them the big song and dance number or making it rain indoors on command. Whatever it is your product or service can do . . . as Nike says, "Just do it."

- Make sure everything is ready to go when you need it. Waiting until the site loads or warming up the launching pad will detract from your presentation.

- Have a big finish, one that makes your point very clear.

to the success of the firm. Without actual examples of the ads, it may be difficult for readers to grasp the appeal and power of your marketing ideas.

Screenshots of your website or Facebook page or links to your television spots along with copies of print ads can all help demonstrate how you will reach your audience. However, keep in mind that this information is optional. If you have an unimpressive advertising campaign, it won't help you to expose investors to the fact.

In the Media

Articles in influential publications and mentions in prominent blogs or on television shows can drive product sales. If your new software program got rave reviews in a major computer magazine, by all means include it here. Readers knowledgeable about the industry will recognize the power of such press. Generating favorable publicity is one of the more valuable things you can do for your business. You can find sample press releases online or get a book such as Paul Clifford's *Press Release Power: How to Write a Press Release for Online Distribution.* Jason Little's *How to Write SEO-Friendly Press Releases That Get Your Brand Noticed* is another good option. There are also publicists, but many will charge far more money than they are worth. If you're looking for a publicist, start with a short-term deal, but only after you see what they've done for other clients. Even if you are using a miniplan or a deck, a good publicist can slip in an article that he or she has placed for you online or someplace in the media.

You may also want to include complimentary ratings, certifications, or other endorsements by entities such as travel guides, associations, and watchdog groups. If your hotel got an impressive number of stars from the AAA, Mobil, or Michelin guides, or your restaurant got great reviews in Zagat or Yelp, you'll probably want to mention it more prominently in your plan, such as in your main marketing or concept sections. And it might not be a bad idea to include a copy of the actual certificate bearing the seal.

Other Appendix Contents

There is no one correct or comprehensive list of what you should include in your appendices. Your business, your intended use of the plan, and your audience will all affect what you want to put in. Photos of a building or a sketch of a proposed development might appeal to a real estate investor. Keep your audience in mind. Ask yourself what additional information they might like you to include. Then provide it.

Facility Photos

Few real estate investors will buy a property without firsthand knowledge of its appearance, state of repair, and general impression. When an investor is being asked to put money into your company, perhaps in exchange for partial ownership of your plan or, often, for the specific purpose of purchasing a building, it's a good idea to calm any concerns about the facility's condition by providing a few photos.

Make sure any facility photos you provide are more informative than glitzy. Skip over the sculpture at the entrance in favor of an outside shot illustrating that the property is in overall good repair.

Site Plans

You may want to include basic factory layouts and store floor plans in the operations section of your plan. If your site plan is complex and you feel some readers would benefit from seeing some of the additional details, provide them here rather than cluttering up the main part of the plan with them. If you have a number of store locations with varying layouts, for instance, you could give an idea of how several of them will look.

Credit Reports

Credit reports could be included in the financial statements section of your plan. However, because bankers are the main ones who will be interested in credit reports, you may want to place them in a separate appendix, or simply bring them as necessary.

Leases

The devil is in the details when it comes to leases. It's not appropriate to discuss every last clause of even an important lease in the main section of your plan. However, there's a chance that diligent readers will have questions about any especially significant leases that can only be answered by reading the actual documents. For these discriminating plan readers, you can include the actual leases or at least the more important sections.

plan pointer

If you don't have an eye-popping contract with a marquee client, but you have a lot of lesser arrangements with more or less impressive customers, include some of your key customers. Nobody is going to want to read a laundry list of names.

Customer Contracts

Few things are better to include in a plan than a long-term contract to supply an established customer. If you're lucky enough to have such a powerfully appealing deal in your pocket, you'll surely want to refer to it early on in your plan.

Like leases, however, the value of a contract may lie in its details. So it might be a good idea to include copies of relevant sections of any really significant contracts as appendices. If the deal is as good as you think (it had better be—otherwise, you wouldn't highlight it in your plan), then exposing potential investors to the beneficial details can only do you good. Make sure this is a contract that should result in sales and profits.

There's no hard-and-fast rule about the overall length of a plan. Most new-venture plans should be under 20 pages. And though plans for complicated enterprises can legitimately run much longer, it's probably a good idea to exercise restraint when it comes to packing things into an appendix. Recall the idea of diminishing returns, and make sure that anything you put in your plan contributes significantly to presenting a clear, compelling picture of your business. If it looks like you are padding the plan or adding in extraneous details, you can blow your chances of funding from investors or your credibility with others.

>> Expert Advice <<

Sometimes the most interesting insights into a proposed investment come from the supporting documents. Most business plan writers know enough about the way bankers and investors read plans to provide marketing, management, and financial information. A few go further and use the appendices to provide extra pieces of information that just don't fit into the main text.

Resumes are obviously important. Financial and credit information on the business and its principals, especially for a very small venture, can make a difference in the investment decision.

Here are a few suggestions:

> Quotes and estimates from suppliers of goods and services
> Letters of intent from qualified prospects
> Letters of support (or names and addresses) of references
> Key marketing information that is more general than the specifics included in the plan itself
> Economic data and predictions that might impact the business
> Leases and other legal documents relevant to the business
> Marketing materials such as brochures, advertisements, fliers, and so on
> Flow charts (work flow, distribution)
> Screenshots, especially if your business is web-based

Ask yourself what other information your prospective investors might wish to see. The easier you make it for them the better. Their time is valuable. You can't do their due diligence for them, but they will appreciate your helping them by providing the sources of your information and the grounds of your assumptions.

14

You Only Make a First Impression Once

I t does not matter how compelling your story is if the reader starts with a negative impression. A shopworn plan reeks of failure from the get-go. Make sure that the cosmetics are right: clean paper, crisp font, clear pictures, and a professional (noncolloquial) presentation go a long way toward securing a fair reading or hearing of your business plan.

As always, keep your audience in mind. Businesslike is almost always best as a fallback decision on how to make a good first impression.

Ask, in advance, if the recipient wants a hard copy or an e-copy of your plan. In the digital age, we want to give the people what they want.

Letter of Introduction

A letter of introduction should be emailed (or mailed) to whomever you would like to read your business plan. In the current business world, sending unsolicited, unanticipated business plans with a mere cover letter will typically not get your plan read. Not only are most people too busy to read whatever comes across their desk or lands in their inbox, they also do not want to be sued someday for "stealing your ideas," even if they never read your plan.

Your letter of introduction is your way of asking them if they would be interested in reading your business plan. Within the letter you explain why you have selected them and what you have to offer, in a brief compelling manner.

You should also explain generally what you're looking for—an investor, a loan, a long-term supplier relationship, or something else. Often this will be obvious from the circumstances. The introductory letter provides a valuable forum for you to explain why you're contacting this particular person. If you've received a personal referral, you'll want to include who gave you the referral very early on, probably in the first sentence following the salutation. Never underestimate the power of a personal referral from a friend, colleague, or acquaintance. It may not land you an investor, but it gets your foot in the door. When emailing the individual, you might put the referral in the subject line. BUT, don't send a plan without a letter of inquiry first.

NOTE: Some investors (VCs or even angels) do request plans on their websites. Hint: Read the website and make sure you follow its guidelines. For example, if it says send a plan of no more than 20 pages, do not send a 42-page plan.

plan pointer

Remove "To Whom It May Concern" from your vocabulary. Program your computer to explode if this phrase is typed into it. Never address a plan cover letter to something as vague as "Loan Department." Strive to get the name of an actual person whom you can identify as a "Mr." or "Mrs." or "Ms.," and use the proper honorific. If this person is not the right one, he or she will forward the plan to the right person. "To Whom It May Concern" is off-putting and amateurish. Don't use it.

In a world of "who you know" and networking, many of the people you will be sending to are referred by others. In some cases you may even have some personal connection to the person other than a referral. For instance, perhaps you once met this individual while networking. Perhaps you even worked together at a company or organization. A shared interest, such as a hobby, is of less value, but it may be worth mentioning if your shared interest is unusual or marked by a close degree of identification among those who share it. For instance, it may not mean much to point out that you, like the reader, are a fan of professional basketball. In fact, it may sound a little like you are grasping at straws to make a connection. However, if you both have competed as crew members on long-distance ocean-racing sailboats, this might be worth mentioning. In any case, the cover letter, not the plan, is obviously the place to bring up this type of personal connection.

Finally, the letter of introduction may detail the terms under which you are presenting your plan. You may, for instance, say that you are not submitting the plan to any other investor. You may explicitly point out that you are currently seeking financing from a number of sources, including this one. If there is a deadline for responding to your plan, if you wish to stress that the plan is confidential and must be returned to you, or if you would like to ask the recipient to pass it on to someone else who may be interested, this is the place to do so. Somewhere between sending the introductory letter and sending the plan—if the person agrees to see it—is where you can email a non-disclosure agreement if you plan to include one.

The letter of introduction gives you a chance to provide updated, expanded, or other important information that isn't in your plan. But mostly, it is a letter of introduction and designed to whet their appetite. See Figure 14–1 on page 250.

Cover Letters and Cover Sheets

A cover letter is a brief letter stating that you are including the business plan that the recipient has acknowledged and asked you to send over after reading your letter of introduction. It goes in the email that includes the plan or on top of a hard copy, and thanks the recipient for agreeing to take a look at the plan. It is a thank you—basically a brief note to accompany the plan and thank them for taking a look.

Sample Cover Letter

Leonard Mineo

Mineo Capital

123 Bankston Blvd., Ste. 100

Tulsa, OK 74138

Dear Mr. Mineo:

Alf Walton suggested I contact you to alert you to an investment opportunity in a new enterprise I am starting up. He discussed with me your interest in finding new, up-and-coming businesses in which to invest.

I would like to send you a copy of my business plan, which details the strategy and concept behind Pairing Off, the new internet dating service I have been building for just over a year. Initial reception to the plan among focus-group members, industry experts, and prospective suppliers has been excellent. We are now at the point where it is appropriate to seek additional equity investors, which is why I am writing to you at this time.

The market for online dating services continues to expand, as evidenced by the growth of Match.com and J-Date. However, we offer not only dating but also the unique opportunity for individuals to use our dating app to determine what qualities they are seeking in another person and then use our online service to pair up in person at safe locations in each of the 12 cities we serve.

In addition, we have just signed recent deals with three well-established bloggers, all of whom are experts in the areas of dating and relationship advice. Each will serve a different demographic group with advice on dating and relationships.

I would be very pleased if you would read our business plan and consider coming onboard with Pairing Off. I can be reached at my office during business hours at Leonard@Pairingoff.com or on my business line at (918) 555-5555. I look forward to hearing from you.

Sincerely,

Figure 14-1. Sample Cover Letter

The first thing anyone looking at your business plan will see is the cover page. After that, they may never look at it again.

A few cover-page components are essential, whether you are using an email or sending a hard copy. You should definitely have your company name, address, phone number, email address, Twitter handle, and other contact information. Other good items to include are the date as well as a notice that this is, indeed, a business plan. Format this information in a large, black, easily readable font. You want, above all else, for a plan reader to know which business this plan is for and how to contact you.

> *"If you have a striking, well-designed corporate logo, it's also a good idea to include that on the cover page."*

If you have a striking, well-designed corporate logo, it's also a good idea to include that on the cover page. A corporate slogan, as long as it's not too long, is also a good identifying mark that does something to communicate your strategy as well.

It's tempting to put all kinds of stuff on the cover page, but you should probably resist it. Your business concept, the amount you're trying to raise, and other details can go on the inside. The cover page must identify the company. More than that is likely to be too much.

Layout

Formatting your plan is easy in Microsoft Word® and easier in business software. The key is that everything has its own section, is easy to read, and does not look cluttered. You also want to check that you can read the plan on various mobile devices, so test it by checking it out on your iPhone or any other device available.

Keep colors to a minimum, and look at photos to see how they appear on other devices and other operating systems.

White space on a page is not your enemy.

Use 1.5 or double spacing. Keep the background white, and use black type. Convert the document into a PDF file, with Adobe Acrobat, and keep the file in one document. Include a table of contents, and make sure to

fact or fiction ⚡

If a plan is used for internal purposes only, it doesn't matter what it looks like as long as it's functional, right? That's true to some extent, but it's also true that part of a plan's functionality is to convince and persuade. A plan that looks shabby and casually thrown together won't command as much respect among other managers and employees as one that's polished and professional looking.

check that what you have in there shows up on the specified pages. Also try to align headings so that they do not start at the bottom of a page. You can use tabs for addendums or a separate document for the additional materials such as an appendix.

Also make sure any graphics are clear and do not take too long to load.

Hardcopies

Yes, you may still be asked for a hardcopy, so be ready to send one. Use good-quality white paper, then bind pages together permanently into a booklet. Any copy shop or printer can do such a binding for you, or you may purchase a do-it-yourself binding kit at an office supply store. Cover your plan with a clear plastic binder so that the cover page shows, or print your cover page information on a heavy piece of paper to serve as a cover for the binder.

Permanent binding helps plan readers keep all the pages of your plan together and makes it easier to read. It's important to keep these reasons for permanent binding in mind—it's a decision that improves the functionality of the plan, not its looks. Spending a lot of money creating a beautiful, perfectly bound plan is not a wise investment. Plan readers are interested in information, not entertainment.

The same thing goes for choosing the paper and typeface you'll use in your plan. Pick white paper, or at most perhaps gray, cream, or some shade of off-white, but leave the colored paper to fliers from the pizza place down the street. To make a businesslike impression, use businesslike stationery.

>> Expert Advice <<

Some people have lots of success in presenting business plans, while other do not. But nobody is always successful. Even a talented entrepreneur with a long track record of starting up winners will run up against an

>> Presenting–Your Business Plan!

Once you've prepared your plan for presentation, put it in front of the right people. There are six steps:

1. *Obtain leads and referrals.* Find names, addresses, and telephone numbers of investors of the type you wish to target. Ask people you know for referrals. Network as much as possible.

2. *Research your target.* Learn as much as possible about how much money people have to invest, industries they're interested in, and other requirements. Search venture capital directories, Who's Who, news articles, websites, and similar sources.

3. *Make your pitch.* First, email or mail an introductory letter to your target letting him know you have a plan you would like to send. If you do send an email or a letter asking him to read your plan and do not hear from him within a short time, send a follow-up email in a week, and try once more about two weeks later (in case he was out of town or swamped with other work). If this doesn't produce a meeting, look elsewhere.

4. *Try to meet people in person.* Despite the fact that we are living in a text, email, and conference-call age, you should still try to meet your recipient face to face, especially if you are seeking any type of funding. It's very hard to get such a commitment through a few texts or by email. Skype may work, but meeting in person for a major financial commitment is best. Nonetheless, if they want to keep all communication electronic, then follow their lead.

5. *Defuse objections.* Although you may think you've answered everything in your plan, you haven't. Prepare a list of possible objections— potential competitors, hard-to-buttress assumptions, and the like— that your investor may raise. Then prepare cogent answers. Have friends, co-workers, and your team play devil's advocate and provide every possible objection or ask tough question—then formulate your answers.

>> **Presenting-Your Business Plan!,** continued

6. *Get a commitment.* You won't get an investment unless you ask for it. When all objections have been answered, be ready to offer one last concession—"If I give your representative a board seat, can we do this today?"—and go for the close.

investor who doesn't want to play. Investors may not be interested in your particular industry, may not have any funds to invest at the moment, may need a larger or smaller amount to invest, or may have any of a hundred other reasons for turning you down.

As an example, your bank may be "loaned up" in your industry. If your proposal for a restaurant is turned down, it may be because your bank already has sufficient exposure in the hospitality sector. If so, ask your banker to refer you to another interested lender.

So the question is not: Will you get turned down? The question is: What do you do when it happens?

The first thing you should do is try to find out why, really, you got the thumbs-down. Is it truly because the person is out of the country, or is it something else?

plan pointer

Use as many charts, tables, and other graphic elements as it takes to get your point across. But don't count on lavish visuals to sway a skeptical reader. Some readers actually are put off by plans that seem to be trying to wow them through the presentation.

Your purpose is not to uncover someone's evasion or white lie. An investor has the right to turn you down for any reason whatsoever (unless, of course, you're dealing with an institution, such as a bank, that must abide by equal opportunity lending guidelines). Instead of pointing fingers at the investors, you should really be interested in pointing fingers at your plan.

If there is a problem with your plan, you want to know about it. If the projected return to investors is so low that nobody is going to take you seriously, now's the time to find out, not after you've presented it unsuccessfully dozens of times.

So gently probe, asking questions that focus on your plan, to find out whether you've made a mistake or just hit an unreceptive audience. If you identify a failing, of course, fix it before submitting your plan to another party.

Also, be ready to compromise. Perhaps they will give you 50 percent of what you are seeking in funding until they see some result. Consider the offer. You can always go for more funding elsewhere or scale down the size of your endeavor for the time being.

Get a Referral

Even a total refusal to consider your plan is helpful if the person suggests another place where you might be successful. You should always ask for a referral from anyone who turns your proposal down. It can't hurt—you've already been nixed. And a referral from a knowledgeable, respected investor can carry a lot of weight when you use it as an introduction (even if he or she is just trying to get rid of you).

Venture investing is very much a network-driven business. Venture capitalists are always asking for referrals, and they're usually willing to give them as well. Often they know someone else who might be interested. The same goes for angel investors.

Keep the Door Open

Leigh Steinberg, the well-known sports agent who has negotiated more than $2 billion worth of contracts for star athletes, says you should always keep in mind that one negotiation leads to the next. Keep that next negotiation in mind while working toward and planning for the one at hand. What that means in a business plan context is don't burn any bridges.

If an investor doesn't respond to your plan, brushes you off, or even rudely tells you to get lost, your response should still be unfailingly courteous and professional. If you let your frustration, disappointment, hurt feelings, and anger show, it could cost you plenty. That investor may be having a bad day and change her mind tomorrow. She may recall your name and the way you behaved so well under pressure and mention it to a more open-minded associate the next week. Or perhaps next year, when you're promoting a more exciting concept, she'll be willing to back the improved idea.

None of these scenarios is certain or even probable in any individual instance. But considering the aggregate potential to help or hurt you that all the people you'll present your plan to will possess, any of these scenarios is quite likely. And they're only possible if you keep the door open for the future.

Information
Creates
Capital

Much of the business-planning process involves research and communication—research about your product, its market, financial resources, your customers, and your competition along with communication with others in your line of work: industry experts, suppliers, and prospective customers. That's why the internet is an invaluable tool for small-business owners. Whether you're writing a business plan for a new business or for one that's already established, the web is a gold mine of information, as well as an indispensable link to future customers, investors, and market opportunities.

Market Research

Thanks to the internet, market research for business-planning purposes has become much easier and less time consuming.

> *"You can garner a wealth of valuable information via the web on your competitors—and on businesses similar to yours operating in other markets."*

For example, by logging on to the U.S. Census Bureau website (www.census.gov), you can learn everything you need about population trends in your market, which helps you determine market share—a key piece of information in any business plan. Using your site or email, you can set up an online focus group to get a handle on what prospective customers want from a product or service like yours, how they'd use it, where they'd like to buy it, and how often they'd purchase it. This kind of information will help you establish pricing, distribution, and promotional strategies.

You can garner a wealth of valuable information via the web on your competitors—and on businesses similar to yours operating in other markets. Visit these companies' websites to see what their product/service lines are, what their unique selling propositions are, who their target markets are and what media are used to reach them, what their prices are, and where and how their product is distributed. If their websites have a section called "News" or "Upcoming Events," you can learn about their plans for future marketing efforts and determine how they'll affect your business.

Trade Associations: Key Source of Targeted Information

Trade associations are an excellent source of specific trade and industry information. Suppose you are an artisan specializing in concrete countertops and related items. Is there a trade association? Sure, see www.concretenetwork.com/newsletter.htm for specialized information.

Because there are more than 30,000 trade associations in the United States, you will be hard-pressed not to find one that will include your business. Most have periodicals—magazines or newsletters—whose editors are eager to justify their positions by providing the membership with up-to-date information of all kinds. You can call the editor directly (they like to hear from members) or send him an email with your particular questions.

Trade associations often sponsor trade shows, which can help you get information on suppliers, industry trends, consultants, and even seminars directly related to your business. The people you meet and the informal exchange of knowledge that results provide the greatest value: production tips, problem solutions, contacts, and ideas.

> *"By reading publications and reports available online, you can stay current with what's happening in your industry as well as plan for your business' future."*

Communication

If your business is already established, use your website and social-media presence to solicit valuable feedback from your customers. Stay in touch with them to foster customer loyalty. After a sale is made, ask them whether they're satisfied or if more service is needed. Let them know about upcoming events and specials. Ask them what changes, if any, they'd like to see made in your product or service and how it's delivered.

Keep in mind the 80-20 principle in business which says that 80 percent of your business comes from repeat customers and 20 percent from new customers. Too many businesses spend an inordinate amount of money trying to lure new customers when their repeat customers and the friends, neighbors, colleagues, and family members of those regular customers are the backbone of most successful businesses.

Use the web and email to get the information you need about vendors and suppliers. Get a list of customers you can email, text, or phone, so you can assess their business relationships before you make any commitments.

If you don't yet have your business up and running, you may want to tap into the social media on your own to discuss your upcoming business—don't give too many secrets away, but go to online groups, discussions, or Facebook pages where you may find your demographic audience and start a conversation. See what they think in general about your ideas—get feedback.

Financing

If your business plan will double as a financing proposal, visit the U.S. government's Small Business Administration site at www.sba.gov to learn more about the many different types of financing programs available. In addition to financial assistance through guaranteed loans, the SBA also offers counseling services, help in getting government contracts, management assistance through programs like SCORE (Service Corps of Retired Executives), and lots of publications.

Other government organizations also offer financing to small businesses,

plan of action

Small Business Development Centers are one-stop shops set up by the Small Business Administration to give entrepreneurs free to low-cost advice, training, and technical assistance. There are SBDCs in each state and territory. Learn more online at www.sba.gov or call (800) 8-ASK-SBA.

including the U.S. Department of Agriculture (www.rurdev.usda.gov) and the U.S. Department of Commerce's Export Assistance Centers (www.ita.doc.gov/uscs/domfld/html). To find nongovernment organizations that provide financing to small businesses in your area, visit the Association for Enterprise Opportunity (AEO) at www.microenterpriseworks.org, and ask which programs serve businesses in your area. Your banker and state economic development office can also help.

Books and How-To Manuals

Scores of books have been written on how to write a business plan. Most provide skimpy treatment of the issues while devoting many pages to sample plans. Sample plans are useful, but unless planners understand the principles of the planning process, they can't really create sophisticated, one-of-a-kind plans. The following books will help you with the details of various sections in your plan:

■ *Dictionary of Business and Economics Terms* (Barron's). In its fifth edition, this compact, 800-page dictionary is a cure for jargon over-exposure. It provides concise definitions of business and has appendices that explain common business acronyms, provide tables of compounded interest rate factors, and more. It's the kind of book you'll turn to again and again.

■ *Guerrilla Marketing in 30 Days, 3rd. ed.* (Entrepreneur Press), by Jay Conrad Levinson and Al Lautenslager. The most recent edition of this marketing classic provides updated marketing techniques for those with little cash but high hopes. Levinson's insistence on the central role of planning and his simple but effective explanations of how to do it will serve business planners well.

■ *What Every Angel Investor Wants You to Know: An Insider Reveals How to Get Smart Funding for Your Billion Dollar Idea,* by Brian Cohen and John Kador. If you want an inside and honest look at what angel investors think, this is a good book to get the perspective from the other side of the table. Cohen is chairman of the New York Angels, an independent consortium of individual accredited angel investors.

Websites

The internet provides a virtually inexhaustible source of information for and about small business, including numerous sites with substantial databases of tips and ideas concerning business planning. Some of the best include the following:

■ *Entrepreneur.com.* This is the website of Entrepreneur Media, the nation's premier source for information for the entrepreneur and small-business community and the parent corporation of this book's publisher. The site contains a vast array of information resources, practical advice, interviews with experts, profiles of successful entrepreneurs, product and service reviews, and more.

The site offers resources for new entrepreneurs, including sample business plans and sections on startups, marketing, and technology, all of which can be helpful while in your planning process.

The Entrepreneur website also hosts Entrepreneur Media's EntrepreneurBookstore.com, a source for books—including this one—that offer expert advice on starting, running, and growing a small business. These include business startup guides, step-by-step startup guides to specific businesses, and business management guides, which offer in-depth information on financing, marketing, and more.

- *Small Business Administration (www.sba.gov).* The SBA's website is a vast directory to services provided by the federal agency devoted to helping small businesses. These include special lending programs, electronic databases of minority- and disadvantaged-owned businesses, directories of government contracting opportunities, and more.

>> Homemade, But Not Half-Baked

Lindsay Frucci created a fat-free brownie mix and built it into a home-based business success. No Pudge! Foods Inc. began in January 1995 with Frucci baking in her home kitchen in Elkins, New Hampshire. The startup notched just $6,000 in first-year sales, reached $42,000 the second year, and exploded to $253,000 the third year.

Frucci's secret ingredient was a pair of SCORE (Service Corps of Retired Executives) counselors who told her to find outside manufacturing and get No Pudge! out of her kitchen. The flexibility and increased capacity allowed Frucci to handle large orders, package products with UPC codes, and devote her own energy to product development and marketing.

Frucci had faith in the SCORE counselors' advice because they'd already helped her draft a business plan when she needed more money to expand the home-based firm. They had faith in her, as they showed when they advised her to turn down a bank's offer of a loan because the bank required her husband to cosign. Insisting the business should be financed on its own merits, without personal guarantees, they went to a second bank, which saw the light.

Frucci says flexibility is her watchword, and it's reflected in the way she runs and plans her business. "Sometimes businesses fail because they have a business plan that says, 'This is the way I'm going,' and they don't consider changing midstream," she says. "Allow your business plan to change. It's not set in stone."

There is also a generous selection of answers to frequently asked questions, tip sheets, and other advice. You can get a list of questions to ask yourself to see if you have the personality of an entrepreneur, find help with selecting a business, and browse an entire area devoted to help with your business plan.

■ *BPlan.com.* Bplans offers a very comprehensive website with a host of information about all aspects of business plans, as well as starting and growing a business. Funding, business plan, tools for creating a plan, and numerous business plans and templates are all included on Bplan.

Trade Groups and Associations

You're not in this alone. There are countless local and national organizations, both public and private, devoted to helping small businesses get up and running. They provide services ranging from low-rent facilities to financial assistance, from help in obtaining government contracts to help with basic business-planning issues. Many of these services are provided for free or at nominal cost.

■ *SCORE.* The Service Corps of Retired Executives, known as SCORE, is a nonprofit group of mostly retired businesspeople who volunteer to provide counseling to small businesses at no charge. SCORE has been around since 1964 and has helped more than three million entrepreneurs and aspiring entrepreneurs. SCORE is a source for all kinds of business advice, from how to write a business plan to investigating marketing potential and managing cash flow.

SCORE counselors work out of nearly 400 local chapters throughout the United States. You can obtain a referral to a counselor in your local chapter by contacting the national office. For more information, visit Score.org or call (800) 634-0245.

■ *National Business Incubation Association.* The NBIA is the national organization for business incubators, which are organizations specially set up to nurture young firms and help them survive and grow. Incubators provide leased office facilities on flexible terms, shared business services, management assistance, help in obtaining financing, and technical support. For more information, visit NBIA.org or call it at (740) 593-4331.

- *Chambers of Commerce.* The many chambers of commerce throughout the United States are organizations devoted to providing networking, lobbying, training, and more. If you think chambers are all about having lunch with a bunch of community boosters, think again. Among the services the U.S. Chamber of Commerce offers is a web-based business solutions program that provides online help with specific small-business needs, includ-

>> Hire Power

If you decide to hire a consultant to help you prepare your plan, take care that you select the right person. Here are guidelines:

1. *Get referrals.* Ask colleagues, acquaintances, and professionals such as bankers, accountants, and lawyers for the names of business-plan consultants they recommend. A good referral goes a long way to easing concerns you may have. Few consultants advertise anyway, so referrals may be your only choice.

2. *Look for a fit.* Find a consultant who is expert in helping businesses like yours. Ideally, the consultant should have lots of experience with companies of similar size and age in similar industries. Avoid general business experts or those who lack experience in your field.

3. *Check references.* Get the names of at least three clients the consultant has helped to write plans. Call the former clients and ask about the consultant's performance. Was the consultant's final fee in line with the original estimate? Was the plan completed on time? Did it serve the intended purpose?

4. *Get it in writing.* Have a legal contract for the consultant's services. It should discuss in detail the fee, when it will be paid, and under what circumstances. And make sure you get a detailed, written description of what the consultant must do to earn the fee. Whether it's an hourly rate or a flat fee isn't as important as each party knowing exactly what's expected.

ing planning, marketing, and other tasks such as creating a press release, collecting a bad debt, recruiting employees, and creating a retirement plan.

The U.S. Chamber of Commerce is the umbrella organization for local chambers, of which there are more than 1,000 in the United States. If you're planning on doing business overseas, don't forget to check for an American chamber of commerce in the countries where you hope to have a presence. They are set up to provide information and assistance to U.S. firms seeking to do business there. Many, but not all, countries have American chambers. You can find the national chamber of commerce at USChamber.gov or call its Washington Headquarters at (202) 659-6000.

Business Plan Consultants

Businesspeople tend to fall into two camps when it comes to consultants. Some believe strongly in the utility and value of hiring outside experts to bring new perspective and broad knowledge to challenging tasks. Others feel consultants are overpaid yes-men brought in only to endorse plans already decided upon or to take the heat for unpopular but necessary decisions.

Who's right? Both are, depending on the consultant you hire and your purpose for hiring one. Most consultants are legitimate experts in specific or general business areas. And most consultants can be hired to help with all or part of the process of writing a business plan.

The downside is you have to spend a lot of time on communication before and during the process of working with a consultant. Be sure you have fully explained, and the consultant fully understands, the nature of your business, your concept and strategy, your financial needs, and other matters such

plan pitfall

Working with a consultant isn't exactly like working with a member of your staff, a partner, an investor, or a banker, lawyer, or other professional you're retaining. Consultants are often freelancers, moving from assignment to assignment without looking back. That helps them bring a valuable outside perspective, but it can also make them more difficult to manage.

>> The Lowdown on Consultants

A good consultant should provide the following:

1. *She should lay out expectations.* In any working relationship, you need to know exactly what is expected of whom you are hiring.

2. *The consultant should only make promises she can keep.* Hold her to her word. Business is about making and keeping promises.

3. *All plans should be made in advance and make promises that were inherently discussed beforehand.* Without a concrete plan a consultant can "wing it," leaving you without any way to look at milestones and keep tabs on her progress.

4. *A consultant should provide regular, specific updates.* You need to set up a schedule and a means of regular communication. You want to know—specifically—what she is doing, and this means regular ongoing communication, which is an integral part of a healthy business relationship.

5. *She should not have a personal agenda.* If the consultant is not acting in the best interest of your company, then she is not doing the job ethically. Make sure anyone you're hiring is working for your needs, not theirs.

as control, future plans, and so on. Refer to these important issues throughout the process—you don't want to pay for a beautifully done plan that fits somebody else's business, not yours. And when the work is done, debrief the consultant to find out if there's anything you can learn that wasn't included in the plan.

Business Plan Competitions

If you happen to be a business student, you may be able to enter your business plan in a college business plan competition. These competitions, of which there are more than three dozen in the United States, confer a measure of fame and even some money on the winners. A panel of plan experts including college professors, venture capitalists, and bankers usually judge entries.

Winners are the plans that best lay out a convincing case for a business's success. Judges can be tough; contestants can expect scathing criticism of poorly thought-out plans.

Moot Corporation is the name of the best known of the nation's business plan competitions. It's sponsored each May by the University of Texas at Austin. Moot Corporation calls itself the "Super Bowl of world business-plan competition" and is the oldest of the approximately three dozen business school-sponsored plan competitions. More than two dozen plan-writing teams from as far away as Australia participate in the contest, which began in 1983. For more on the history of this competition visit www.businessplans.org/history.html.

Another major competition is the Rice Business Plan Competition. This very prestigious three-day competition is the largest and richest graduate-level student startup competition with more than $1 million in cash and prizes. As of 2013, there were more than 1,200 applications submitted, over 130 companies involved as sponsors, and more than 250 judges. More information is at http://alliance.rice.edu/rbpc.aspx.

You'll also find competitions that are not sponsored by universities or business schools such as New York Start Up, an annual competition for New Yorkers starting for-profit businesses that offers cash prizes totaling up to $30,000. Sponsored by the New York Public Library and the Citi Foundation, the competition began in 2010. For more go to www.nypl.org/locations/tid/65/node/95979.

There are numerous state competitions such as the Rhode Island Business Plan Competition. Started in 2000 by Garrett Hunter, then president of the Business Development Company of Rhode Island, the annual competition is designed for new businesses as well as those in the early development stages. Categories include three tracks for entrepreneurs, students, and technical companies with prizes in the $39,000 to $43,000 range for first place winners.

For more competitions throughout the country go to www. bizplancompetitions.com. Review the requirements, deadlines, and details very carefully.

Hackathons

Also known as hack days, a hack weekend, or a hackfest, a hackathon is an event (usually lasting a weekend) in which programmers, software developers, interface designers, and others team up to create software, apps, or some useful technology. Typically, the process emerges from brainstorming sessions to explore and discuss ideas. Then they move to implementing the best ones. In the end there are hackathon winners in competitions such as Hack MIT, presented by the university, or Hack NY, co-organized by NYU and Columbia University.

In a slight variation of the hackathon, the hackaplan has emerged. In short, the goal of a Hackaplan is the same as a hackathon, but with diverse business teams as opposed to programmers. The objective is for each team to create a business plan, rather than software or an app. While there may certainly be a lot of tweaking of the final product, a weekend of brain storming on a business plan can jump-start the process.

What Does It All Mean?

In the end, consultants can only help you know what it is you're looking to accomplish with your business. Business plan competitions can give you a

>> Elevator Pitch

Sometimes there is simply not enough time for someone to read your business plan or even hear a full presentation. Therefore, you need an elevator pitch. It is the ultra-short version of your plan featuring only the most significant of significant information, all presented in the time it takes for an elevator ride. The perfect example of an elevator pitch came from the 1988 movie *Working Girl*, when Melanie Griffith pitched her great business idea in an elevator to the radio station executives. Of course, the elevator pitch cannot replace the well-though-out, detailed business plan, but it can drum up interest in reading one. Have such a pitch written, rehearsed, and ready to go. And, keep in mind, it can be harder to write the 20- to 30-second elevator pitch than the entire business plan. Each and every word carries more weight because (like on Twitter) you are very limited.

leg up on the competition, but you will then need to use that edge wisely by putting your award-winning plan into the right hands. SCORE and other organizations can benefit you in the business-planning process, if you are ready to listen, learn, and ask questions.

Remember, though, there is no magic formula for success. Your business plan should lay down the foundation from which you will do everything you can to build and sustain a successful business. It should tell the story of your business going forward and help you think hard about every aspect of your business. It should help you make the key decisions as you proceed. It should also keep you thinking about all of the possibilities.

Writing a business plan is not easy, but neither is starting and running a successful business. Many new businesses (as well as older ones) fail every year. Some have no concrete plan, others have drifted from the plan, and many have lost the motivation to grow and change to keep pace with the changing marketplace. Complacency stops many businesses from taking the next steps.

A business plan means what you want it to mean. It can be a way of guiding you through the process, a means of getting investors, a way of finding advisors, a document to help lure new talent, or all of the above. It is not something that you finish and forget to look at, but instead something you can go back to, just as you would do with a blueprint of a house or a building as you plan to add on a new room or rewire the facility.

Of course, the business plan is worthwhile only if you are honest in what you put on paper, meaning honest to yourself. If you are writing down an idealized version of what you'd like to see without including well-researched facts and forecasts that are based on due diligence, then your business plan will simply lead you to disappointment. Therefore, as you write the plan, stop and look at it periodically to make sure you are being realistic and have other people you know and trust read it to confirm that you are being forthright and not overly optimistic.

The real optimism of a business plan is creating something that you can accomplish and make successful over time. It's fine to use the business plan to shoot for the stars, but start with one star at a time.

Sample Business Plans

The sample plans in Appendices A, B, C, and D were chosen to represent a cross section of companies and the variety of reasons for writing a plan. Please note that these companies are fictitious and that their concepts may or may not be applicable to your business. For the purposes of this book, they show how business owners can approach various issues relating to a business plan depending on the type of industry, size of the company, characteristics of the market, caliber of management, and other factors.

Read these sample plans with an eye toward seeing whether any of the approaches taken in them fits what you're trying to do.

Appendices

Business Plan for a Retailer Seeking Startup Capital

W aterWorks Inc. is a retail food-service operation seeking startup capital. Its business plan is succinct, carefully thought out, and well-documented. Particular attention has been paid to studying the national sales trends for the beverages WaterWorks will serve. The plan provides adequate financial data, including a three-year income statement projection and a month-by-month cash flow projection for the first year.

The primary purpose of this plan is to facilitate a $30,000 bank loan so the two partners can launch their business and get through the first six months. From that point on, the business will be able to sustain itself on cash flow. When the partners need additional financing to open their second location in a couple of years, they should have little difficulty in obtaining a second loan for expansion.

There are several strengths to this business plan. First is the fact that management is experienced in the hospitality industry. Second, the partners are providing a significant portion of the startup capital themselves, which delights bankers. Third is that demand for WaterWorks's products appears to be growing, with little or no direct competition in its market. Most important from a financier's point of view is that the plan shows enough cash generated from sales to pay off the loan in 12 months.

Among the weaknesses revealed by this business plan are that the idea is unproven, at least in its geographic market. Second, the partners are paying themselves salaries. Some lenders would prefer to see borrowers do without salaries, at least in the beginning. This is somewhat offset by the facts that the partners are not taking a draw—a dividend paid from profits in addition to salary—and that the salaries will be modest.

Business Plan

for

WaterWorks Inc.

WaterWorks Inc.

12709 Enfield Terrace

Austin, TX 78704

(512) 555-1212

Albert Walter, President

Matthew Strang, CEO

September 1, 2013

Contents

2

I. Executive Summary

Market

According to *Beverage Digest* (April 2012), still, or noncarbonated, water beverages are the trendiest new drinks since gourmet coffee. The market for still-water drinks has been building steadily for three years and now appears ready to enter an accelerated period of growth.

Still-water drinks are different from the mass-produced carbonated beverages sold by the soft-drink giants like Coca-Cola. They are usually produced in small quantities by small operations, product quality is high, and they often include functional additives, such as nutriceuticals, that differentiate them from mass-market soft drinks and appeal to health-conscious consumers.

Business Description

WaterWorks will sell still-water beverages through a retail outlet in Austin, Texas. The store will have a bar and seating area as well as a service counter and will serve beverages prepared on the premises for consumption there or off-site, along with prepackaged products like baked goods.

The store, which will also include a drive-through window, will be located in an existing facility near the intersection of Loop 1 and Enfield Road in central Austin.

Products

The product line, all purchased from outside vendors, will consist of approximately 20 different still-water and functional beverages, in addition to a selection of freshly baked breads, muffins, cookies, and other locally produced foods.

3

Management

WaterWorks is registered as a partnership owned in equal shares by Albert Walter and Matthew Strang. Mr. Walter will serve as President and Mr. Strang as Chief Executive Officer. Mr. Walter and Mr. Strang are both experienced in food-service operations. (See "Management" for more information.)

Financing Needs

WaterWorks needs $30,000 in short-term financing to cover startup costs, purchase necessary equipment, and provide working capital until the business can support itself from cash flow. The owners will invest $20,000 of their own cash and would like to borrow $20,000 initially, with the remaining $10,000 available as a line of credit over the next 180 days. Interest payments will begin after the first month. After 10 months, operations will generate sufficient cash to pay down the balance of the loan in two balloon payments, which will result in the loan being paid off by the end of the first year. The owners are prepared to pledge personal assets as collateral for this loan.

4

II. Business Mission and Strategy

Mission Statement

WaterWorks will sell still water and functional beverages to health-conscious consumers in Austin, Texas. Customers will include students, faculty, and staff from the nearby University of Texas, the nation's largest institution of higher education, and residents of the well-educated, affluent surrounding neighborhoods.

Strategic Elements

The WaterWorks strategy embodies several key elements:

- The store will be the first of its kind in Austin, a major metropolitan area of more than one million people.
- The location is near Sixth Street and Lamar Boulevard, one of the city's busiest intersections and hottest retail environments.
- Only products of the highest quality will be offered.
- Austin has one of the country's highest per-capita rates of consumption of natural foods and beverages.

Strategic Objectives

- To repay initial bank loans by the end of the first year of operation.
- To produce a net profit of at least $75,000 by the third year of operation.
- To expand to three additional retail locations by the end of the fifth year of operation.
- To explore additional expansion through the creation of more company-owned or possibly franchised outlets after year five.

5

III. Sources and Uses of Funds

Startup Costs Summary

Startup costs will be approximately $55,000, which includes initial lease payments, leasehold improvements, inventory, permits, and other expenses. Startup costs will be financed primarily through a combination of bank borrowing and investment by the partners.

Sources and Uses of Funds

USE OF FUNDS

Capital Expenditures

Leasehold Improvements	$10,000
Equipment	10,000
Total Capital Expenditures	**$20,000**

Working Capital

Legal	$1,000
Permits and Licenses	1,500
Printing	1,000
Graphic Design	1,000
Insurance	2,500
Rent (three months)	10,000
Salaries	10,000
Startup Inventory	5,000
Other Business Activities	3,000
Total Working Capital	**$35,000**
TOTAL USE OF FUNDS	**$55,000**

SOURCES OF FUNDS

Partner Investments	$20,000
Trade Credit	5,000
Bank Loan	30,000
Total Sources of Funds	**$55,000**

6

IV. Products

WaterWorks will sell still-water drinks and baked goods to customers in Austin, Texas.

Company Locations and Facilities

WaterWorks will be located near the intersection of Loop 1 and Enfield Road in Austin, Texas, an attractive retail location near desirable residential areas, the state capitol complex, and the University of Texas main campus.

An existing 900-square-foot facility with seating and a drive-up window will be leased. Improvements will include additions to the seating area, a water bar, and landscaping. A second location is planned for the third year of operation at a site to be determined.

Products

The primary products sold through WaterWorks will be functional still-water drinks in three categories:

1. *Nutriceuticals.* Nutriceutical waters include still waters to which minerals such as potassium and calcium, vitamins including C or D, or other substances such as caffeine have been added.
2. *Bacteria-Free Still Water.* Bacteria-free still waters are processed using techniques that eliminate microorganisms, including associated flavors and particles, from the water.
3. *Exotic Waters.* Exotic waters are bottled and imported from locations such as Alaska, Canada, France, Hawaii, Sweden, and Russia.

7

V. Markets and Competition

Still-Water Sales Trends

Still water is the fastest-growing segment of the alternative beverage industry. Sales for 2013, the most recent year available, were up 25 percent, almost double the industry average of 13 percent. Other alternative beverages include juices, teas, sport drinks, sparkling waters, and natural sodas.

Still-water sales totaled 731 million cases, making the category the dominant one in alternative beverages, whose total sales neared 1.9 billion cases. Still water's share of the alternative beverage market exceeded 39 percent, up 3.7 percent from the previous year, when 585 million cases of still waters were sold. Other strong categories included sport drinks and teas. *Source: Beverage Digest*, February 2013.

Industry Analysis

Alternative beverage producers include some of the beverage industry's largest companies. The graph on the following page shows the top alternative beverage producers and their respective market shares.

Suppliers

The following products will be supplied by various vendors: Aqua Health, Water for Life, Nutri-Water, Hydration Technologies, Guava Cool, and Soft Beverages. Vendors supply a variety of beverages with features such as nutriceutical content, bacteria-free processing, and a number of organic flavorings including berries, other fruits, and spices.

Suppliers are for the most part located in the continental United States. While they are not currently available for wholesale distribution in Austin, which partially explains the lack of local retail distribution, all operate existing distribution systems with representatives in other Texas cities, including Houston, San Antonio, and Dallas. No problems in obtaining adequate supplies of important products are anticipated.

8

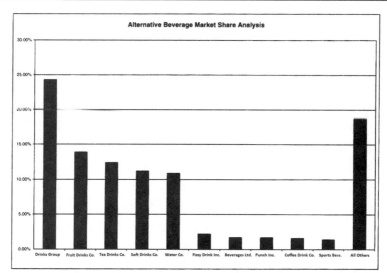

Source: Beverage Week

Market Analysis Summary

Austin, the capital of Texas, is located near the center of the state, approximately 70 miles north of San Antonio and 200 miles south of Dallas. The city has a population of nearly 2 million people and was the fastest-growing city in America in 2014, as listed in *Forbes* magazine. Austin is home to the nation's largest university, many offices related to the state government, and a booming business community that includes the headquarters of Dell Computer Corporation and Whole Foods Market, the nation's largest retailer of natural foods.

Austin has one of the highest percentages of adults with college degrees of any American city and is generally regarded as a center of progressive lifestyles in the Southwest.

WaterWorks is an ideal business for Austin given a market of this size and demographics. Based on average individual transactions of approximately $2.25, including still-water drinks and related products, the business has the potential to gross more than $400,000 in sales by the third year of operation.

9

Competitive Analysis

No other business in Austin focuses exclusively on the still-water market. This opportunity provides considerable flexibility in pricing and allows WaterWorks to create a great deal of customer awareness and brand loyalty.

While no retail businesses devoted exclusively to water beverages exist in Austin, water beverages are sold at Whole Foods, Whole Earth Provision, Randall's Markets, and other grocery retailers.

Research in San Francisco reveals information on six still-water beverage retail locations. The oldest has been in operation for slightly more than two years. These businesses are thriving, selling still-water drink units at prices ranging from $1.25 for small, counter-prepared beverages to be consumed on the premises to $24 for larger bottles to be installed off-premises in water coolers.

The owner of one of the older San Francisco businesses indicated that first-year sales in his market, which, like the WaterWorks location, is near a university and an affluent residential district, were 200 units per day, yielding a first-year revenue potential of $117,000, assuming minimal average transaction value of $1.75. Considerable price flexibility is likely to exist in markets where competition is lower or nonexistent.

Competition and Buying Patterns

Still-water retailing will be new to Austin. Competitors primarily sell mass-market waters through grocery-store-type locations and do not focus on the still-water beverage market. There are no retail providers of counter-prepared still-water beverages for consumption on the premises—so-called water bars.

WaterWorks' success will come from educating consumers about the appeal and benefits of still-water beverages and from providing high-quality products not available in grocery stores. Price competition will be a minimal concern given current market conditions.

10

VI. Marketing

Marketing Strategy

WaterWorks's overall marketing strategy will be to educate consumers about the benefits of still-water beverages and to promote the availability of these products through WaterWorks. Customers will be reached through fliers, newspaper advertisements, and special events.

Location also plays an important role in marketing and promotion, with the business being located near a high-traffic retail area in central Austin.

Target Markets and Market Segments

WaterWorks will target health-conscious and generally well-educated and affluent consumers who are interested in trying new products and dissatisfied with the limited selection and lack of personal service found in grocery-store-type water retailers.

Pricing Strategy

Still-water fountain drinks will be offered at the following prices:

Small: $1.50
Medium: $2.25
Large: $3.75

In addition, larger sizes of water will be sold for customer carryout or delivery. They will range in size from one-liter bottles to 20-liter plastic jugs at prices from $3.75 to $35.00.

Products will be sold on a cash basis to retail customers. Corporate customers, expected to represent an insignificant proportion of sales at the beginning, will be invoiced and given 30 days to pay.

Promotion Strategy

WaterWorks will promote its still-water drinks to customers through:

- Regular newspaper advertisements focusing on the benefits of still-water beverages.

11

- A publicity campaign that will spotlight company owners on health-related TV and radio broadcasts and position them as experts in print publications.
- Educational and promotional fliers that are distributed to residences within a one-mile radius.
- Discounts offered to groups such as health-food cooperatives, organic gardening clubs, and cultural associations.

Distribution Strategy

- Primary distribution of still-water drinks will be through the retail facility.
- Secondary distribution will consist of deliveries of bottled water to restaurants, retailers, and corporate locations.
- Additional distribution will be through temporary booths set up at athletic and cultural events such as bicycle races and concerts.

Sales Projections

Sales will start in January 2015. Sales forecasts are based on experiences of similar startups in San Francisco. Forecasts include retail sales consistent with similar markets with significant competition and may be considered conservative. Corporate sales include sales of bottles for office water coolers and beverages for corporate parties. Special-events sales include products sold through booths set up at concerts, races, and other events. Third-year sales are projected to include partial results from opening a new retail location.

Sales Forecast

Year	2015	2016	2017
Retail walk-in	$147,000	$183,000	$390,000
Corporate	0	6,000	12,000
Special events	15,000	18,000	30,000
Total	$162,000	$207,000	$432,000

12

VII. Management

Albert Walter has five years' experience in the retail restaurant industry. He served for three years as manager of the Java Coffee Beanery and for two years as assistant manager of the Travis Bagel Shop. He is a 1999 graduate of the University of Texas at Austin business school, where he earned an MBA.

Matthew Strang has seven years of experience in the hospitality industry. He served as assistant general manager of the Hill Country Bed & Breakfast in Fredericksburg, Texas, for five years and as manager of Bee Cave Bar & Grill in Austin for two years.

WaterWorks will hire one part-time employee to assist with the business. The partners will perform the bulk of the duties required to operate the initial store.

13

VIII. Financial Data

Financial Plan

WaterWorks will finance growth through cash flow. Expansion will begin in year three and will include the opening of a second location, an increase in corporate sales, and added emphasis on special-event promotions.

Seasonal Data

As a result of Austin being a "college town," seasonal variations will be most pronounced in June, July, and August. During these months, many between-term college students leave the city, causing a significant—but temporary—reduction in the size of Austin's market.

Break-Even Analysis

The following table and chart show break-even analysis for year one. The owners have determined that the business will require sales of approximately $12,591 per month to break even during the first year of operation. Assumptions include average monthly fixed expenses of $9,443 (general and administrative expenses less depreciation divided by 12) and a gross profit margin of 75 percent.

Break-Even Analysis

$$\frac{\$9,443}{75\%} = \$12,591$$

Projected Profit and Loss

Profits for the next three years are projected to equal:

> 2015: $1,581
> 2016: $24,086
> 2017: $78,022

14

Projected Income Statement

	2015	2016	2017
INCOME			
Gross Sales	$157,500	$207,000	$432,000
Less Returns and Allowances	0	0	0
Net Sales	157,500	207,000	432,000
Cost of Sales	40,500	49,653	99,360
Gross Profit	$117,000	$157,347	$332,640
Gross Profit Margin	74%	76%	77%
OPERATING EXPENSES			
General & Administrative Expenses			
Salaries and Wages	$45,360	$54,750	$121,500
Employee Benefits	2,721	3,285	7,290
Payroll Taxes	2,268	2,738	6,075
Sales Commissions	0	0	0
Professional Services	1,725	1,725	2,400
Rent	29,400	29,400	58,800
Maintenance	1,350	1,350	2,250
Equipment Rental	1,650	2,250	3,375
Furniture and Equipment Purchase	1,875	2,400	3,375
Insurance	2,820	3,000	6,300
Interest Expenses	2,025	2,025	3,000
Utilities	3,225	3,375	3,840
Office Supplies	1,350	1,425	1,800
Postage	1,125	1,388	1,575
Marketing and Advertising	15,225	19,875	26,138
Travel	825	1,125	1,500
Entertainment	375	450	600
Bad Debt	0	0	0
Depreciation and Amortization	2,100	2,700	4,800
TOTAL OPERATING EXPENSES	**$115,419**	**$133,261**	**$254,618**
Net Income before Taxes	$1,581	$24,086	$78,022
Provision for Taxes on Income	608	2,406	7,802
NET INCOME AFTER TAXES	**$973**	**$21,680**	**$70,220**

15

Notes to projected income statement:

1. Figures for 2015 include added income and operating expenses from second location.

2. Cost of Sales reflects slight but steady increase in gross profit margins.

3. Salaries and Wages include one part-time employee the first two years of operation, three part-time employees the third year of operation (when two locations will be staffed), and the following annual salaries for each partner in lieu of draw:

   2015: $18,000

   2016: $22,500

   2017: $45,000

Projected Cash Flow

Projected cash flow for the next three years is estimated as follows:

   2015: $6,750

   2016: $22,300

   2017: $93,000

16

Projected Cash Flow Statement for 2015

	Jan.	Feb.	Mar.	Apr.	May	Jun.	Jul.	Aug.	Sep.	Oct.	Nov.	Dec.	TOTAL
CASH RECEIPTS													
Income from Sales													
Cash Sales	$3,000	$7,500	$10,500	$10,500	$16,500	$15,000	$15,000	$15,000	$16,500	$16,500	$18,000	$18,000	$162,000
Collections	0	0	0	0	0	0	0	0	0	0	0	0	$0
Total Cash from Sales	$3,000	$7,500	$10,500	$10,500	$16,500	$15,000	$15,000	$15,000	$16,500	$16,500	$18,000	$18,000	$162,000
Income from Financing													
Interest Income	0	0	0	0	0	0	0	0	0	0	0	0	$0
Loan Proceeds	15,000	0	0	3,750	0	0	3,750	0	0	0	0	0	$22,500
Total Cash from Financing	15,000	0	0	3,750	0	0	3,750	0	0	0	0	0	$22,500
Other Cash Receipts	15,000	0	0	0	0	0	0	0	0	0	0	0	$15,000
Total Cash Receipts	$33,000	$7,500	$10,500	$14,250	$16,500	$15,000	$18,750	$15,000	$16,500	$16,500	$18,000	$18,000	$199,500
CASH DISBURSEMENTS													
Expenses													
Cost of Goods	750	1,875	2,625	2,625	4,125	3,750	3,750	3,750	4,125	4,125	4,500	4,500	$40,500
Operating Expenses	18,750	6,225	6,600	7,200	7,538	9,488	7,875	8,587	9,825	9,975	10,087	10,350	$112,500
Loan Payments	0	225	225	225	225	225	225	225	225	225	11,362	11,363	$24,750
Income Tax Payments	0	0	0	0	0	0	0	0	0	0	0	0	$0
Equipment Purchase	7,500	0	0	3,750	0	0	0	0	0	0	0	0	$11,250
Contingency	0	0	0	0	0	0	0	0	0	0	0	3,750	$3,750
Owner's Draw	0	0	0	0	0	0	0	0	0	0	0	0	$0
Total Cash													
Disbursements	$27,000	$8,325	$9,450	$13,800	$11,888	$13,463	$11,850	$12,562	$14,175	$14,325	$25,959	$29,963	$192,750
Net Cash Flow	6,000	-825	1,050	450	4,612	1,537	6,900	2,438	2,325	2,175	-7,950	-11,963	$6,750
Opening Cash Balance	0	6,000	5,175	6,225	6,675	11,288	12,825	19,725	22,163	24,488	26,663	18,713	$0
Cash Receipts	33,000	7,500	10,500	14,250	16,500	15,000	18,750	15,000	16,500	16,500	18,000	18,000	$199,500
Cash Disbursements	-27,000	-8,325	-9,450	-13,800	-11,887	-13,463	-11,850	-12,562	-14,175	-14,325	-25,950	-29,963	-$192,750
Ending Cash Balance	$6,000	$5,175	$6,225	$6,675	$11,288	$12,825	$19,725	$22,163	$24,488	$26,663	$18,713	$6,750	$6,750

Notes to projected cash flow statement:

1. Cash sales reflect summer slowdown due to college students being out of town.

2. Other Cash Receipts consist of investment by partners.

3. Contingency fund set up at year-end to provide cash reserves.

4. Owners receive nominal salaries instead of draws.

5. Loan Payments cover interest at 10 percent on $30,000 loan until balance of principal and interest are repaid in two third-quarter balloon payments.

6. April equipment purchase is for trailer, portable equipment, and booth, to prepare for promotions at outdoor events.

Balance Sheet Projection

Projected shareholders' equity and net worth after one year of operation is $29,250.

18

Projected Balance Sheet
for Year Ending
December 31, 2015

ASSETS	
Current Assets	
Cash	$6,750
Accounts Receivable	0
Inventory	4,125
Prepaid Expenses	3,750
Total Current Assets	**$14,625**
Fixed Assets	
Land	$0
Buildings	0
Equipment	3,000
Furniture	7,500
Fixtures	7,500
Less Accumulated Depreciation	3,375
Total Fixed Assets	**$21,375**
Other Assets	**0**
TOTAL ASSETS	**$36,000**
LIABILITIES	
Current Liabilities	
Accounts Payable	$4,125
Accrued Payroll	2,250
Taxes Payable	375
Short-Term Notes Payable	0
Total Current Liabilities	**$6,750**
Long-Term Liabilities	
Long-Term Notes Payable	$0
Total Long-Term Liabilities	**$0**
Net Worth	**$29,250**
Retained Earnings	0
Total Net Worth	**$29,250**
TOTAL LIABILITIES & NET WORTH	**$36,000**

Note to projected balance sheet:

1. Accounts receivable will be minimal in the first year because all business will be conducted on a cash basis.

19

Business Plan for a High-Tech Company Seeking Financing for Growth

The following business plan is for a high-tech company looking for a second round of financing to enable it to market and distribute its product nationwide. The strongest parts of this plan are the industry analysis and management sections. Management is clearly experienced enough to achieve the objectives set in its plan. Two other positive indicators are the industry's strong growth and trends favoring the introduction of this company's product.

The plan's weakness relates to the amount of money being requested. The $750,000 that the owners are asking for reduces the expected return, based purely on net income projections, to a rate below that at which most venture capitalists are likely to be interested.

It's possible that another company might be interested in buying out Software Solutions or that the company may go public after a few more years. For now, the owners need to make a stronger case for an enticing cash-out or to ask for less money.

Software Solutions

Helping to Make

Automobile Dealerships More Productive

26209 Fairfax Ave.
Cincinnati, OH 45207
513-555-7272
Bradley Regent, CEO

The information contained in this document is confidential. If you are not authorized to view it, please immediately return it to the above address.

Table of Contents

2

Executive Summary

Software Solutions is a one-year-old software manufacturer. Our initial product is an inventory management system for automobile dealers on customizable websites that will be accessible through a brand new app compatible with most popular smartphones. The system will be Cloud-based for safe storage.

Many automobile dealers complain about the lack of good inventory-management systems. Even today, many dealerships use paper stock cards, sales slips, and invoice books. However, these are frequently out-of-date and inaccurate and always time-consuming to maintain.

Additional problems with existing inventory management systems include employees' inability to access inventory records while on the showroom floor or away from the office. This can result in missed sales opportunities, as employees must return to the office or call a prospect later to provide information about the availability of a particular model.

Software Solutions's DriversSeat inventory management system is designed specifically for mobile usage, running on smartphones

Software Solutions was created specifically to produce the web-based format with the app that would work on all smartphones.

The founder and CEO, Bradley Regent, spent ten years as an information systems manager for automobile dealerships in Ohio and Pennsylvania. Mr. Regent understands dealership information issues and has many contacts with those responsible for purchasing information technology for dealerships. Other members of his team include a marketing manager, a programmer, and an office assistant.

Nine months were spent developing the DriversSeat product, including market research, programming, and testing. Initial sales of the product have been encouraging. Several of the largest dealers in the Cincinnati area have tested the programs, and at least two regional chains are also trying them out.

3

Software Solutions was launched with $80,000 provided by the founder and is now seeking an additional $750,000 to market and distribute DriversSeat nationwide. The company anticipates no difficulty raising this sum through a private equity placement of preferred stock, based on strong initial acceptance of the product and numerous pending sales.

4

Software Solutions's Management Team

One of Software Solutions's strengths is its management team's industry experience.

Bradley Regent, CEO

Prior to founding Software Solutions, Mr. Regent worked for several large automobile dealerships as a programmer, systems analyst, and information systems manager. A native of Cincinnati, Mr. Regent graduated from Ohio State University with a degree in computer science. After two years with a large systems integrator in Cincinnati, Mr. Regent began working in the automobile dealership industry.

Mr. Regent has extensive experience in analyzing, developing, and maintaining inventory management systems for automobile dealerships. He has received professional training and certification as a developer in Oracle, SAP, Microsoft SQL, and DB2 database environments and has managed information systems departments of up to seven people.

Mr. Regent's primary responsibilities at Software Solutions will be long-term planning, participating in product development, managing company growth, and meeting with investors, customers, and suppliers. Mr. Regent is now the primary owner of Software Solutions and holds 80 percent of the corporation's stock.

Wanda McIntire, Vice President of Marketing

Ms. McIntire has worked for five years as a marketing specialist for two companies serving automobile dealerships' information-systems needs in Kentucky and Indiana. Ms. McIntire has experience positioning and marketing new information systems products geared to automobile dealers. She developed the initial marketing plan for Parts Perfect, a parts inventory management system created by Autosoft Systems that is now used by more than 500 dealerships nationwide. Ms. McIntire graduated from Tulsa University in 1999 with a degree in business.

5

Ms. McIntire's responsibilities at Software Solutions are formulating and implementing marketing strategy, participating in product development, and working with customers and prospects. She holds 5 percent of the corporation's shares.

Perry Honeywell, Program Developer

Mr. Honeywell was one of the first 20 employees of Helping Hand Systems, a Palo Alto, California, company that was the largest third-party supplier of software for the PalmPilot computer system during Mr. Honeywell's tenure. He led the team that designed and produced Third Hand, a data -collection system running on the PalmPilot that is now used in ISO 9000 quality-control programs around the world. He received computer science degrees from San Francisco University and the University of California at Berkeley.

Mr. Honeywell's responsibilities at Software Solutions are overseeing program operation and interface design and creating and testing code. He holds 10 percent of the corporation's shares.

Steven Wise, Human Resources and Administrative Manager

Mr. Wise has expertise in interviewing, screening, and hiring applicants for positions with information-systems firms. For the past three years, he has been in charge of staffing and administration for Staple Systems, a Cincinnati electronic commerce software firm that grew from three to more than 40 employees during the time that the leading-edge software became well received in the marketplace.

Mr. Wise's responsibilities at Software Solutions are managing office operations, including bookkeeping and accounts receivables and payables, as well as dealing with outside suppliers. As the company grows, he'll be responsible for recruiting and hiring program designers, programmers, testers, and other employees. Mr. Wise holds 5 percent of the corporation's shares.

6

The DriversSeat Product

DriversSeat is a web-based inventory system that works through mobile devices to make managing inventory from anywhere a reality. The program was created in the mobile environment. The following table summarizes DriversSeat features and benefits to customers.

DriversSeat Features and Benefits

Features	Benefits
• Thoroughly tested app using iOS and Android app platforms	• Enables salespeople, whether they're offsite or away from their desk, to quickly and easily provide customers with accurate information on the availability of specific automobile models
• A customizable website that allows each auto dealership to easily input its data or transfer data from another online location	• Design reflects thorough understanding of the needs of automobile dealerships

7

DriversSeat Marketing Strategy

Software Solutions's marketing strategy takes advantage of two trends: the rapid growth of mobile systems for industrial and commercial applications and the increasing need for more sophisticated and flexible inventory management as the automobile dealership industry consolidates and grows in size.

Recent figures from the National Automobile Dealers Association show:

- Total sales for auto dealerships are almost $700 billion annually and growing.
- More than 17,850 new-car dealerships exist, as of 2013 a number that has grown slightly (.055) over the previous two years.
- Mobile information systems have become increasingly important to the industry.
- Apps and mobile devices have become a part of our culture. The numbers don't lie. Nearly 103 billion apps were downloaded in 2013, which was up by 59 percent from the previous year. It is estimated that by the end of 2014, mobile will have surpassed desktop internet usage.
- According to IDC, the smartphone market is now larger than the PC market.

Software Solutions is using email marketing to auto dealership information systems managers, followed up with telemarketing and personal sales calls as its primary marketing method. This approach takes maximum advantage of the company principals' reputations and visibility in the Ohio automobile dealership community.

As marketing for the DriversSeat is rolled out nationwide to all 21,650 prospective auto dealer customers, additional marketing dollars will be required to produce conduct telemarketing follow-up calls, arrange for personal sales calls to prospects, and staff these functions with appropriately skilled personnel.

8

Software Solutions believes it can achieve a 9 percent market share within four years. Sales of systems to approximately 2,000 dealerships, at an average purchase price of $10,000, indicates total sales through 2018 of approximately $2 million, with more than half that amount occurring in the final year as the effect of prior marketing efforts begins to be felt.

9

Program Development and Operations

One of Software Solutions's biggest advantages is the expertise of its principals in the design, development, and maintenance of software for portable applications, particularly those in the automobile dealer industry.

The principal technologists, Bradley Regent and Perry Honeywell, combine years of experience in, respectively, auto dealership information systems and portable platform software development. In addition to extensive training in industry-standard database management systems, which allows Mr. Regent to effectively interface DriversSeat data with existing dealership computer systems, he maintains a network of beta testers, consisting primarily of auto dealership IS managers, sales managers, salespeople, and inventory management personnel, to help with testing, product development, feature refinement, and other tasks.

Mr. Honeywell is recognized as an expert in app development. He serves on the advisory board for developing and maintaining standards for mobile applications for smartphones. His contacts and experience ensure that Software Solutions will have ongoing access to the latest and best technology for developing its products.

Management believes its combination of industry-specific and technical expertise makes it unique among companies addressing the inventory management needs of automobile dealerships. Other competitors include EDS, Digital Dealership, Microsoft, and SAP. All these companies are much larger than Software Solutions and capable of bringing much greater resources to bear on the market. However, Software Solutions's management believes that its lead time in developing applications for this market, plus the market segment's small size relative to those its competitors are primarily interested in, will provide the company with an opportunity to secure a solid foothold.

Software Solutions operates out of offices at 26209 Fairfax Avenue in Cincinnati, Ohio. The offices measure approximately

10

5,000 square feet and offer adequate room for expansion over the next five years. Leasing terms are flexible, and management believes rent is competitive with comparable office space in the city.

In addition to office furniture and fixtures, Software Solutions's primary physical assets consist of five computer workstations used for application development.

11

Historical Financial Statements and Projections

Software Solutions's startup was financed by $80,000 from Bradley Regent. The current financial plan anticipates raising an additional $750,000 to market and distribute DriversSeat nationwide. Following this financing, equity ownership would be distributed as shown below.

Pro Forma Statement of Equity Ownership

Owner	Stock Class	Shares	Amount
Mr. Regent	Common	350,000	$660,000
Ms. McIntire	Common	2,000	44,000
Mr. Honeywell	Common	4,000	88,000
Mr. Wise	Common	2,000	44,000
Investors	Preferred	100,000	500,000
Total		**458,000**	**$1,336,000**

The proceeds of this financing will allow Software Solutions to distribute and market DriversSeat nationwide.

12

Software Solutions's Income Statement

	2015	2016
Net Sales	$0	$83,400
COGS	0	48,713
Gross Margin	$0	$34,687
Operating Costs		
Development	$41,799	$20,831
SG&A	7,253	26,478
Other	1,985	2,694
Total Operating Costs	$51,037	$50,003
Operating Earnings	−51,039	−15,315
Interest Expense	−1,479	−2,138
Pretax Earnings	−52,518	−17,453
Income Tax	0	0
Net Income	−$52,518	−$17,453

Notes to income statement: Software Solutions's income statement for the first two years of operation reflects no sales revenues the first year, when the founder's efforts were devoted to developing the product. Development costs that year were correspondingly high. Sales the second year took off nicely, and gross margin was also in line. However, heavy marketing expenses took their toll, and the company has produced a net loss of more than $66,000 for its first two years in operation.

13

Software Solutions's Current Balance Sheet
December 31, 2014

ASSETS	
Cash	$54,000
Accounts Receivable	17,780
Inventory	1,181
Prepaid Expenses	4,194
Other Current Assets	1,674
Total Current Assets	$78,829
Fixed Assets	$26,346
Intangibles	1
Other Noncurrent Assets	0
Total Assets	**$105,175**
LIABILITIES	
Notes Payable	$11,435
Accounts Payable	3,411
Interest Payable	1,175
Taxes Payable	978
Other Current Liabilities	2,376
Total Current Liabilities	**$19,375**
Long-Term Debt	0
Other Noncurrent Liabilities	3,182
Total Liabilities	**$22,557**
Net Worth	**$82,618**
Total Liabilities & Net Worth	**$105,175**

Note to balance sheet: Assets included $54,000 in cash from the founder's $80,000 initial capitalization.

14

Software Solutions's Cash Flow Statement

Sources of Cash	
Sales	$83,400
Total Cash In	**$83,400**
Uses of Cash	
COGS	$48,713
SG&A	26,478
Other	2,694
Interest	2,138
Taxes	0
Equipment Purchase	6,480
Total Cash Out	**$86,503**
NET CHANGE IN CASH	**−$3,103**
Beginning Cash on Hand	**$55,801**
Ending Cash on Hand	**$52,698**

15

Software Solutions's Pro Forma Income Statement

INCOME PROJECTION				
	2015	**2016**	**2017**	**2018**
INCOME				
Net Sales	$191,250	$286,875	$788,907	$1,577,814
Cost of Sales	95,625	137,700	362,897	788,907
Gross Profit	$95,625	$149,175	$426,010	$788,907
OPERATING EXPENSES				
General & Administrative Expenses				
Salaries and Wages	$116,288	$143,438	$236,672	$263,063
Sales Commissions	9,562	14,344	39,445	78,891
Rent	4,800	5,040	5,292	5,556
Maintenance	1,913	2,009	2,109	2,214
Equipment Rental	1,687	1,771	1,860	1,953
Furniture and Equipment Purchase	9,000	3,333	2,343	3,960
Insurance	2,280	2,394	2,514	2,998
Interest Expenses	1,875	1,970	2,068	3,909
Utilities	1,650	1,732	1,819	1,911
Office Supplies	975	1,239	3,266	1,466
Marketing and Advertising	150,225	98,250	120,000	135,000
Travel	15,750	18,750	22,500	26,250
Entertainment	900	450	640	830
Bad Debt	750	287	789	485
Depreciation and Amortization	2,700	4,050	6,075	9,113
TOTAL OPERATING EXPENSES	**$320,355**	**$299,057**	**$447,392**	**$537,599**
Net Income before Taxes	−$224,730	−$149,882	−$21,382	$251,308
Provision for Taxes on Income	0	0	0	37,697
NET INCOME AFTER TAXES	**−$224,730**	**−$149,882**	**−$21,382**	**$213,610**

Notes to income projections: Sales projections reflect assumptions of progressively greater rollout into the national market, with accordingly higher levels of sales. Heavy first-year marketing expenses level off as national distribution is achieved. Sales increase in subsequent years as the effect of initial marketing efforts is felt. Wage and salary increases reflect need to hire additional programmers, salespeople, and administrative personnel to cope with higher sales.

Sustained profitability is achieved in 2015. Projected income tax reflects effects of applying net operating loss from prior years to 2015 profits.

16

Software Solutions's Pro Forma Balance Sheet

	2015	% Sales	2016 (projected)
Sales	$83,400		$191,250
ASSETS			
Cash	$54,000	64.7%	$123,739
Accounts Receivable	17,780	21.3%	40,736
Inventory	1,181	1.4%	2,678
Prepaid Expenses	4,194	5.0%	9,563
Other Current Assets	1,674	2.0%	3,825
Total Current Assets	**$78,829**	**94.5%**	**$180,541**
Fixed Assets	26,346	31.6%	60,435
Intangibles	1	0.0%	0
Other Noncurrent Assets	0		0
Total Assets	**$105,175**		**$240,976**
LIABILITIES			
Notes Payable	$11,435	13.7%	$26,201
Accounts Payable	3,411	4.1%	7,841
Interest Payable	1,175	1.4%	2,678
Taxes Payable	978	1.2%	2,295
Other Current Liabilities	2,376		2,506
Total Current Liabilities	**$19,375**		**$41,521**
Long-Term Debt	0		0
Other Noncurrent Liabilities	3,182		4,833
Total Liabilities	**$22,557**		**$46,354**
Net Worth	**$82,619**		**$194,622**
Total Liabilities & Net Worth	**$105,176**		**$240,976**

Note to balance sheet projection: Balance sheet projections were based on relationships among various items reflected in 2014 actual results. Intangibles include goodwill, proprietary technology, and long-term service and maintenance contracts.

17

Software Solutions's Pro Forma Cash Flow Statement
Projected Cash Flow for 2015

	Jan.	Feb.	Mar.	Apr.	May	Jun.	Jul.	Aug.	Sep.	Oct.	Nov.	Dec.	TOTAL
CASH RECEIPTS													
Income from Sales													
Sales	$11,475	$11,475	$13,387	$13,388	$15,300	$15,300	$17,212	$17,213	$17,213	$19,125	$19,125	$21,037	$191,250
Total Cash from Sales	11,475	11,475	13,387	13,388	15,300	15,300	17,212	17,213	17,213	19,125	19,125	21,037	$191,250
Financing Income													
Net Offering Proceeds	649,500	0	0	3,750	0	0	0	0	0	0	0	0	$653,250
Interest Income	5,250	5,250	3,750	3,750	3,000	3,000	2,625	2,625	2,250	2,250	1,875	1,875	$37,500
Total Cash Receipts	666,225	$16,725	$17,137	$20,888	$18,300	$18,300	$19,837	$19,838	$19,463	$21,375	$21,000	$22,912	$882,000
CASH DISBURSEMENTS													
Expenses													
COGS	5,738	5,737	6,693	6,693	7,648	7,649	8,605	8,606	8,605	9,561	9,561	10,518	$95,614
SG&A	18,150	15,832	13,842	9,037	13,125	12,333	14,336	14,287	12,333	15,750	13,125	14,258	$168,178
Taxes	0	0	0	0	0	0	0	0	0	0	0	0	$0
Equipment Purchase	12,000	0	0	0	0	0	6,000	0	0	0	0	0	$18,000
Dividends	0	0	0	0	0	0	0	0	0	0	0	0	$0
Total Cash	35,888	21,569	20,535	15,730	20,773	19,982	28,941	22,893	20,938	25,311	22,686	24,776	$281,792
Disbursements													
Net Cash Flow	$630,337	-$4,844	-$3,398	$5,158	-$2,473	-$1,682	-$9,104	-$3,055	-$1,475	-$3,936	-$1,686	-$1,864	$600,208
Opening Cash Balance	54,000	684,337	679,493	676,095	681,253	678,780	677,098	667,994	664,939	663,464	659,528	657,842	$0
Cash Receipts	666,225	16,725	17,137	20,888	18,300	18,300	19,837	19,838	19,463	21,375	21,000	22,912	$882,000
Cash Disbursements	-35,888	-21,569	-20,535	-15,730	-20,773	-19,982	-28,941	-22,893	-20,938	-25,311	-22,686	-24,776	-$281,792
Ending Cash Balance	$684,337	$679,493	$676,095	$678,780	$677,098	$677,098	$677,994	$664,939	$663,464	$659,528	$657,842	$655,978	

Note to cash flow projection: Cash flow projections for 2015 reflect offering proceeds, net of fees, of $649,500. Interest income is generated from investing excess proceeds of offering.

Business Plan for a Service Firm Seeking Working Capital

The following business plan is for an established company in need of working capital. Draper Rains Associates, a public relations and marketing firm, has grown steadily for 15 years—it employs 109 people and has a solid base of customers and billings. Recently, the company began expanding its operations to other cities in order to attract new and larger clients. The result has been an increase in expenses and a clear need for working capital, which the company is looking for in the form of a bank loan.

The company is forward thinking and prudent to seek this type of loan now. Its cash flow is positive, and its expenses will increase as its geographic expansion efforts gather steam.

Confidential Business Plan

Draper Rains Associates

14479 Jackson St.
San Francisco, CA 94115
415-555-6968

Alice Draper, Chairman, President, and CEO

Executive Summary

Draper Rains Associates is a 15-year-old public relations and marketing firm serving the health-care industry in the San Francisco Bay area.

Draper Rains offers integrated public relations and marketing consulting services to its clients, which consist of large hospitals, clinics, and health maintenance organizations. While the majority of the services Draper Rains offers are available from other firms, the company believes its execution is superior. This is evidenced by the fact that the majority of its clients have been active with the firm for more than five years, some have been active more than ten years, and one client has been with the firm since its founding.

After several years of steady growth as a regional services provider, the company is now poised to break out into the national scene. In pursuit of this strategy, the company has expended a substantial proportion of its capital reserves in opening new offices, increasing staff, and acquiring necessary equipment and technology.

The strategy has been successful so far, and the firm has acquired several national accounts whose billings are much larger than the average client the firm has worked with in the past. These larger clients, many of whom are also slower in cycling invoices than other clients, are causing increases in accounts payable and accounts receivable. As a result, the company is now seeking additional funding to provide working capital during this period of expansion.

Bank financing of $525,000 is currently being sought. The objective is a line of credit in that amount, with approximately $262,500 paid out immediately and the balance paid out in equal installments for the next five quarters. At the end of two years, payments against principal will begin, and the entire principal amount will be paid off after four years.

2

Product

Draper Rains provides integrated public relations and marketing services to large hospitals, clinics, and health maintenance organizations.

The company's services consist of planning marketing strategy, writing and editing marketing materials and press releases, conducting publicity and media placement campaigns, media training for key executives, and related services. The company arranges for production of videotapes and printed materials, conducts on-premises briefings and seminars, and participates in high-level strategy sessions with its clients' executives.

The mission of the company is to provide its clients with positive, integrated public images in the marketplace, with the ultimate goal of increasing client sales and profits.

Draper Rains competes with numerous other companies for customers. Many of these competitors provide similar services. However, the company believes that its reputation for quality service and its long-established relationships with existing clients will allow it to maintain and expand its current level of sales in this competitive environment.

3

Industry

The health-care industry is undergoing monumental shifts as changes in payer policies, declining bed-utilization rates, and increasingly expensive new medical technology combine to make marketing more important than it has been previously.

The marketing and public relations industry is also undergoing a period of consolidation as numerous global advertising and marketing firms establish large, U.S.-based public relations divisions. These same competitors are targeting health care for much the same reasons as is Draper Rains.

If current trends play out as expected, the business of providing marketing and public relations services to large health-care clients will become increasingly consolidated among a few sizable firms. To remain competitive in this market, Draper Rains must develop a national presence to attract large, new clients.

In pursuit of this goal, Draper Rains has opened new offices on the East and West coasts as well as in the Midwest and the Southeast. It has also increased employees by approximately 25 percent, or 16 people, to staff these offices.

4

Marketing

Draper Rains obtains clients almost exclusively through word-of-mouth. Because of the large size of its typical client—average clients are billed approximately $30,000 annually—and the long-standing conservatism of health-care institutions in matters of marketing, personal referrals, informal testimonials, and an excellent reputation among hospital administrators and professionals in the health-care marketing field continue to be the best marketing tools available.

Draper Rains has a formal program for generating and disseminating positive word-of-mouth, informal testimonials, and referrals in the marketplace. While this program is difficult to track for effectiveness, the company believes its program is working and will continue to use it.

For the company to compete effectively in new geographic markets, it must establish and maintain a physical presence in those markets. To that end, the company has in the past year opened new offices in several cities, each of which serves as a hub for its region of the United States. New offices are located in Miami, Chicago, New York, and Los Angeles.

The company's headquarters in San Francisco consist of approximately 8,000 square feet of leased space in a modern office building, with a staff of 80. In each of the new cities, the firm has begun with small facilities and small staffs. Offices average approximately 600 square feet and have staffs of five people in order to control expenses while providing a marketing foothold in the new markets. Each of the new offices has adjoining space suitable for expansion. Draper Rains has acquired formal options to lease adjoining space in New York, Miami, and Los Angeles and has an informal understanding with its landlord in Chicago.

In addition to establishing a physical presence in the new cities, Draper Rains is mounting a modest advertising campaign. The effort includes placing advertisements in the printed programs for

5

meetings of local health-care marketing organizations, advertising groups, and the like. The firm has purchased outdoor advertising space on one or more billboards in each of the cities for a term of approximately one year to build name recognition among its target group.

Another key element of the company's marketing campaign consists of personal sales calls by the principal and other personnel. These sales calls are scheduled with hospital administrators, hospital marketing directors, HMO chief executives and marketing vice presidents, and similar individuals. The initial intent of these sales calls is to introduce our firm to potential clients and to begin a dialogue. We anticipate that these sales calls, the increased frequency of which is indicated in the growing travel budget, will yield significant numbers of new clients and increased billings over time.

6

Management

Alice Draper

Chairman, CEO, and President

Ms. Draper, a resident of San Rafael, California, since 1976, is one of the best-known figures in the field of public relations and marketing in the Bay area. She is past president of Northern California Media Relations Professionals, was a delegate from the Public Relations Society of America to a global conference in London, England, in 1996, and has taught marketing at San Jose State University as an adjunct professor since 1994. Ms. Draper founded the firm as a home-based business in 1999 in San Francisco. During the next 15 years, she grew the firm to its present size of 109 employees. She is a graduate of San Jose State University.

Charles Allen

Vice President, Marketing

Mr. Allen is the firm's chief marketing officer and handles many of the marketing duties that are beyond the scope of the president's duties. He and his staff are responsible for developing marketing strategy and preparing and executing the marketing plan. Mr. Allen has been employed by Draper Rains for seven years and is a graduate of the University of Colorado.

Cheryl Plant

Vice President, Technology

Ms. Plant is Draper Rains's chief information officer. She is responsible for developing technology strategies; selecting hardware, software, and vendors; staffing the information office; and preparing a budget for information technology expenditures. Her role has become more important as information management becomes essential to providing the firm's services and as remote offices are incorporated into the firm's technology network. Ms. Plant joined

7

the firm last year from Intel Corporation, where she served as assistant director of information services for a major division. She is a graduate of Carnegie Mellon University.

8

Facilities

Draper Rains's headquarters are at 14479 Jackson Street in San Francisco, with additional offices in New York, Miami, Chicago, and Los Angeles. Until 2006, the firm's only office was in San Francisco. The additional offices were opened as part of the long-range expansion plan.

One of the company's key operational resources is the integrated communications and computing network that links all personnel in its headquarters, as well as those in the remote offices. This network allows the company to quickly and effectively compose, edit, reproduce, and disseminate client marketing materials. The investment in technology provides the company with a significant edge over competitors in terms of increased quality and reduced turnaround time to complete assignments.

The company's physical assets consist primarily of the computers, modems, cabling, and other equipment required to construct this network. Other assets are furniture, equipment, and fixtures in its headquarters office. Most fixtures and furnishings in the new offices are leased rather than purchased.

9

Financial Statements

Income Statement 2014

Sales Receipts	$8,176,635
Interest Income	16,068
COGS	5,396,579
Gross Margin	2,796,124
Expenses	2,044,160
Depreciation	38,528
Operating Earnings	713,436
Interest Expense	113,487
Pretax Earnings	599,949
Income Tax	179,985
Net Income	**$419,964**

10

Balance Sheet

June 30, 2014

ASSETS	
Cash	$267,798
Accounts Receivable	651,678
Prepaid Expenses	204,858
Other Current Assets	113,741
Total Current Assets	**$1,238,075**
Fixed Assets	385,281
Total Assets	**$1,623,356**
LIABILITIES	
Notes Payable	$215,784
Accounts Payable	170,346
Interest Payable	9,458
Taxes Payable	44,997
Other Current Liabilities	1,479
Total Current Liabilities	**$442,064**
Long-Term Debt	380,334
Other Noncurrent Liabilities	1,734
Total Liabilities	**$824,132**
Net Worth	**$799,224**
Total Liabilities & Net Worth	**$1,623,356**

Note to balance sheet: The company operates on a June 30 fiscal year.

11

Cash Flow Statement

Sources of Cash	
Sales	$7,767,804
Other Sources	
Interest	16,068
Short-Term Borrowings	150,000
Total Cash In	$7,933,872
Uses of Cash	
COGS	$5,126,750
SG&A	2,044,160
Interest	113,487
Taxes	179,985
Equipment Purchase	80,313
Debt Principal Payments	38,763
Dividends	0
Total Cash Out	$7,583,458
NET CHANGE IN CASH	$350,414
Beginning Cash on Hand	$81,581
Ending Cash on Hand	$431,995

Note to cash flow statement: The company intends to reduce short-term borrowings in favor of less costly long-term debt.

12

Pro Forma Income Statement

INCOME PROJECTION

	2015	2016	2017	2018 (projected)
INCOME				
Net Sales	$7,379,414	$7,767,804	$8,176,635	$8,994,299
Interest Income	9,528	12,813	16,068	17,286
Cost of Sales	4,796,619	5,049,072	5,396,579	5,846,294
Gross Profit	$2,592,323	$2,731,545	$2,796,124	$3,165,291
OPERATING EXPENSES				
General and Administrative Expenses				
Salaries and Wages	$969,656	$1,020,690	$1,058,466	$1,181,851
Sales Commissions	368,970	388,391	490,598	449,715
Rent	33,816	35,506	37,283	62,634
Maintenance	73,794	77,484	82,133	137,982
Equipment Rental	5,773	6,062	6,424	10,792
Furniture and Equipment Purchase	4,848	5,091	5,346	8,982
Insurance	10,467	13,083	16,353	19,623
Interest	54,375	57,237	113,487	214,491
Utilities	73,794	77,677	81,767	128,782
Office Supplies	47,966	50,490	53,966	52,617
Marketing and Advertising	125,450	132,052	139,004	10,806
Travel	26,164	32,706	40,883	1,500
Entertainment	22,139	23,304	24,529	831
Bad Debt	8,193	8,622	9,078	486
Depreciation and Amortization	24,657	30,822	57,792	57,792
TOTAL OPERATING EXPENSES	$1,850,062	$1,959,217	$2,217,109	$2,338,884
Net Income before Taxes	$742,261	$772,328	$579,015	$826,407
Provision for Taxes on Income	222,680	231,699	179,985	247,021
NET INCOME AFTER TAXES	$519,581	$540,629	$399,030	$579,386

13

Pro Forma Balance Sheet

	2015	% Sales	2016 (projected)
Sales	**$8,176,635**		**$8,994,299**
ASSETS			
Cash	$267,798	3.3%	$296,812
Accounts Receivable	651,678	8.0%	719,544
Prepaid Expenses	204,858	2.5%	224,857
Other Current Assets	113,741	1.4%	125,920
Total Current Assets	**$1,238,075**	**15.1%**	**$1,367,133**
Fixed Assets	385,281	4.7%	422,732
Total Assets	**$1,623,356**		**$1,789,865**
LIABILITIES			
Notes Payable	$215,784	2.6%	$233,852
Accounts Payable	170,346	2.1%	188,880
Interest Payable	9,458	0.1%	8,994
Taxes Payable	44,997	0.6%	53,966
Other Current Liabilities	1,479	0.0%	0
Total Current Liabilities	**$442,064**	**5.4%**	**$485,692**
Long-Term Debt	380,334	4.7%	422,732
Other Noncurrent Liabilities	1,734		2,202
Total Liabilities	**$824,132**		**$910,626**
Net Worth	**$799,224**		**$879,211**
Total Liabilities & Net Worth	**$1,623,356**		**$1,789,837**

Note to pro forma balance sheet: Long-term debt projected includes $262,500 in loan proceeds.

14

Pro Forma Cash Flow Statement
Projected Cash Flow: 2016

	Jan.	Feb.	Mar.	Apr.	May	Jun.	Jul.	Aug.	Sep.	Oct.	Nov.	Dec.	TOTAL
CASH RECEIPTS													
Income from Sales													
Cash Sales	$719,544	$656,585	$728,538	$800,493	$683,567	$764,516	$674,573	$791,499	$746,528	$818,481	$800,493	$818,481	$9,003,298
Total Cash from Sales	$719,544	$656,585	$728,538	$800,493	$683,567	$764,516	$674,573	$791,499	$746,528	$818,481	$800,493	$818,481	$9,003,298
Income from Financing													
Loan Proceeds	262,500	0	0	0	0	0	0	0	0	0	0	0	$262,500
Other Cash Receipts	1,440	1,440	1,440	1,440	1,440	1,440	1,440	1,440	1,440	1,440	1,440	1,440	$17,280
Total Cash Receipts	$983,484	$658,025	$729,978	$801,933	$685,007	$765,956	$676,013	$792,939	$747,968	$819,921	$801,933	$819,921	$9,283,078
CASH DISBURSEMENTS													
Expenses													
COGS	$474,899	$433,345	$480,835	$528,325	$451,018	$504,580	$404,718	$522,390	$492,708	$540,198	$528,325	$540,198	$5,901,539
SG&A	179,886	164,146	182,134	200,124	170,892	191,128	168,643	197,875	186,631	204,621	200,124	204,621	$2,250,825
Interest	17,874	17,874	17,874	17,874	17,874	17,874	17,874	17,874	17,874	17,874	17,874	17,874	$214,488
Taxes	20,585	20,585	20,585	20,585	20,585	20,585	20,585	20,585	20,585	20,585	20,585	20,585	$247,014
Equipment Purchase	8,250	0	8,250	0	8,250	0	8,250	0	8,250	0	8,250	0	$49,500
Debt Principal Payments	3,000	3,000	3,000	3,000	3,000	3,000	3,000	3,000	3,000	3,000	3,000	3,000	$36,000
Dividends	0	0	0	0	0	0	0	0	0	0	0	0	$0
Total Cash Disbursements	$704,494	$638,950	$712,678	$769,908	$671,619	$737,167	$623,070	$761,724	$729,048	$786,278	$778,158	$786,278	$8,699,366
Net Cash Flow	278,990	19,075	17,300	32,025	13,388	28,789	52,943	31,215	18,920	33,643	23,775	33,643	$583,712
Opening Cash Balance	267,798	546,788	565,863	583,163	615,188	628,576	657,365	710,308	741,523	760,443	794,086	817,861	$0
Cash Receipts	983,484	658,025	729,978	801,933	685,007	765,956	676,013	792,939	747,968	819,921	801,933	819,921	$9,283,078
Cash Disbursements	-704,494	-638,950	-712,678	-769,908	-671,619	-737,167	-623,070	-761,724	-729,048	-786,278	-778,158	-786,278	$8,699,366
Ending Cash Balance	$546,788	$565,863	$583,163	$615,188	$628,576	$657,365	$710,308	$741,523	$794,086	$794,086	$817,861	$851,504	

Business Plan for a Startup Needing an Equipment Loan

The primary purpose of this business plan is to secure a loan for equipment, which the business needs to begin operation. Although the idea for this type of business is new in this particular market, it has been successful in other, similar markets. The owner and his partners are helping to fund the business's working-capital needs with their equity stake, which helps bolster the business's debt-to-equity ratio, strengthens its balance sheet, and makes the business more attractive to prospective lenders. Other funding comes from two low-interest, three-year loans—one from a state development agency to help bring jobs to the area and another from a vendor to fund initial marketing expenses.

The strengths of this plan include the business's solid balance sheet and the owner's years of experience in the food industry.

He's also done considerable market research, which helps him make a strong case for starting this business.

The primary weakness of this plan is that it assumes cash flow will be strong through the first year, enabling the business to begin paying the owner a salary in the second year and retiring the two short-term loans the following year.

Confidential Business Plan
for

JAVA MOBILE

Eugene's Only Cellular Café

Cale Bruckner
President
1435 10th Street
Eugene, Oregon 97403
(541) 555-7654

EXECUTIVE SUMMARY

Java Mobile, is a unique café for mobile phone users who not only text but also converse. Eugene's first café of its kind will provide unique seating with soundproof separations so that customers can enjoy a bite to eat while catching up on business calls or reaching out to chat with friends and loved ones.

According to market research conducted by Java Mobile president Cale Bruckner, between texting and using popular apps, people also like to talk on their mobile phones, but other diners do not appreciate being a part of their neighbor's conversations. Java Mobile is place where those who want to talk can do just that. The latest in secure wifi connections will also allow those who want to be online and even Skype to do so from their own private booths.

Java Mobile's goal is to provide the community with a setting for the mobile set, including enough space for conference-call meetings and larger seating areas. In a more traditional seating area, the nonphone users can also come in to enjoy local entertainment while sipping a variety of international blends of coffee on weekends.

This business plan requests a $21,000 equipment loan that the business projects repaying in four years. Additional financing has already been secured for $20,000 from the Oregon Economic Development Fund to support our efforts to create new jobs, $19,000 from majority owner Cale Bruckner, $36,000 from three investors, and $5,000 from Microsoft to help fund startup marketing expenses.

Java Mobile will be incorporated as a limited liability corporation, which offers the business all the benefits of a corporation but allows Mr. Bruckner and his partners to be taxed as if they were in a partnership. The partners—Luke Walsh, Doug Wilson, and John Underwood—will not be involved in the day-to-day management of Java Mobile.

As shown in the company's financial statements, the financial arrangement allows Java Mobile to launch the business, provide

2

customers with a unique café experience, and maintain operations through 2016. Mr. Bruckner believes that successful operation in the first year will provide Java Mobile with a sufficient and loyal customer base so that the company can sustain itself on income from operations in the second year.

Java Mobile's Mission

Java Mobile's goal is to create a unique, upscale, comfortable, innovative environment that will allow businessmen and women to enjoy pastries and coffee at a location out of the office where they can catch up on their calls while being free from interruptions.

Keys to Success

In order to succeed, Java Mobile must create a unique space and differentiate itself from other local coffee shops in which phone conversations are a distraction to other customers. Mobile service must be excellent and soundproofing is essential to create privacy for cell phone conversations. It must also encourage customer loyalty by promoting itself as a hub for good coffee and entertainment. Finally, Java Mobile needs to provide outstanding bakery items.

Risks

The main question is: Will enough cell phone users duck into Java Mobile to make their calls?

3

COMPANY SUMMARY

Java Mobile will be located in downtown Eugene on 10th and Oak Streets in a major business district and will provide soundproof booths with upscale seating, mobile phone access, and, of course, with the more common wifi access with security codes for online security. Java Mobile will also provide customers with a pleasant environment in which to enjoy great coffee, specialty beverages, and baked goods.

Java Mobile will offer two conference rooms for groups that need access to conference-call capabilities. This option will get them out of the boardroom and into a more congenial setting, with the same food, beverages, and internet connectivity available in the rest of the store.

Company Ownership

Java Mobile is a privately held limited liability corporation registered in Oregon. Cale Bruckner, the founder of Java Mobile, is the majority owner (70 percent), and Luke Walsh, Doug Wilson, and John Underwood are minority shareholders (10 percent each).

Startup Expenses

Java Mobile's startup costs include coffee-making equipment; site modification; funds to cover first-year operations and the hardware, software, and other equipment necessary to get its customers online and provide uninterrupted cellular and conferencing access. Soundproofing materials will also be purchased from a local building-supply corporation in Eugene.

Coffee-making equipment includes one espresso machine, an automatic coffee grinder, and minor additional equipment that will be purchased from Allann Brothers.

4

Sources and Uses of Funds at Startup

Startup Expenses	
Legal	$ 3,000
Letterhead, business cards	2,000
Brochures	1,000
Consultants	2,000
Advertising	5,000
Insurance	2,400
Rent	6,000
Automatic coffee machine	1,700
Bean grinder	795
Conference room design, furniture and connection capabilities (2x)	17,000
Computer connectivity	3,000
Communication lines	840
Furniture, other equipment	11,695
Soundproofing	11,605
Inventory	5,000
Working capital for payroll	18,750
Total Startup Expenses	**$91,785**

5

Sources of Startup Funds

Investors	
Cale Bruckner	$19,000
Luke Walsh	12,000
Doug Wilson	12,000
John Underwood	12,000
Total Investment	$55,000
Short-Term Liabilities	
Oregon Development Fund	$20,000
Microsoft	5,000
Total Short-Term Liabilities	**25,000**
Long-Term Liabilities	21,000
Total Liabilities	$46,000
Total Funds Available at Startup	**$101,000**
Profit/(Loss) at Startup	**$9,215**

Location and Facilities

The site at 10th and Oak in downtown Eugene was chosen for its:

- Proximity to the downtown business community.
- Proximity to trendy, upscale restaurants, such as West Brothers and Allegra.
- Abundance of parking.
- Low-cost rent.
- High visibility.

6

Java Mobile's Services

Java Mobile customers will have access to private booths, surrounded on three sides with soundproofing, in which to talk and drink coffee or other beverages, while enjoying pastries. Customers can also use their laptops or other mobile devices through secure wifi connections.

Two fully functional conference room settings will be designed for conference calls and include video-conferencing capabilities. Both rooms will be able to accommodate up to 12 attendees comfortably. Prebooking, up to two weeks in advance, will assure the meeting space availability. Hourly packages will include coffee and pastries.

7

THE MARKET

Java Mobile is faced with the exciting opportunity of being the first of its kind.

Market Segmentation

Java Mobile's customers can be divided into two groups. The first are typical cell phone users looking to find a place to talk while they are out and a bite to eat at the same time. The other are local businesses that need to escape the usual boardroom for a conference call or simply a less formal place to meet. Java Mobile's target market falls between the ages of 18 and 50. Within these two broad categories, Java Mobile's target market can be further divided into specific market segments, the majority of whom are students and businesspeople. See the Market Analysis table below for more specifics.

Potential Customers	Growth	2015	2016	2017	2018	2019
University Students	4%	$15,000	$15,600	$16,224	$16,873	$17,548
Office Workers	3%	25,000	25,750	26,523	27,319	28,139
Seniors	5%	18,500	19,425	20,396	21,416	22,487
Teenagers	2%	12,500	12,750	13,005	13,265	13,530
Others	0%	25,000	25,000	25,000	25,000	25,000
Total	2.68%	$96,000	$98,525	$101,148	$103,873	$106,704

Strategy for Reaching Our Target Market

Java Mobile will cater to anyone who has ever been told to "shush" when talking on the phone in a public location. It will cater to business professionals and students who need a quiet place during the day in which to talk while having coffee. Java Mobile will be a magnet for local and traveling professionals who want to work and use their computers and cell phones in a comfortable, quiet setting.

8

Factors such as current trends and historical sales data ensure that the demand for coffee will remain constant over the next five years. The need of millions of mobile-phone users for a suitable place to talk without disturbing others and to be able to hear the other party clearly is a growing concern.

Java Mobile's customers can be divided into two groups. The first is the typical cell-phone user looking for a place to talk and a bite to eat at the same time. The other is the local business that needs to escape the usual boardroom for a conference call or simply find a less formal place to meet.

Mr. Bruckner hired Rumblefish Marketing to conduct a market survey in Eugene 2012. Key findings include:

- More than 70 percent of mobile-phone users say they have trouble finding a suitable place to carry on a conversation when they are shopping or at work.
- Nearly 75 percent of office employees and managers agree that having a place outside of the office to meet for conferencing and video conferencing would be a refreshing change and morale booster. The retail coffee industry in Eugene experienced rapid growth in the early 1990s and is now moving into the mature stage of its life cycle. Many factors contribute to the still-healthy demand for good coffee in Eugene. The biggest is university students and staff.

Business Vendors

There are approximately 16 coffee wholesalers in Lane County. These wholesalers distribute coffee and espresso beans to more than 20 retailers in the Eugene area. Competition in both channels creates a balance of bargaining power between buyers and suppliers, resulting in extremely competitive pricing for coffee beans and related products.

In Eugene there is a positive relationship between price and quality of coffee. Some coffees retail at $8/pound while other, more

9

exotic beans may sell for as much as $16/pound. Wholesalers sell beans to retailers at a 50 percent discount on average. For example, a pound of Sumatran beans wholesales for $6.95 and retails for $13.95. As in most industries, price decreases as volume increases.

Competition

There are 14 Starbucks locations in Eugene, all of which offer wifi connections. None offers enclosed booths for private mobile conversations. Other competing coffee cafes include Full City, Coffee Corner, and Cuppa Joe. These businesses are located in or near the downtown area and target a market segment similar to Java Mobile's (students and businesspeople). However, none of these competitors has made the investment in soundproofing part of their establishment nor do any offer business conferencing capabilities.

Marketing Strategies

Java Mobile's plans on attracting customers by:

- Providing a setting for meetings that require state-of-the-art conference calls or video conferencing, and assisting business members attending meetings in the conference rooms. If a customer has any type of question or concern, a Java Mobile employee will always be available to help.
- Java Mobile will place print ads in *The Register Guard, The Eugene Weekly*, and *The Emerald* to help build customer awareness.
- A website, Facebook page, and Twitter feed will update discounts, allow for booking the conference rooms, and list local entertainers, such as folksingers, who will appear on weekends.

10

Pricing Strategy

Java Mobile bases its prices for coffee and specialty drinks on the "retail profit analysis" provided by our supplier, Allann Brothers Coffee Co. Inc. Allann Brothers has been in the coffee business for 22 years and has developed a solid pricing strategy.

Determining a fair-market hourly price for conference room facilities is more difficult because there is no direct competition from another café in Eugene. Therefore, Java Mobile considered three sources to determine the hourly charge rate. First, we considered the cost of using conferencing technology and then the value of both the food and the coffee included in the package.

Promotion Strategy

Initially, Java Mobile will budget $5,000 for promotional efforts, which will include advertising with coupons for free pastries. Java Mobile's manager and chief technician realizes that in the future, when competition enters the market, additional revenues must be allocated for promotion in order to maintain market share.

Sales Strategy

Customer service, common sense, and the ability to help with any technical needs for customers using their laptops or other mobile technology, as well as helping meeting attendees, are required for all Java Mobile employees. There will be training in all conference room equipment and in basic computer and wifi technology.

11

Sales Forecast

Sales forecast data is presented in the table below.

UNIT SALES	2015	2016	2017
Coffee (based on average)	$12,015	$14,068	$15,475
Specialty Drinks (based on average)	6,654	7,913	8,705
Email Memberships	8,704	10,505	11,556
Hourly Internet Fees	38,270	46,365	51,002
Baked Goods (based on average)	32,673	42,150	46,365
Other	0	0	0
Total Unit Sales	**$98,316**	**$121,001**	**$133,103**

UNIT PRICES	2015	2016	2017
Coffee (based on average)	$1.00	$1.00	$1.00
Specialty Drinks (based on average)	2.00	2.00	2.00
Email Memberships	10.00	10.00	10.00
Conference Room Rental Hourly Rates	$50	$50	$50
Baked Goods (based on average)	1.25	1.25	1.25
Other	**0.00**	**0.00**	**0.00**

SALES	2015	2016	2017
Coffee (based on average)	$12,015	$14,068	$15,475
Specialty Drinks (based on average)	13,308	15,826	17,409
Email Memberships	87,038	105,053	115,558
Conference Room Rental Hourly Rates	95,676	115,913	127,505
Baked Goods (based on average)	40,841	52,688	57,957
Other	0	0	0
Total Sales	**$248,878**	**$303,548**	**$333,904**

12

DIRECT UNIT COSTS	2015	2016	2017
Coffee (based on average)	$0.30	$0.30	$0.30
Specialty Drinks (based on average)	0.50	0.50	0.50
Email Memberships	2.50	2.50	2.50
Conference Room Rental Hourly Rates*	5.92	5.92	5.92
Technology usage per person	0.19	0.19	0.19
Baked Goods (based on average)	0.31	0.31	0.31
Other	0.00	0.00	0.00

* Based on 12 people including food / coffee or specialty drinks

DIRECT COST OF SALES	2015	2016	2017
Coffee (based on average)	$3,004	$3,517	$3,869
Specialty Drinks (based on average)	3,327	3,957	4,352
Email Memberships	21,759	26,263	28,890
Conference Room Rental Hourly Rates*	23,919	28,978	31,876
Baked Goods (based on average)	10,210	13,172	14,489
Other	0	0	0
Subtotal Direct Cost of Sales	**$62,219**	**$75,887**	**$83,476**

13

Milestones

The Java Mobile management team has established milestones to keep the business-planning process on target. Mr. Bruckner is responsible for meeting the following deadlines, which will be revised as needed.

Milestone	Start Date	End Date
Business Plan	1/1/2014	2/1/2015
Secure Startup Funding	2/15/2014	3/1/2014
Site Selection	3/1/2014	3/15/2014
Architect Designs	4/1/2014	5/1/2014
Designer Proposal	4/1/2014	4/15/2014
Technology Design	4/1/2014	4/15/2014
Year 1 Plan	6/1/2014	6/5/2014
Personnel Plan	7/1/2014	7/10/2014
Accounting Plan	7/1/2014	7/5/2014
Licensing	9/1/2014	9/15/2014

14

MANAGEMENT SUMMARY

Java Mobile is 70 percent owned and 100 percent operated by Mr. Cale Bruckner, who makes all major management decisions. Mr. Bruckner's three partners—Luke Walsh, Doug Wilson, and John Underwood—each owns 10 percent of the corporation, and none is involved in the day-to-day management of Java Mobile.

After earning his MBA at the University of Oregon, Mr. Bruckner worked for ten years at Peet's, a worldwide distributor of fine teas based in San Francisco. He worked his way up to vice president, marketing (a position he held for five years), and was responsible for all market-planning efforts, including the company's successful foray into the e-business arena.

Java Mobile's Personnel Plan

Java Mobile's staff will consist of six part-time employees, each working 20 hours a week at $10 per hour for the first two years. In 2017, raises will be given to $12 per hour. One full-time manager/technician (who can handle minor terminal repairs/inquiries) will be on duty 40 hours a week at $20 per hour for 2015, $21.50 per hour for 2015, and $24 per hour in 2017.

Personnel	2014	2015	2016
Owner	$0	$25,000	$40,000
Part Time 1	10,400	10,400	12,480
Part Time 2	10,400	10,400	12,480
Part Time 3	10,400	10,400	12,480
Part Time 4	10,400	10,400	12,480
Part Time 5	10,400	10,400	12,480
Part Time 6	10,400	10,400	12,480
Technician	41,600	44,720	49,920
Total Payroll	104,000	132,100	164,800
Java Mobile share of FICA and Medicare	7,958	10,105	12,607
TOTAL PAYROLL EXPENSE	**$111,958**	**$142,205**	**$177,407**

15

FINANCIAL PLAN

Sales

Java Mobile is basing its projected coffee and espresso sales on information from Allann Bros. Coffee Co. Internet sales were estimated by calculating the total number of hours each terminal will be active each day and then generating a conservative estimate as to how many hours will be purchased by consumers.

First Year

Fixture Costs $43,000

Payroll Expense $104,000

Rent $24,000 ($2,000 per month for 2 years).

Java Mobile is leasing a 1,700-square-foot facility for $2,000/month for a total of 24 months at which time it holds the option for a third year. At the end of the third year, the lease is open for negotiation, and Java Mobil may or may not re-sign the lease depending on the demands of the lessor.

Utilities $19,000

Insurance $9,600

Advertising & Marketing $40,000

Java Mobile has allocated $5,000 to run advertisements in local newspapers in order to build consumer awareness and $35,000 to spend on web and social media marketing to businesses and local college students.

Insurance $9,600

Java Mobile acquired a $21,000 loan from a bank at a 10 percent interest rate. It will be paid back at $750/month over the next four years. The $5,000 loan from Microsoft and the $20,000 from the Oregon Economic Development Fund will be paid back over three years at an interest rate of 4 percent.

16

Financial Projections

Profit and Loss (Income Statement)

	2015	2016	2017
Sales	$313,317	$406,323	$560,856
Direct Cost of Sales	93,330	113,830	125,214
Other	$0	$0	$0
Total Cost of Sales	**$93,330**	**$113,830**	**$125,214**
Gross Margin	19,987	29,493	41,642
Operating Expenses			
Advertising/Marketing	$40,000	$44,000	$48,000
Office, Inventory	18,000	20,000	22,000
Fixture Costs	43,000	8,000	8,000
Payroll Expense	111,958	142,205	177,407
Utilities	19,200	21,120	23,230
Insurance	9,600	11,520	13,820
Rent	24,000	24,000	24,000
Legal & Accounting	4,000	3,000	3,000
Total Operating Expenses	**$265,758**	**$273,845**	**$319,457**
Profit Before Interest and Taxes	(45,771)	18,648	116,185
Interest Expense Long-Term	2,820	1,785	1,050
Taxes Incurred	($5,511)	$309	$3,782
Net Profit	**($43,080)**	**$16,554**	**$111,253**

17

Business Plan for a Freelance Artisan/ Contractor

This business plan was written while Geoff Crosby, the owner of Construct Design, was making the decision to leave an executive job with a high-tech company and go into business for himself. He has since rented and fitted out appropriate industrial space and is in business full-time. Pay particular note to his careful and thorough analysis of both the industry and the competition and to the composition of his advisory board. While he doesn't need additional capital (the business became cash-flow positive and self-financing within ten months of startup), he would have no problem finding investors.

His financial statements are confidential. However, his projections clearly justified his decision to go out on his own, and experience has shown the decision to be a good one.

Construct Design, LLC

Business Plan

Geoffrey K. Crosby
Revised March 3, 2014

Table of Contents

2

Executive Summary

Construct Design is transitioning from a part-time to a full-time business. The purpose of this plan is provide a framework to a) evaluate the business potential of Construct Design and b) project a series of financial scenarios to determine the amount of capital needed to get Construct Design up and running. At this time no additional funds are sought.

Section One: The Business

What We Do

We build high-quality custom concrete counters and tables. We work with customers and designers to create counters not available anywhere else, and we do so with passion, good design sense, and fun. We want to be a pleasure to do business with, and we want to create high quality, highly functional concrete art.

Construct Design—bringing highly functional concrete art into home and office.

Location

We are located in Portsmouth, New Hampshire, and plan to offer products and services within a 20-mile radius of Portsmouth, but focused on the Seacoast corridor up into Maine. However, we will accept jobs within a 50-mile radius.

Products and Services

We will start initially with our strength—custom residential countertops, which require custom samples, custom templates, custom molds, and installation. As we grow, we will add additional products and services.

3

Initial Products and Services

- Custom concrete counters for residential customers and contractors
- Custom pieces for small commercial installations
- Refinishing/sealing services

Future Products and Concepts

- Production tables supplied to furniture stores
- Outdoor tables, benches, etc.
- Cabinet pulls and interior doorknobs
- Large commercial installations
- Production sinks for local supply, (i.e., Sonoma Cast Stone)
- Other countertop materials, (i.e., copper, zinc, or soapstone)
- Alignment with bigger firm, (i.e., Cheng or Stone Soup, to produce products for them in this area or perform installations)

The Market

Our primary market is high-end art- and design-focused local architects, kitchen designers, interior designers, and high-end contractors, who are executing kitchen or bath remodels or new construction. Our secondary market is the actual end user: high-income, art[and design-focused home or business owners.

"Industry advances will be fueled by a trend toward higher value added styles of laminates and tiles, as well as a shift in the overall product mix toward more expensive countertops such as solid surface and natural and engineered stone." (*Source*: Freedonia Focus on Countertops, July 2012.)

Natural stone (primary competitor) is composed of granite, marble, slate, limestone, soapstone, lavastone, and bluestone. Granite accounts for 92 percent of natural stone countertop demand. While each stone has unique characteristics, these countertops are in general high maintenance and expensive. Demand stems from

4

growing consumer interest in the luxurious appearance of natural materials.

Other: Other types of countertops include stainless steel, wood butcher block, engineered stone, concrete, miscellaneous cast polymers, copper, and zinc. Stainless steel has been the largest of this group, due to the popularity of the professional kitchen look and its heat and stain resistance. Engineered stone, introduced to the United States in the late 1990s, by far the fastest growing, is durable, requiring low maintenance, and mimics the look and feel of natural stone.

Eighty percent of the $11.7 billion market is in remodeling, 20 percent in new construction.

Business SIC Code 3281 Cut Stone and Stone Products

Marketing Plan: Awareness, Interest, Desire, Action

We plan to focus our business within a 20-mile radius of Portsmouth on the Seacoast corridor up into Maine, but we will accept jobs within a 50-mile radius. We could also explore south to Boston, but this market already has some formidable competition.

Why We Will Win

- We provide a high-quality, highly personalized product.
- We have good design sense.
- It will be a pleasure to do business with us.
- We have good experience.
- We will deliver on schedule, and we are reliable.
- We will continually learn and improve and explore.
- We will network with the design and contractor communities.
- We are expensive, but justified by all the above.

5

Target Audience: All High-End Businesses

- Kitchen designers
- Architects
- Interior designers
- Contractors
- High-end artsy furniture stores

Initial Goals of Customer Contact

- Find out what their wants and needs are
- Create awareness of Construct Design capabilities
- Create interest in concrete as a medium

Initial Marketing Tactics

- Direct mailings and phone follow-up
- Personal visits with samples and portfolio
- Website and Facebook page
- Yellow Pages listing

Pricing Strategy

- We will start at $100 per square foot for direct business.
- We will evaluate 10–15 percent discounts for contractors.
- We will evaluate kitchen design businesses as dealers.
- We will position ourselves against quality granite and soapstone surfaces.
- The website, concretenetwork.com, states prices range from $65 to $125 per square foot.
- We will undertake a new pricing study for installed price per square foot.

Options to Increase Credibility and Publicize Contact Information

- Join chamber of commerce
- Become a member of the Concrete Exchange?
- Become a member of the Concrete Network?

6

- Become a member of the Decorative Concrete Council?
- Become a member of the American Society of Concrete Contractors?
- PR through local magazines, newspapers, and blogs
- Create pieces and retail displays for display showrooms

Competition

Competition here comes primarily from manufacturers of other countertop material, such as granite and soapstone. I need to do pricing research on local suppliers for these products as installed. There are a limited quantity of concrete counter suppliers in the area, with limited experience and capabilities. The national concrete counter suppliers can ship nationally, but this seriously hampers the personal and creative touch.

Local Concrete Countertop Suppliers

- Form/Function, Rowley, MA, Ray Iacobacci, (978) 432-1093 $65 to $75 per square foot, www.formfunctionconcrete.com. Good article in the *Boston Globe*, looks like good quality stuff, on Concretenetwork.com.
- Marathon Concrete, Bellingham, MA, Mark Brunelle, (508) 509-5247, On Concrete Exchange.
- Distinctive Concrete of New England, Rowley, MA, Bill Guthro, (978) 948-2970, www.distinctiveconcrete.com. Counters look rough, looks primarily like stamping business. On Concretenetwork.com.
- Stone Soup Concrete, Florence, MA, (413) 582-0783, www. stonesoupconcrete.com. Very sharp, excellent design, and quality look. Counters, sinks, tubs. On Concrete Exchange and Concretenetwork.com
- Dimensional Creations, Dover, NH, Owen Whisnant, (603) 750-0055. On Concrete Exchange.

7

- Stonecraft, Portland, ME, Scott Chasse, (207) 699-2422 $60 per square foot, www.astonecraft.com. Not many examples, looks very new, not great quality. On concretenetwork.com.
- Ocho Furniture, Kittery, ME, Bradlee Hall Kirkpatrick. Concrete-topped tables, available through Nahcotta and Lekkers in Boston.
- Reye Studio, Eliot, ME, Richard Webber, (207) 748-1084 $55 to $75 per square foot, plus $11 per square foot for installation, www.reye-studio.com.

Local Granite and Soapstone Countertop Suppliers

- W.S. Goodrich, Epping, NH
- Home Depot, Newington, NH
- Arens Stoneworks, Greenland, NH
- Eno Building Supply, Hampton, NH
- Stoneyard, Eliot, ME
- National Concrete Countertop Suppliers
- Buddy Rhodes, San Francisco, CA
- Cheng Design, Berkeley, CA
- Soupcan Inc., Chicago, IL

Management

Geoff Crosby is the owner of Construct Design. Geoff first started building concrete countertops in 1998 as a result of a lack of local supply and has been experimenting and building counters on a part-time basis since. He has completed projects for Portsmouth area kitchen designers, contractors, architects, and individual home owners.

Geoff has an extensive background in sales and marketing, having worked in retail sporting goods, consumer products, industrial capital equipment, and laboratory equipment sales and marketing positions over the past 16 years.

8

He also has experience in the operations and construction side, having supervised commercial renovations and industrial equipment installation, as well as having two years' experience remodeling homes professionally.

Geoff has a Bachelor of Science degree in Molecular Biology with a Management minor, and has continuing education credits in Project Management, Product Management, and Services Selling. He has also worked with P&L statements and other financial business models and controls for 15 years.

Advisory Board/Board of Directors–Wish List

Chairman	Geoff Crosby
Human Resources/Personnel	Amanda Telford
General Business	David H. Bangs, Jr.
Finance/M&A	Aaron Gowell
Engineering	Chris Dundorf
Production	Ric Hayes
Construction/Industry	Ben Auger, Lisa DeStefano
Marketing/Sales	Deb Ludington, Tim LeFebvre
Customer Member	Laura Ludes, Jeannie Ryan? Mehalls?
Options	Jay Prewitt, Stewart Johnson, Penny Stevens, Drew Wilson

Personnel

Initially, Geoff will perform all work, but as volume increases, he will add on labor for production purposes. Construct Design will use the legal services of George Venci Law PLLC and the accounting services of Edward R. Caito, CPA.

For installation purposes, which typically require two to three additional people to transport slabs, we will reach agreements with individual contractors, set up barter agreements with contractor friends, and rely on friends.

9

Production Capabilities

At start up, we will have 370 square feet of production space, broken down into 190 square feet of heated space, and 180 square feet of unheated space. These spaces contain five pouring tables, four heated, one unheated. As we currently estimate 17 hours of labor per average slab, we are limited by pouring tables, able to produce roughly 70 slabs per year on our tables at full capacity, which is roughly 30 weeks of labor.

Quoted lead times on custom counters will be five to six weeks from receipt of deposit. This includes time to template, build custom molds, pour, cure, finish, and schedule installation.

Future capabilities should consider larger space for material and tool storage, mold production, pouring tables, and a gallery/office space. Production space should consider heating capabilities, air handling/filtration capabilities, and material handling (i.e., overhead crane) for pallets of supplies and large slabs.

Estimated production space should require roughly 1,000 square feet for nine pouring tables' capacity, which could produce 156 counter slabs per year, or $240,000 of revenue. Office space requirements are flexible but should be around 200 to 300 square feet for an office, customer meeting area, and bathroom.

Suitable commercial space in the Portsmouth area is typically available at $8 to $12 per square foot per year. This would result in a yearly lease of $8,000 to $18,000 for the space. We have looked at space in Newington, NH, and $10 per square feet per year in Greenland, NH. (Note: Deb is paying $1,025/month in Greenland for 1,200 square feet of space).

Cost for labor for production is currently $11 to 15 per hour in Portsmouth and similar in surrounding towns. Additional benefits/costs?

10

Summary

Construct Design will offer high-quality, design-oriented concrete countertops to a focused, local audience of high-end customers. We will use our existing network of architects, designers, and contractors to continue to build our reputation, and we will market to new architects, designers, and contractors. We will rely upon our reliability, quality, timeliness, fair pricing, and personalized service to win business.

11

Section Two: Financials

Sources and Applications of Funding

Capital Equipment List	
Existing Capital Equipment	
2004 Ford F-150	$4,500
Four pouring tables	1,200
Concrete mixer	200
Miscellaneous tools	1,600
Computer and software	2,000
Office supplies and phones	350
Total existing capital equipment	**$9,850**
Future Purchases	
Trailer and hitch	$3,000
Color laser printer	700
Phones	200
Miscellaneous tools	200
Accounting software	400
Air filtration/dust collection	500
Total future purchases	**$5,000**

12

Balance Sheet {confidential}

Break- Even Analysis {confidential}

Projected Income Statement {confidential}

Cash Flow Projection {confidential}

Deviation Analysis {confidential}

Historical Financial Information

This will be a summary of previous jobs, their prices, material costs, and labor estimates.

Appendix

    A. Freedonia Focus on Countertops, 2012
    B. Exit Strategies
- Sell to local contractor
- Sell to local concrete supplier
- Sell to local counter supplier
- License to established national supplier such as Cheng or Sonoma Stone
- Sell out to employees
- Close up shop

13

Government
Listings

Government Agencies

Copyright Clearance Center
222 Rosewood Drive
Danvers, MA 01923
(978) 750-8400
www.copyright.com

U.S. Copyright Office
Library of Congress
101 Independence Avenue, SE
Washington, DC 20559-6000
(202) 707-3000
www.copyright/gov

Department of Agriculture
1400 Independence Avenue, SW
Washington, DC 20250
(202) 720-7420
(201) 720-2790 Information
hotline
www.usda.gov

Department of Commerce
1401 Constitution Avenue, NW
Washington, DC 20230
(202) 482-2000
www.doc.gov

Department of Energy
1000 Independence Avenue, SW
Washington, DC 20585
(202) 586-5000, (800) 342-5363
www.energy.gov

Department of the Interior
1849 C Street, NW
Washington, DC 20240
(202) 208-3100
www.doi.gov

Department of Labor
200 Constitution Avenue, NW
Room S-1004
Washington, DC 20210
(866) 487-2365
www.dol.gov

Department of the Treasury
Main Treasury Building
1500 Pennsylvania Avenue, NW
Washington, DC 20220
(202) 622-2000
www.treasury.gov

Export-Import Bank of the United States
811 Vermont Avenue, NW, #911
Washington, DC 20571
(800) 565-3946
www.exim.gov

Internal Revenue Service
1111 Constitution Avenue, NW
Washington, DC 20224
(202) 622-5000
www.irs.gov

U.S. Patent & Trademark Office
600 Dulany Street
Alexandria, VA 22314
(800) 786-9199
www.uspto.gov

U.S. Government Printing Office
710 North Capitol Street, NW
Washington, DC 20402
(202) 512-1800
www.gpo.gov

Securities & Exchange Commission
100 F Street, NE
Washington, DC 20549
(202) 942-8088
www.sec.gov

Small Business Administration
409 Third Street, SW
Washington, DC 20416
(800) 827-5722
www.sba.gov

SBA District Offices

Alabama
801 Tom Martin Drive
Birmingham, AL 35211
(205) 290-7101

Alaska
420 L Street, #300
Anchorage, AK 99501
(907) 271-4022

Arizona
2828 N. Central Avenue, #800
Phoenix, AZ 85004-1093
(602) 745-7200

Arkansas
2120 Riverfront Drive, #250
Little Rock, AR 72202
(501) 324-7379

California
Fresno District
801 R Street, #201
Fresno, CA 93721
(559) 487-5791

Los Angeles District
330 N. Brand Blvd., #1200
Glendale, CA 91203-2304
(818) 552-3201

Sacramento District
6501 Sylvan Road, #100
Citrus Heights, CA 95610
(916) 735-1700

San Diego District
550 W. C Street, # 550
San Diego, CA 92101
(619) 557-7250

San Francisco District
455 Market Street, #600
San Francisco, CA 94105
(415) 744-6820

Santa Ana District
200 W. Santa Ana Blvd., #700
Santa Ana, CA 92701
(714) 550-7409

Colorado
721 19th Street, #426
Denver, CO 80202
(303) 844-2607

Connecticut
330 Main Street, 2nd floor
Hartford, CT 06106
(860) 240-4700

Delaware
1001 N. Orange Street, #720
Wilmington, DE 19801
(302) 573-6294

District of Columbia
409 Third Street, SW, 2nd floor
Washington, DC 20416
(202) 205-8800

Florida
South Florida
100 S. Biscayne Blvd., 7th floor
Miami, FL 33131
(305) 536-5521

North Florida
7825 Baymeadows Way, #100B
Jacksonville, FL 32256
(904) 443-1900

Georgia
233 Peachtree Street, NE, #1900
Atlanta, GA 30303
(404) 331-0100

Hawaii
500 Ala Moana Blvd., #1–306
Honolulu, HI 96850
(808) 541-2990

Idaho

Boise District
380 East Parkcenter Blvd., #330
Boise, ID 83706
(208) 334-9353
Also see Seattle, Washington,
district office

Illinois

500 W. Madison Street, #1150
Chicago, IL 60661
(312) 353-4528

Indiana

8500 Keystone Crossing, # 400
Indianapolis, IN 46204
(317) 226-7272

Iowa

210 Walnut Street, #749
Des Moines, IA 50309
(515) 284-4422

Kansas

Wichita District
220 W. Douglas Avenue, #450
Wichita, KS 67202
(316) 269-6566

Kansas City District
1000 Walnut Street, #500
Kansas City, MO 64106
(816) 426-4900

Kentucky

600 Dr. Martin Luther King Jr.
Place, #188
Louisville, KY 40202
(502) 582-5971

Louisiana

365 Canal Street, #2820
New Orleans, LA 70130
(504) 589-6685

Maine

Edward S. Muskie Federal Bldg.
68 Sewall Street,# 512
Augusta, ME 04330
(207) 622-8277

Maryland

10 S. Howard Street, #6220
Baltimore, MD 21201
(410) 962-6195

Massachusetts

10 Causeway Street, # 265
Boston, MA 02222
(617) 565-5590

Michigan

McNamara Building
477 Michigan Avenue, # 515
Detroit, MI 48226
(313) 226-6075
Fax: (313) 226-4769

Minnesota

100 North Sixth Street, #210-C
Butler Square
Minneapolis, MN 55403
(612) 370-2324

Mississippi

210 E. Capitol Street, #900
Jackson, MS 39201
(601) 965-4378

Missouri

Kansas City District

1000 Walnut Street, # 500

Kansas City, MO 64106

(816) 426-4900

St. Louis District

1222 Spruce Street, #10.103

St. Louis, MO 63103

(314) 539-6600

Montana

Federal Building

10 W. 15th Street, #1100

Helena, MT 59626

(406) 441-1090

Nebraska

10675 Bedford Avenue, #100

Omaha, NE 68134

(402) 221-4691

Nevada

300 S. Fourth Street, #100

Las Vegas, NV 89101

(702) 388-6611

New Hampshire

55 Pleasant Street, #3101

Concord, NH 03301

(603) 225-1400

New Jersey

2 Gateway Center, #1501

Newark, NJ 07102

(973) 645-2434

New Mexico

P.O. Box 2206

Albuquerque, NM 87103

(505) 248-8225

New York

Buffalo District

130 S. Elmwood Avenue, #540

Buffalo, NY 14202

(716) 551-4301

New York City District

26 Federal Plaza, #3100

New York, NY 10278

(212) 264-4354

Syracuse District

224 Harrison Street, 5th Floor

Syracuse, NY 13202

(315) 471-9393

North Carolina

6302 Fairview Road, #300

Charlotte, NC 28210

(704) 344-6563

North Dakota

657 2nd Avenue, N, #218

Fargo, ND 58108

(701) 239-5131

Ohio

Cleveland District

1350 Euclid Avenue, #211

Cleveland, OH 44115

(216) 522-4180

Columbus District

401 Front Street, #200

Columbus, OH 43215

(614) 469-6860

Oklahoma
301 NW Sixth Street
Oklahoma City, OK 73102
(405) 609-8000

Oregon
601 SW Second Avenue
Portland, OR 97204
(503) 326-2682

Pennsylvania
Philadelphia District
Parkview Tower 1150 First
Avenue, #1001
King of Prussia, PA 19406.
(610) 382-3062

Pittsburgh District
411 Seventh Avenue, #1450
Pittsburgh, PA 15219
(412) 395-6560

Puerto Rico
273 Ponce de Leon Blvd., #510
San Juan, PR 00917
(787) 766-5572

Rhode Island
380 Westminster Street, #511
Providence, RI 02903
(401) 528-4561

South Carolina
1835 Assembly Street, #1425
Columbia, SC 29201
(803) 765-5377
Fax: (803) 765-5962

South Dakota
2329 N. Career Avenue, #105
Sioux Falls, SD 57107
(605) 330-4243

Tennessee
2 International Plaza Drive, #500
Nashville, TN 37217
(615) 736-5881

Texas
Dallas/Fort Worth District
4300 Amon Carter Blvd., #114
Fort Worth, TX 75155
(817) 684-5500

El Paso District
211 N. Florence Street, #201
El Paso, TX 79901
(915) 834-4600

*Lower Rio Grande Valley
District*
2422 E. Tyler Avenue, Suite E
Harlingen, TX 78550
(956) 427-8533

Houston District
8701 S. Gessner Drive, #1200
Houston, TX 77074
(713) 773-6500

Lubbock District
1205 Texas Avenue, #408
Lubbock, TX 79401
(806) 472-7462

San Antonio District
615 E. Houston Street, #298

San Antonio, TX 78205

(210) 472-5900

Utah

125 S. State Street, #2231

Salt Lake City, UT 84138

(801) 524-3209

Vermont

87 State Street, #205

Montpelier, VT 05601

(802) 828-4422

Virginia

Federal Building

400 N. 8th Street, #1150

Richmond, VA 23219

(804) 771-2400

Washington

2401 Fourth Avenue, #450

Seattle, WA 98121

(206) 553-7310

West Virginia

320 West Pike Street, #330

Clarksburg, WV 26301

(304) 623-5631

Wisconsin

310 West Wisconsin Avenue, #580W

Madison, WI 53203

(414) 297-3941

Wyoming

Federal Building

100 E. B Street, #4001

4001 Box 44001

Casper, WY 82602

(307) 261-6500

SBA Small Business Development Centers also offer assistance to small businesses and new entrepreneurs all over the United States. Many of the development centers are located on the campuses of major universities and are funded in part by the SBA.

The SBA web directory(www.sba.gov/tools/local-assistance/sbdc) includes 27 pages of listings including states and U.S. Territories.

State Commerce and Economic Development Departments

Alabama
Department of Commerce
P.O. Box 304106
Montgomery, AL 36130
(800) 248-0033
madeinalabama.com

Alaska
Department of Commerce,
   Community and Economic
   Development
P.O. Box 110800
Juneau, AK 99811
(907) 465-2500
commerce.alaska.gov/

Arizona
Commerce Authority
333 N. Central Avenue,
   Suite 1900
Phoenix, AZ 85004
(602) 845-1200
azcommerce.com

Arkansas
Economic Development
   Commission
900 West Capitol Avenue, # 400
Little Rock, AR 72201
(800) ARKANSAS
arkansasedc.com

California
California Chamber of Commerce
1215 K Street, #1400
Sacramento, CA 95814
(916) 444-6670
calchamber.com/

Colorado
Office of Economic Development
   and International Trade
1625 Broadway, #2700
Denver, CO 80202
(303) 892-3840
advancecolorado.com/contact-us

Connecticut
Economic Resource Center
805 Brook Street, Bldg. 4
Rocky Hill, CT 06067
(860) 571-7136,
cerc.com

Delaware
Economic Development Office
99 Kings Highway
Dover, DE 19901
(302) 739-4271
dedo.delaware.gov/

District of Columbia
Office of the Deputy Mayor
   for Planning and Economic
   Development
1350 Pennsylvania Ave., NW, #317
Washington, DC 20004
(202) 727-6365
dcbiz.dc.gov/

Florida
Enterprise Florida
800 North Magnolia Avenue, # 1100
Orlando, Florida 32803
(407) 956-5600
www.enterpriseflorida.com

Georgia
Department of Community Affairs
60 Executive Park S., NE
Atlanta, GA 30329
(404) 679-4940
georgia.gov

Hawaii
Department of Business, Economic
   Development & Tourism
No. 1 Capitol District Building
250 S. Hotel Street
Honolulu, Hawaii 96813

P.O. Box 2359
Honolulu, Hawaii 96804
(808) 586-2355
dbedt.hawaii.gov/

Idaho
Idaho Commerce
700 W. State Street
P.O. Box 83720
Boise, ID 83720
(208) 334-2470
commerce.idaho.gov/

Illinois
Department of Commerce and
   Economic Opportunity
500 East Monroe Street

Springfield, IL 62701
(217) 782-7500
www.illinois.gov/dceo

Indiana
Economic Development
  Commission
1 N. Capitol Avenue, #700
Indianapolis, IN 46204
(800) 463-8081
http://iedc.in.gov/

Iowa
Department of Commerce
commerce.iowa.gov
No other contact information
  provided

Kansas
Department of Commerce and
  Housing
Business Development Division
1000 SW Jackson Street, #100
Topeka, KS 66612
(785) 296-3481
kansascommerce.com/

Kentucky
Cabinet for Economic Development
Old Capitol Annex
300 West Broadway
Frankfort, KY 40601
(800) 626-2930
thinkkentucky.com/

Louisiana
Louisiana Economic Development
1051 North Third Street

Baton Rouge, LA 70802
(800) 450-8115
opportunitylouisiana.com

Maine
Department. of Economic and
  Community Development
59 Statehouse Station
Augusta, ME 04333
(207) 624-9800
maine.gov/decd/

Maryland
Department of Business and
  Economic Development
401 East Pratt Street
Baltimore, MD 21202
1-888-ChooseMD
http://business.maryland.gov/

Massachusetts
Office of Business Development
One Ashburton Place, #2101
Boston, MA 02108
(617) 788-3610
mass.gov/hed/economic/eohed/bd/

Michigan
Pure Business/Michigan Economic
  Development
300 N. Washington Square
Lansing, MI 48913
(888) 522-0103
michiganbusiness.org

Minnesota
Department of Employment and
  Economic Development

First National Bank Building
332 Minnesota Street, # E-200
Saint Paul, MN, 55101
Twin Cities (651) 259-7114
Greater Minnesota (800) 657-3858
mn.gov/deed

Mississippi
Development Authority
P.O. Box 849
Jackson, MS 39205
(601) 359-3449
mississippi.org

Missouri
Department for Economic
    Development
P.O. Box 1157
Jefferson City, MO 65102
(573) 571-4962
http://ded.mo.gov/

Montana
Business Resources Division
P.O. Box 200505
Helena, MT 59620
(406) 841-2730
http://businessresources.mt.gov/

Nebraska
Department of Economic
    Development
301 Centennial Mall S
P.O. Box 94666
Lincoln, NE 68509
(402) 471-3111, (800) 426-6505
neded.org/

Nevada
Governor's Office of Economic
    Development
555 E. Washington Avenue, #5400
Las Vegas, NV 89101
(702) 486-2700
diversifynevada.com

New Hampshire
Division of Economic
    Development
172 Pembroke Road
P.O. Box 1856
Concord, NH 03302
(603) 271-2591
Fax: (603) 271-6784
nheconomy.com

New Jersey
Economic Development Authority
36 West State Street
Trenton, NJ 08625
(609) 858-6700
njeda.com

New Mexico
Economic Development
    Department
Joseph M. Montoya Building
1100 St. Francis Drive
Santa Fe, NM 87505
(505) 827-0300
gonm.biz

New York
Economic Development Council
111 Washington Avenue, 6th Floor

Albany, New York 12210
(518) 426-4058
nysedc.org

North Carolina
Small Business and Technology
   Development Center
5 West Hargett Street, #600
Raleigh, NC 27601
(919) 715-7272, (800) 258-0862
sbtdc.org

North Dakota
Department of Commerce
1600 E. Century Avenue, #2
Bismarck, ND 58503
(701) 328-5300
commerce.nd.gov

Ohio
Ohio Development Services
P.O. Box 1001
77 S. High Street, 28th floor
Columbus, OH 43216
(800) 848-1300
development.ohio.gov/

Oklahoma
Department of Commerce
900 N. Stiles Avenue
Oklahoma City, OK 73126
(405) 815-6552, (800) 879-6552
okcommerce.gov

Oregon
Business Oregon
775 Summer Street NE, #200
Salem, OR 97301-1280

(503) 986-0123, (800) 233-3306
Fax: (503) 581-5115
Oregon4biz.com

Pennsylvania
Department of Community and
   Economic Development
Commonwealth Keystone Bldg.
400 N Street, 4th floor
Harrisburg, PA 17120
(866) 466-3972
newpa.com

Rhode Island
Commerce Corporation
315 Iron Horse Way, #101
Providence, RI 02908
(401) 278-9100
commerceri.com

South Carolina
Department of Commerce
1201 Main Street, Suite 1600
Columbia, SC 29201-3200
(803) 737-0400, (800) 868-7232
sccommerce.com

South Dakota
Governor's Department of
   Economic Development
711 E. Wells Avenue
Pierre, SD 57501
(605) 367-4518
www.sdreadytowork.com/

Tennessee
Department of Economic and
   Community Development

312 Rosa L. Parks Avenue, 27th
Floor
Nashville, Tennessee 37243
(615) 741-1888
www.tn.gov/ecd

Texas
Economic Development Council
1011 San Jacinto, #650
Austin, TX 78701
(512) 480-8432
texasedc.org

Utah
Governor's Office of Economic
Development
60 East South Temple, 3rd Floor
Salt Lake City, UT 84111
(801) 538-8680
business.utah.gov/

Vermont
Agency of Commerce and
Community Development
1 National Life Drive, 6th Floor
Montpelier, VT 05620
(802) 828-5765
accd.vermont.gov/business

Virginia
Economic Development
Partnership
901 East Byrd Street
P.O. Box 798
Richmond, VA 23218
(804) 545-5600
Yesvirginia.org

Washington
Department of Commerce
1011 Plum Street SE
P.O. Box 42525
Olympia, WA 98504
(360) 725-4000
commerce.wa.gov/

West Virginia
Economic Development
Partnership
Capitol Complex, Bldg. 6
1900 Washington St. Street E.,
#525
Charleston, WV 25305
(800) 982-3386, (304) 558-2234
wvcommerce.org/business/default.
aspx

Wisconsin
Economic Development
Corporation
201 W. Washington Avenue
Madison, WI 53703
(855) 469-4249
inwisconsin.com

Wyoming
Wyoming Business Council
214 West 15th Street
Cheyenne, WY 82001
(307) 777-2800, (800) 262-3425
wyomingbusiness.org

Business and Business Plan Resources

Websites

Angelcapitalassociation.org—
for locating angel investors

Angel-investor-network.com

Bizfilings.com—Information
for small-business owners

Bizplan.com

Bizplancompetitions.com—
Listings of nationwide
business plan competitions

Bplans.com

Businessweek.com

CNNMoney.com

Economist.com

Entrepreneur.com/bestbanks—
Leading banks for small-
business owners

Entrepreneur.com/businessplan

Forbes.com

FundingPost.com—Events that
include angel investors and
VCs

Gust.com—Angel investor networks

Inc.com/business-plans

Nolo.com—Legal forms and information

Nvca.org—National Venture Capitalist Association

Online-business-plan-services-review.toptenreviews.com/ —Reviews of business plan software

SBA.org—Small Business Association

Score.org—Volunteer mentors and advisors. They also have business plan templates at: Score.org/resources/business-plan-template-startup-business

Books

Anatomy of a Business Plan: The Step-by-Step Guide to Building a Business and Securing Your Company's Future by Linda Pinson, 7th edition, Out Of Your Mind and into the Market, 2008

Cash from the Crowd by Sally Outlaw, Entrepreneur Press, 2013 (ebook)

How to Write a Business Plan by Mike McKeever, 11th edition, NOLO, 2012

Legal Forms for Starting & Running a Small Business by Fred S. Steingold, NOLO, 2012

The Marketing Plan Handbook by Robert Bly, Entrepreneur Press, 2009

Networking Like a Pro by Ivan Misner, Ph.D., Entrepreneur Press, 2010

Start Your Own Business: The Only Startup Book You'll Ever Need by the Staff of Entrepreneur Media, Inc., 6th edition, Entrepreneur Press, 2015

Start Your Own e-Business by Entrepreneur Press and Rich Mintzer, Entrepreneur Press, 2014

Successful Business Plan: Secrets & Strategies by Rhonda Abrams, 5th edition, Planning Shop, 2010

Ultimate Startup Directory by James Stephenson, Entrepreneur Press, 2007

Your First Business Plan by Joseph A. Covello and Brian Hazelgren, Sourcebooks, 2005

FYI: All books from Entrepreneur Press can be found at EntrepreneurBookstore.com

Online Business Plan Courses

New Hampshire Small Business Development Center—Crafting a Business Plan: www.nhsbdc. org/need-business-plan

The Right-Brain Business Plan® Home Study e-Course: www. rightbrainbusinessplan.com/ courses

SBA Small Business Learning Center—How to Write a Business Plan:

www.sba.gov/tools/sba-learning-center/training/how-write-business-plan

Udemy.com—Create a Damn Good Business Plan:

www.udemy.com/create-a-damn-good-business-plan

Universal Class—How to Write a Business Plan 101:

www.universalclass.com/i/course/how-to-write-a-business-plan.htm

Glossary

balloon payment–A single, usually final, payment on a loan that is much greater than the payments preceding it; some business loans, for example, require interest-only payments the first year or two, followed by a single large payment that repays all the principal.

branding–The marketing practice of creating a name, symbol, or design that identifies and differentiates a product from other products; well-known brands include Tide, Dockers, and Dell.

business concept–The basic idea around which a business is built. For instance, FedEx is built on the idea of overnight delivery, while Amazon.com was originally built around the idea of selling books over the internet.

cash conversion cycle–The amount of time it takes to transform your cash outlays into cash income; for a manufacturer, the number of days or weeks required to purchase raw materials and turn them into inventory, then sales, and, finally, collections.

competitive advantage–Factor or factors that give a business an advantage over its competitors. This can be based on the quality of products or services, lower prices, better customer service, faster delivery, and/or all of the above.

co-op promotion–Arrangement between two or more businesses to cross-promote their enterprises to customers.

current assets–Assets likely to be turned into cash within a year.

current liabilities–Amounts you owe and are to pay in less than a year, such as accounts payable to suppliers and short-term loans.

due diligence–Doing research to find data on a business, company, customers, lender, vendor, or any individual or group with whom you may potentially do business.

EBIT–An accounting term for a company's operational earnings separate from the effects of interest payments and taxation.

ecommerce or electronic commerce–Selling products and services through sites on the internet.

executive summary–Section of a business plan that briefly describes what the rest of the plan contains; also the first section of the plan, often written after the other sections.

factoring–The flip side of trade credit; what happens when a supplier sells its accounts receivables to a financial specialist called a factor. The factor immediately pays the amount of the receivables, less a discount, and receives the payments when they arrive from customers; an important form of finance in many industries.

forecast–To forecast is to use prior data to determine upcoming trends. Forecasting can prove very helpful for budgeting and marketing purposes. In a business plan for a startup, forecasting can indicate that you have utilized historical data within your industry to predict future results.

Initial Public Offering (IPO)–The first sale of stock by a private company to the public. Typically IPOs are issued by smaller, younger companies seeking capital to expand. However, established companies can issue one later on to generate additional funding.

limited liability corporation–Business legal structure resembling an S corporation but allowing owners more flexibility in dividing up profits while still providing protection from liability; abbreviated LLC.

liquidity–A company's ability to convert noncash assets, such as inventory and accounts receivable, into cash; essentially, the company's ability to pay its bills.

logistics–The science of moving objects, such as product inventory, from one location to another.

management team–The key personnel that have significant roles in managing and running the business. They need to be profiled in the management section of a business plan.

marketing plan–Part of your business plan, and something that you will update regularly. Such a plan outlines how you will spread the word about your product and/or services. It includes everything from advertising to promotional messages to web presence to giveaway items with your company name or logo.

mission statement–A sentence or two describing a company's function, markets, and competitive advantages.

objectives–Long-term aims, frequently representing the ultimate level to which you aspire.

organization, functional–A company or other entity with a structure that divides authority along functions such as marketing, finance, etc.; these functions cross product lines and other boundaries.

organization, line–A company or other entity with a structure divided by product lines, means of production, industries served, etc.; each line may have its own support staff for the various functions.

organization, line and staff–A company or other entity with a structure calling for staff managers, like planners and accountants, to act as advisors supporting a line manager, such as the operations vice president.

outsourcing–Having a component or service performed or supplied by an outside firm or individual; used to reduce time and money costs for support work and add flexibility in production staffing.

positioning–Marketing tool that describes a product or service in reference to its position in the marketplace; for example, the newest, smallest, cheapest, or second-largest.

rate of return–The income or profit earned by an investor on capital invested into a company; usually expressed as an annual percentage.

search engine optimization (SEO)–Utilizing keywords and other strategies in order to position your website to come up higher during an online web search.

target market–The audience most likely to buy your goods or services, usually found as the result of demographic research

turnaround–A reversal in a company's fortunes, taking it from near death to robust health or the revival of a failing company to more profitable status.

unique selling proposition–The factor or consideration presented by a seller as the reason that one product or service is different from, and better than, the competition.

vision statement–A sentence or two describing a company's long-range aims, such as achieving a dominant market share or attaining a reputation for world-class quality.

working capital–The amount of money a business has in cash, accounts receivable, inventory, and other current assets; normally refers to net working capital, which is current assets minus current liabilities.

Index